Titles published by Zed Books in association with ACDESS

Africa Within the World:
Beyond Dispossession and Dependence
(1993)

South Africa and Africa:
Within or Apart?
(1996)

Nigeria: Renewal from the Roots?
The Struggle for Democratic Development
(1997)

Comprehending and Mastering African Conflicts:
The Search for Sustainable Peace and Good Governance
(1999)

African Development and Governance Strategies in the 21st Century:
Looking Back to Move Forward:
Essays in honour of Adebayo Adedeji at Seventy
(2003)

African Development and Governance Strategies in the 21st Century
Looking Back to Move Forward

Essays in Honour of
Adebayo Adedeji
at Seventy

Lawrence O. C. Agubuzu
Olu Ajakaiye
Yves Ekoue Amaïzo
Peter Anyang' Nyong'o
A. I. Asiwaju
Julia A. Duany
Mbaya Kankwenda
Khadija Yaya Mansaray
Mike I. Obadan
Oluwafemi Odediran
Bade Onimode
Elsie Onubogu
Ejeviome Eloho Otobo
Hassan A. Sunmonu
O. W. Tomori
S. O. Tomori

Zed Books
LONDON & NEW YORK

**African Centre for Development
& Strategic Studies** (ACDESS)
IJEBU-ODE

African Development and Governance Strategies in the 21st Century
was first published in 2004 by
Zed Books Ltd, 7 Cynthia Street, London N1 9JF, UK and
Room 400, 175 Fifth Avenue, New York, NY 10010, USA
www.zedbooks.co.uk

in association with

The African Centre for Development and Strategic Studies (ACDESS)
PO Box 203, Ijebu-Ode, Nigeria

Cover design by Andrew Corbett
Designed and set in 10/13 pt Bembo
by Long House, Cumbria, UK
Printed and bound in Malta by Gutenberg Ltd

Distributed in the USA exclusively by Palgrave Macmillan, a division of
St Martin's Press, LLC, 175 Fifth Avenue, New York, NY 10010

A catalogue record for this book
is available from the British Library

US Cataloging-in-Publication Data
is available from the Library of Congress

ISBN   Hb 1 84277 408 5
Pb 1 84277 409 3

Contents

Tables

Figures

Contributors

Lawrence O. C. Agubuzu is Assistant Secretary-General of the Community Affairs Department of the African Union (formerly the Organisation of African Unity).

Olu Ajakaiye is Professor of Economics and Director-General of the Nigeria Institute for Social and Economic Research.

Yves Ekoue Amaïzo is Economic Affairs Officer of the United Nations Industrial Development Organisation (UNIDO).

Peter Anyang' Nyong'o is Professor of Political Science at the University of Nairobi, Fellow of the African Academy of Science and a member of Kenya's Parliament.

A. I. Asiwaju is Professor of History at the University of Lagos.

Julia A. Duany is a Sudanese refugee and currently a research associate in the Workshop in Political Theory and Policy Analysis, Indiana University.

Mbaya Kankwenda was formerly Professor of Economics at the University of Kinshasa and is currently Resident Representative of the United Nations Development Programme (UNDP) and UN Coordinator in Nigeria.

Khadija Yaya Mansaray is a UN consultant on gender.

Mike I. Obadan is Professor of Economics and Director-General of the National Centre for Economic Management and Administration (NCEMA).

Oluwafemi Odediran works for the United Nations Children's Fund (UNICEF) as a member of that organisation's senior management staff in Asia.

Bade Onimode, who died while preparing this volume for publication, was Professor of Economics at the University of Ibadan.

Elsie Onubogu is an international lawyer with expertise in gender issues and served as a United Nations peacekeeper in former Yugoslavia.

Ejeviome Eloho Otobo is Chief of Policy Analysis and Monitoring Unit, Office of Special Adviser on Africa, United Nations.

Hassan A. Sunmonu is Secretary-General of the Organisation of African Trade Union Unity.

O. W. Tomori is Lecturer in Economics at the University of Lagos.

S. O. Tomori is Professor of Economics at the University of Lagos.

Abbreviations

AAF–SAP	African Alternative Framework to Structural Adjustment Programmes for Socio-Economic Recovery and Transformation
ACBF	African Capacity Building Foundation
ACDESS	African Centre for Development and Strategic Studies
ACP	Africa, Caribbean and the Pacific
ADB	African Development Bank
AEBR	Association of European Border Regions
AEC	African Economic Community
AERC	African Economic Research Consortium
AMU	Arab Maghreb Union
ANC	African National Congress (South Africa)
APPER	Africa's Priority Programme for Economic Recovery
ASEAN	Association of South-East Asian Nations
ASYCUDA	Automated System of Customs Data Analysis
AU	African Union (successor organisation to the OAU, established in July 2002)
CACG	Commonwealth Association on Corporate Governance
CBN	Central Bank of Nigeria
CBO	Community-based organisation
CEAO	Communauté Economique de l'Afrique de l'Ouest (West African Economic Union)
CEDAW	Convention on the Elimination of All Forms of Discrimination Against Women
CEMAC	Central African Economic and Monetary Community
CEN–SAD	Community of Sahel–Saharan States
CEO	Chief executive officer

CFA	Communauté Financière Africaine
CFR	Commander of the Federal Republic of Nigeria
COMESA	Common Market of Eastern and Southern Africa (formerly PTA)
COMPASS	COMESA Payment and Settlement System
CSO	Civil society organisation
CSR	Corporate social responsibility
CSW	Commission on the Status of Women
DAC	Development Assistance Committee of the OECD
DMS	Development merchant system
DSA	Debt sustainability analysis
EACC	East African Cooperation Commission
ECA (UNECA)	United Nations Economic Commission for Africa
ECCAS	Economic Community of Central African States
ECOMOG	ECOWAS Ceasefire Monitoring Group
ECOWAS	Economic Community of West African States
ESAF	Enhanced Structural Adjustment Facility
FAL	Final Act of Lagos
FDI	Foreign direct investment
FEPA	Federal Environmental Protection Agency (Nigeria)
G7 or G8	Group of the Seven (or Eight) Most Industrialised and Powerful Countries (USA, Japan, Germany, UK, Canada, France, Italy, and Russia)
GCA	Global Coalition for Africa
GDP	Gross domestic product
GNP	Gross national product
HDI	Human Development Index
HIPC	Highly indebted poor country
HPI	Human Poverty Index
IDA	International Development Assistance
IDP	Internally displaced person
IFI	International financial institution
IGAD	Intergovernmental Authority on Development (formerly IGADD)
IGADD	Intergovernmental Agreement on Desertification and Development
IGO	Intergovernmental organisation
ILO	International Labour Organisation
IMF	International Monetary Fund
LDC	Least developed country
LPA	Lagos Plan of Action for the Economic Development of

	Africa, 1980–2000
LTPS	Long-Term Perspective Study
MAI	Multilateral Agreement on Investment
MGS	Import goods and services
NAFTA	North American Free Trade Agreement
NCEMA	National Centre for Economic Management and Administration
NDIC	National Deposit Insurance Corporation (Nigeria)
NEPA	Nigerian Electric Power Authority
NEPAD	New Partnership for Africa's Development
NGO	Non-governmental organisation
NIC	Newly industrialising country
NIEO	New International Economic Order
NISER	Nigerian Institute for Social and Economic Research
NRM	National Resistance Movement (Uganda)
OATUU	Organisation of African Trade Union Unity
OAU	Organisation of African Unity (established in May 1963 and replaced in July 2002 by the AU)
ODA	Official development assistance
OHADA	Organisation pour l'Harmonisation en Afrique du Droit des Affaires
OECD	Organisation for Economic Cooperation and Development
OPEC	Organisation of Petroleum Exporting Countries
PANAFTEL	Pan African Telecommunications Network
PICA	Program on International Cooperation in Africa
PTA	Preferential Trade Area for Eastern and Southern Africa
RDC	Rassemblement Démocratique Congolaise
RDP	Reconstruction and Development Programme (South Africa)
REC	Regional economic community
RPF	Rwandese Patriotic Front
SACU	Southern African Customs Union
SADC	Southern African Development Community
SADCC	Southern African Development Coordination Conference
SAP	Structural Adjustment Programme
SHD	Sustainable human development
SILIC	Severely indebted low-income country
SIMIC	Severely indebted middle-income country
SOE	State-owned enterprise
SSA	Sub-Saharan Africa
TC	Technical cooperation
TDS	Total debt service

TNC	Transnational company
TRIMs	Trade-related investment measures
TRIPs	Trade-related aspects of intellectual property rights
UDEAC	Union Douanière et Economique de l'Afrique Centrale (Central African Customs and Economic Union)
UEMOA	Union Economique et Monétaire Ouest Africaine (West African Economic and Monetary Union)
UNAIDS	Joint United Nations Programme on HIV/AIDs
UNCRD	United Nations Centre for Regional Development
UNCTAD	United Nations Conference on Trade and Development
UNDP	United Nations Development Programme
UNHCR	United Nations High Commissioner for Refugees
UNICEF	United Nations Children's Fund
UNIDO	United Nations Industrial Development Organisation
UN–NADAF	United Nations New Agenda for the Development of Africa in the 1990s
UN–PAAERD	United Nations Programme of Action for Africa's Economic Recovery and Development
USAID	United States Agency for International Development
WCED	World Commission on Environment and Development
WFP	World Food Programme
WHO	World Health Organisation
WTO	World Trade Organisation
XGS	Export goods and services

Preface

Africa continues to be in search of a development paradigm that would rid it of abject poverty, the bug of disease and the quagmire of ignorance after over four decades of such endeavours. In pursuit of that goal a series of theories and concepts of development have been advanced, and tried to no avail. Most of them have been grounded in Western political and development traditions that failed to take cognisance of Africa's cultural and historical background.

Rather than accept this fact, Western experts have continued to back the Structural Adjustment Programme of the Bretton Woods institutions as a ready prescription that they apply to all countries irrespective of differences in economic, socio-cultural and historical background. It is a *gbogbounse* (all-purpose) formula that has yielded no effectual results. The Structural Adjustment Programme itself is reminiscent of the social and political institutions that the colonial masters bequeathed to African countries. Once these institutions are discovered not to have worked, as Basil Davidson once noted, the blame is put not on the institutions but on the persons who have failed to work them. But special pleaders apart, the Structural Adjustment Programme has very few sympathisers among economic experts on the continent.

Foremost among those who challenged the SAP's there-is-no-alternative (TINA) approach is Professor Adebayo Adedeji, CFR, one-time Nigerian Minister for Economic Development and Reconstruction and former United Nations Under-Secretary-General and Executive Secretary of the UN Economic Commission for Africa (ECA). As if responding to the *quare impedit* of Western theoreticians and marabouts of development, Professor Adedeji has continued to advocate African indigenous alternative paradigms for development. Under his leadership, the ECA produced its African Alternative Framework to Structural Adjustment Programme for Economic Recovery and Transformation (AAF–SAP) to win the approval of a historic joint meeting of African Ministers of Finance and Planning Development and the endorsement of the African Heads of State and

Government at the July 1989 Summit meeting of the Organisation of African Unity (now the African Union), and of the General Assembly of the United Nations in December of the same year. In 1980, he had masterminded the Lagos Plan of Action and the Final Act of Lagos.

The thrust of AAF–SAP is that there should be a holistic approach to the issue of adjustment as an integral process of socio-economic transformation based on the principles of self-reliance and self-sustainment advocated in the LPA. Africa, according to AAF–SAP, should be transformed from an economy based primarily on exchange to one based on production, with a simultaneous democratisation of the development process and pervasive accountability on the part of policy makers and public officials. Needless to add, these changes were to be matched by improved financial management, greater agricultural incentives, export diversification, improved external debt management, and other features of an efficient state system.

Adedeji's advocacy of holistic human development is based on the general concept that society can only develop with the mobilisation of its people; hence his statement that Africa would need to set in motion a process that puts the individual at the very centre of a development effort that is both human and humane, without necessarily softening the discipline that goes with development and enhances the human personality. Such a development process should not alienate the African from his society and culture but rather develop his self-confidence and identify his interest with those of his society, thereby strengthening his capacity and desire for self-reliance.

This stance, which links the individual to his society and culture, is what has endeared Adedeji to many people. Despite the fact that he has retired from the international civil service, his opinions on issues affecting African development and the economic perspectives of other developing countries are much sought after and held in high respect. Africa owes a lot to him.

The papers presented at a symposium in December 2000 as part of the activities organised by admirers, friends and former students and colleagues to mark Adedeji's seventieth birthday are a reflection of what he means to individuals in their various callings – economists, political scientists, politicians, women activists, human rights advocates, trade unionists, environmentalists, historians and the Nigerian civil servants, who organised their own separate symposium. In paying tribute to Adebayo Adedeji, the participants were also honouring the wisdom of his view that in order to restructure its institutions Africa will need to reinvent itself. If Africa is to be relevant in this 21st century, it has to look back in order to move forward – not with the idea of returning to the past, but rather by looking to those principles, attitudes and moralities of controlling and sharing power in community that brought success when they were applied and left failure when they were not. Beyond that, Adedeji's efforts in promoting regional integration –

political, social and economic – can be seen as having recourse to older African structures that were vivisected by the colonial administrations. Adedeji's constant advocacy of African economic cooperation and integration, embodied in his successful push for the establishment of ECOWAS, also bore fruit in the establishment of the Preferential Trade Area/Common Market for East and Southern Africa (PTA–COMESA), the Southern African Development Community (SADC) and the Economic Community of Central African States (ECCAS); it culminated in the signing of the treaty establishing the African Economic Community in Abuja in June 1991 – at the end of Adedeji's highly successful career at the UN. This has prompted S. K. B. Asante to view Adedeji as Africa's counterpart of Jean Monnet and Raul Prebisch, respectively the champions of European and Latin American economic integration.

This book hopes to continue the tradition of two earlier, seminal publications put together in appreciation of Adedeji's devotion to Africa's development cause. The first, *African Development: Adebayo Adedeji's Alternative Strategies* was written by S. K. B. Asante and published in 1991. The second, *Issues in African Development – Essays in Honour of Adebayo Adedeji at 65*, appeared in 1995.

But can Africa really claim the 21st century? This is the big challenge that the contents of this book pose. Like Adedeji, the contributors are optimistic of success – but only if African leaders demonstrate the political will to mobilise their peoples with a view to moving them towards self-reliance at the national level and political and economic integration at the regional level. Mobilisation will bring in its trail the empowerment of the people of the continent within a democratic dispensation that is becoming a global phenomenon.

As Adedeji himself once noted, Africa's own vision of socio-economic and political development – cutting across gender, age, ethnicity, religion and national borders and nurturing ties based on the recognition of equality and the need for mutual benefit – can now be pursued with self-confidence, resilience and endurance.

These are challenging times, however, in that the majority of African countries are ranked among the world's poorest. Some African leaders seem to be mesmerised by the New Partnership for Africa's Development (NEPÅD), which most of the stakeholders do not understand. And no economic permutations can yield the desired results without the backing of motivated, democratically empowered collectives guided by their leaders towards economic and political integration at the national and international levels. The optimism that Africa can lift itself from the present morass and take the strides that the century demands is based on the hope that those traditional values that motivate societies can be reactivated, that surviving cultural paradigms, fine-tuned and revitalised, can be operationalised and implemented. Africa should stop shopping for new paradigms and expending valuable energy and time reinventing the wheel.

I cannot conclude this preface without paying homage to Professor Bade Onimode, who not only initiated the ACDESS International Millennium Symposium at which the chapters in this volume were first presented but had also embarked on the editorial task of turning conference papers into this book when the cold hand of death prematurely led him away. His death was a severe blow to ACDESS – of which he was a foundation Senior Fellow – as well as to the University of Ibadan and the wider academic world. During the last two decades – the 1980s and 1990s – he was in the first rank of intellectuals engaged in a tireless and earnest search for alternative development in Africa. His place will be hard to fill. May his gentle soul rest in peace.

Segun Odunuga
University of Ibadan

Professor Adebayo Adedeji, CFR
A Profile

Professor Adebayo Adedeji has had a singularly distinguished academic, managerial, diplomatic and political career in the service of his native country, Nigeria, the wider African continent and the international community for over four decades. Born in 1930 in Ijebu-Ode in Nigeria, he graduated from London University (BSc and PhD in Economics) and Harvard (MPA). At the age of 36, he became a full professor at the University of Ife, now Obafemi Awolowo University. And at the age of 40, in 1971, he was drafted into the government of the Federal Republic of Nigeria by General Yakubu Gowon as the cabinet minister responsible for the economic development and reconstruction of post-civil war Nigeria. He was the founding chairman of the Nigeria National Youth Service Corps (NYSC) and on the larger Pan-African stage in May 1975 established the Economic Community of West African States (ECOWAS) after over three years of arduous negotiation with 16 governments and countries.

In June 1975 he was appointed United Nations Assistant Secretary-General and Executive Secretary of the UN Economic Commission for African (ECA) and was promoted to the rank of United Nations Under-Secretary-General in January 1978 – a position he held until July 1991 when he resigned to return to his native country after 16 years of international service. It should not be forgotten that, at the height of the great African drought and economic crisis of 1984–6, he was designated the UN Secretary-General's Special Representative on Africa's Economic Crisis, in addition to continuing as the executive head of the ECA.

Professor Adedeji's success in establishing ECOWAS in 1975 emboldened him to launch, two years after he became the head of the ECA, parallel integration processes in Eastern and Southern Africa and in Central Africa. This initiative culminated in the establishment of the 18-nation Preferential Trade Area for Eastern and Southern Africa (the precursor of the Common Market of Eastern and Southern Africa, COMESA) in 1981 and the 10-nation Economic Community of Central African States (ECCAS) in 1983. The process culminated in the adoption of the treaty inaugurating the African Economic Community in June 1991 and in the establishment of the African Union in 2000.

Immediately after his resignation from the United Nations, Professor Adedeji established and still currently heads the African Centre for Development and Strategic Studies (ACDESS) – an independent, non-governmental, not-for-profit think-tank dedicated to multidisciplinary and strategic studies on and for Africa. Born out of the need to fill the void in strategic thinking in Africa, ACDESS's raison d'être is to provide and promote policy options for overcoming the marginalisation of the vast majority of African peoples – within local communities, nation states or the global economic and political system – through a holistic, human-centred, political and socio-economic development and transformation process.

Through his engagement in creating, in ACDESS, a viable and sustainable centre for future studies, Professor Adedeji continues to dedicate himself to the struggle for an Africa that is an integral part of and a fully respected partner in the world community. Throughout his career, he has stressed the need for Africa's socio-economic transformation and genuine democratisation based on an indigenously crafted, human-centred holistic development paradigm. The African Alternative Framework to Structural Adjustment Programmes (AAF–SAP, 1989) and the African Charter for Popular Participation (1990) bear his unmistakable imprint. Both were endorsed by the United Nations General Assembly and have become landmarks in Africa's emancipation debate.

Adedeji has been a strong advocate of democracy in Africa and of the democratisation of the development process ever since 1975 – a time in history when it was imprudent to take up that cause. He has consistently argued that Africa's persistent economic crisis – severe as it has been – is but a consequence of the political crisis that manifests itself in a lack of democracy, accountability, good governance and a human-centred development paradigm.

Professor Adedeji's contributions to development theory, strategy and policy suitable for Africa and other developing regions have been presented cogently and systematically in Professor S. K. B. Asante's book *African Development: Adebayo Adedeji's Alternative Strategies* (London and Ibadan, 1991) and in a book of essays written in his honour and edited by Bade Onimode and Richard Synge, *Issues in African Development: Essays in Honour of Adebayo Adedeji at 65* (Ibadan: Heinemann, 1996).

Many national and international honours have been bestowed upon him. He is a Fellow and past President of the Nigerian Economic Society, Fellow of the Nigerian Institute of Management, Fellow of the African Academy of Sciences and Fellow and past President of the African Association for Public Administration and Management. He has been awarded many honorary degrees – at Ahmadu Bello University, Zaria (D Litt); Obafemi Awolowo University, Ile-Ife (DSc Econ); Dalhousie University (LLD); University of Zambia (LLD); University of Calabar

(LLD), University of Ibadan (DSc), and Ogun State University (DSc). He has received national honours from many countries. Among these are the Grand Order of the Mono of the Republic of Togo; Commander of the Order of Merit of the Islamic Republic of Mauritania; Grand Commander of Distinguished Service of Zambia; Commander of the Republic of Gambia; Grand Commander of the Order of the Lion, Senegal; Grand Officer of the National Order of the Niger and Grand Commander of the Most Excellent Order of the Eagle, Namibia. In October 2001, the prestigious Nigerian national honour of Commander of the Federal Republic of Nigeria (CFR) was conferred upon him.

In 1982, he received the International Gold Mercury Award (*ad personam*) and in 1991 the Arthur Houghton Star Crystal Award of the African-American Institute. In a further recognition of his services to Africa and humanity, he was made an honorary citizen of the Republic of Namibia in March 1997.

Since his departure from the United Nations in August 1991, Professor Adedeji has served extensively as consultant to UN organisations, African governments and non-governmental organisations and universities – both African and non-African. For example, he was on the UN Secretary-General's Panel of Independent High-Level Advisers on the future course of UN development activities (1992); served as Chairman of the High-Level Group of Experts on the future of the United Nations Development Programme (UNDP) (1994); and as consultant to the UN on Asia–Africa Cooperation (1997). In 1999 and 2001 he led a three-person team on the evaluation and assessment of the United Nations Development Assistance Framework (UNDAF). Also on behalf of the United Nations, in 2000 he led another team that undertook a study of the Future of the United Nations Staff College. He has been Economic Adviser to the Government of the Republic of Namibia since 1991.

Since January 1998 he has been a member of the Advisory Board of the United Nations African Futures Project – a long-term perspective studies project co-sponsored by the United Nations Development Programme (UNDP), the World Bank, the United Nations Economic Commission for Africa (ECA) and the African Development Bank (ADB).

On the restoration of democracy in Nigeria on 29 May 1999, he organised, at the request of Chief Olusegun Obasanjo, GCFR, President and Commander-in-Chief of the Armed Forces of Nigeria, a series of two-weekly reorientation programmes for over 2,000 senior members of the Federal Civil Service of Nigeria, to assist them in coping effectively with the challenges of governance, development and globalisation in a democratic Nigeria that previously had been subjected to military dictatorship for three decades.

From March to May 2002 he was Nigeria's Special Envoy to Zimbabwe, facilitating reconciliation between the two warring political parties, ZANU-PF and MDC, following that country's controversial elections in March 2002, and from December 2002 to early January 2003 he served as the Chairman and Leader of the 54-nation Commonwealth Observer and Monitoring Group on Kenya's 2002 Presidential and Parliamentary Elections. And between these two assignments, he served as special adviser to the OAU Secretary-General on the transformation of the OAU into the African Union (AU).

It is amazing, though not surprising, that at his ripe old age Professor Adedeji's commitment to the service of his own country, Nigeria, and of his own continent, Africa, the consuming passions of his life, has remained undiminished.

PART I

Mobilisation for the Implementation of Africa's Indigenous Alternative Paradigms

1

Forty Years of Development Illusions: Revisiting Development Policies and Practices in Africa
Mbaya Kankwenda

It is obvious to everyone that Africa has been undergoing a crisis for over 20 years. Solutions in the form of strategies, policies and programmes have been formulated and implemented. Solutions are proffered in one or more of the following policy areas: (1) economic reforms (including the problem of aid and debt); (2) political reforms including governance; (3) environmental protection; and (4) humanitarian assistance. The results of these efforts are not convincing. Africa has yet to get out of the crisis and put itself on the right path of human development.

Development has become big business in the world. It is a market, obedient to supply and demand. On the demand side are the developing countries (especially Africa), and the supply comes from developed countries and their institutions, the producers and marketers of development products: export goods, equipment, project ideas, projects, development policies and programmes, conceptual and practical know-how, human expertise and material technology. The development market also has its wholesalers and retailers.

During the early development decades, the suppliers appeared to be going about it individually, more or less in a scattered manner. But in the last two decades, development business has become more and more organised until it has become, indeed, a development merchant system – DMS – with its institutions, structures, operational mechanisms for opening up markets, development of customer loyalty and business expansion.

The development market has three particularities:

- The suppliers at the level of transnational and big development business institutions sell their products and services by financing the buyer or by advancing money. Whether by grant or loan, the seller always does good business, directly or indirectly, as an individual or as a system.

- The development merchants do not wear the garb of businessmen, but come dressed as gurus, marabouts or prophets of development. They come as do-gooders and humanists preaching the way of salvation, the way out of crisis, and even the way of development, and they finance those who follow their preaching and prescriptions.

- A new category of development merchandise has become more and more important: economic reform policies. These are special goods because they are not exhausted in mere consumption like the others; instead they shape the development route, the future and the destiny of African countries, defining the nature of development and the mode of integration in the global economy. They open and speed up business for the other development products and services, and are therefore financed by the DMS with largesse and urgency.

Africa's right to define its own development path – to chart it, like every other major region, without paternalistic interference, whether from businessman or marabout – is not recognised. Even during the present historic period of democratisation in Africa, this fundamental right is being assailed, despite appearances to the contary.

Methodological Hypotheses

Development policies bought from merchants and prescribed by marabouts cannot but fail, no matter their financial strength, conceptual ability or whatever. Forty years of development effort, led or inspired by these development merchants and by marabouts with doctorates in the subject show that Africa is not yet on the path of sustainable human development. It is our opinion that development is built from within, from conception to implementation. It is owned and mastered as a process by its actors and beneficiaries, more especially at this period of rapid globalisation. The DMS negates this hypothesis. Consequently, it is both faulty and erroneous, making development a business system that benefits the North as it firmly ties the African canoe to the North's neoliberal ship on the waters of globalisation.

The DMS is therefore made up of a combination of institutions: public and private agencies, organisations, programmes and funds. Their procedures and work methods in passing to the developing countries their ideas, advice, services, projects, programmes and development policies; in financing, implementing and evaluating the entire process, are aimed at making economic, financial, political or strategic profit – whether or not the result, in real terms, is human development progress for the countries who buy their products.

In spite of several national and regional development strategies and programmes, and despite general and sectoral development decades proclaimed now and then and here and there, the indicators show that but for a few exceptions of short duration, and notwithstanding the progress made in the social sector during the 1960s and 1970s: (1) real GDP growth has declined on annual variation over a long period for the whole of the continent; (2) a rather negative pattern of real

GDP *per capita* has persisted; (3) there is escalating poverty; (4) the number of African least developed countries (LDCs) has increased, to stand today at 33 out of a total of 48.

Moreover, the global economic context at the dawn of the 21st century is characterised mainly by:

- a growing globalisation process which encompasses not only the economic integration of markets, production, and capital, but also harmonisation of political systems for the desired management of a globalised economy and the uniformity and standardisation of cultures and social systems;
- the strengthening of collective neoliberal ideological and economic dictatorship over the South by the North, with the tendency to strengthen the role of instruments and institutions such as the World Trade Organisation (WTO), the World Bank and the International Monetary Fund (IMF);
- the rise and consolidation of conservative neoliberalism;
- the imposition of the principle of competition in the global market as the guiding principle and the only criterion for production at the national level;
- a fierce struggle between globalisation forces, not only for markets, but more for the scientific and technological control of the information highways, of natural and environmental resources, the resources of outer space and the control of cutting-edge techniques for replacing basic primary products;
- the growing marginalisation of Africa in all these processes of exchange and capital movements.

Faced with this global context, contemporary Africa is characterised by: (1) a development crisis of unprecedented severity; (2) a twin process of economic and political liberalisation; and (3) the absence of a peaceful and stable management framework or governance system that will give a chance to the development process in a large part of the continent.

The continent's crisis has not only contributed to the slowdown of development business on the continent, but has also tended to discredit the marabout of the DMS and to reveal his true identity. The DMS multiplies studies, reports, seminars, workshops and conferences to the point that Africans find themselves flooded with DMS products mapping the continent and the general and sectoral paths to take their countries out of the economic quagmire. These products, so numerous and prolific, are not always coherent; they have ended by confusing and entangling African leaders. Besides, the weight of the crisis in its triple dimension – political, economic and social – has pushed Africa into a tunnel, where it has been confined without ever seeing the light at the end of its entombment, despite the attendance of a multitude of prophets of good fortune.

The DMS is strengthened ideologically by development recipes and policies that justify and underpin the sale of development goods to Africa. The main ideological ingredients of the 1960s and 1970s are, first, the Cold War competition between the East and the West, and with this the development ideology of the South, including Africa; and, second, the emphasis on catching up with the North.

These two decades were thus characterised mainly by the sale of development appurtenances: economic take-offs and miracles were showcased but the continent entered a profound economic and social crisis in spite of the economic reform success stories being paraded. The third decade of the 1980s became one of stabilisation and structural adjustment policies aimed at managing the African crisis, more to ease the pinch on the West (debt repayment, integration into the global market by export growth and opening of frontiers), than to bring African economies out of the crisis. The end of the Cold War and the crisis of liberal economic policies helped to make economic reforms look like the touchstones of development policies. They became the conditionalities imposed on African countries as medicinal regimes enabling their systems to benefit from development aid and loans. Development business entered, therefore, another dimension, because it became enlarged to include development policies and other theoretical entities which, like goods, have their producers, their vendors, their buyers and their financiers. The fourth decade of the 1990s consisted of strengthening the globalisation of the economy (the ultimate reason for economic reform policies) through the globalisation of politics, with demands for political reform and good governance as new conditionalities.

But the result is there, thumbing its nose at Africa as well as its partners: the continent is able to show neither sustainable economic growth nor tangible progress in human development. And yet this is the goal of its partners in the DMS – partners that have sold it projects, economic and social programmes and policies, and financed them for 40 years.

Hence there is an *impasse of the development model in Africa* due to the fact that the basic accumulation sectors – agriculture and the mining industry are the foundations – were undergoing crises. The economic crisis of the continent is, therefore, a *crisis of its accumulation model* in the sense that the latter has come to an impasse: it is crumbling, incapable of reproducing itself, while as yet no replacement has been defined or implemented. While the main structural accumulation function has not changed, therefore, in its place we find crisis management policies.

Development has an ideological dimension and, since independence, Africa has had its ideologists and doctrinaires who, while appearing to be guides in quest of the good of the continent, have in fact been trading in development goods and appearances. And, as in every business, the sellers and the buyers (African political regimes) have profited from the trade.

The development marabout, like his traditional counterpart in Africa, is the one institution that lays claim, by reason of his vast knowledge, to the secret causes of anguish and distress: he alone is recognised, or has made himself known, as the source of relief and healing. Recourse to him is two-pronged: hope of healing and belief in his technical force and quasi-magical power of action. The mere fact of entering into dialogue and friendship with him is reassuring and relieves some of the distress. This is the mental state in which one beckons those whose calling is to be marabouts of development in Africa.

And indeed, the lack of development has drawn numerous marabouts and entire development marabout systems with a grand or chief marabout, imams, local and village marabouts, muezzins and other actors. There is no end to the recipes and prescriptions intended to bring the continent out of its maldevelopment, actualised and reviewed always by the development marabouts and prophets, with all the strength of these pretenders to knowledge who end up confusing the mind the more.

The marabout who comes bearing solutions to the existential distress of development in Africa is well known on the continent. He has been prescribing medicine for the development illness of Africa since independence. His prescriptions may have evolved, but the marabout remains the same, with the same basic canons and paradigms as the foundations of his development doctrine.

The 1960s and 1970s were decades of development by projects: industrial projects (import substitution strategies) as well as agricultural and infrastructural projects, all deeply marked by the climate of the Cold War. By the end of the 1970s, however, it was obvious that the system was in crisis: projects were no longer selling well; Africa was becoming more and more incapable of paying its debts; and exports were not bringing in enough to meet the internal and external expenditures of the system. This led the DMS to launch other recipes in the development market. Consequently, the third and fourth decades became the decades of economic and political reform policies, respectively.

The grand marabout has the power of:

1 information, making him a reference point, and endowing him with the authority this confers;
2 know-how and doctrinal inspiration, through the production of knowledge and analyses which without doubt are biased;
3 inspiration of ideas and (macro-economic and sectoral) development policies;
4 coordination of the development aid and loans system. He initiates development programmes, and determines the nature of the development goods for sale and the approach to follow. He coordinates and oversees the process and the intervention of other actors in the system. That way, he ensures that interventions are not made arbitrarily; more especially, he is able to control development policies in Africa and to choose those better suited to the interests of the DMS, and therefore to be supported. This function is so important that African countries themselves feel obliged to be on good business terms and to obtain a certificate of good conduct from the grand marabout, in order to be in the good books of the other members of the DMS;

5 finally, he has the power of *financial pressure* to ensure that DMS prescriptions are implemented.

At another level, the DMS comprises other marabouts and imams, small, medium and big, who function principally in bilateral exchanges. Over and above the common or integrated activities which they carry out within the system, they also carry out other specific activities according to sectors or geographical zones.

The small and middle-level marabouts do not really have a development doctrine as such. They prefer to leave that to the grand marabout, whom they are sure to have recourse to, at least for the basics and the essence of the doctrine.

The DMS functions especially through an army of small, local and village marabouts, muezzins, and other foot soldiers in the honourable cause of development business:

1 institutions more or less under the patronage of the grand marabout and/or one or several imams;
2 advisory and consultation organisations, to which should be added a multitude of technical cooperation officers;
3 so-called private enterprises for development, whether they be voluntary or non-governmental. The DMS reserves a particular place for such organisations as chartered engineers, research groups and NGOs, who act much like the boy scouts and courtesans of the DMS.

The DMS thus occupies the development terrain in Africa, not only in the domain of capital markets and other classical goods and services, but also in the more crucial area of development policies that have become both goods and framework for vending other development goods. Unfortunately for African countries, these are mainly mere development appearances. Development can be neither brought by nor bought from others, no matter how genuine their missionary zeal. That is why it has become necessary to take a hard look again at the development path of the continent in the 21st century and to redefine the nature and operational modality of the relationship with the DMS.

The DMS Strategic Arsenal

I have chosen to focus on four instruments, which I consider important in the current strategy of the DMS in Africa:

1 development aid and the recent politics of its reform;
2 economic reform policies;
3 political reforms and good governance policies; and, finally,
4 capacity-building policies.

Development aid

Development aid is a response to the theory of resource gaps: Africa lacks experts and technicians, capital, equipment, etcetera. Therefore, these have to be provided and acquired for its development. And the North gives itself this mission. This has been accepted and eagerly demanded by Africa.

However, after 40 years of aided development, the gaps have got wider and the need for development aid has increased. The instruments of aid programmes have been institutionalised and perpetuated, thus justifying and defending their existence, which is nothing but a confession of the failure of the aid programmes.

During the decades, development aid has become complex:

- it covers development and humanitarian work;
- it takes the form of technical cooperation, investment projects, non-project aid, food aid and military assistance;
- it covers the social sector as well;
- as it has evolved over the past 40 years, the first three decades of which were marked by the Cold War and ideological competition, the defining period saw a focus on the sale of infrastructural projects and white-elephant industrial and agricultural projects to countries chosen on the basis of their ideological leaning, the geopolitical situation and the economic interest they represented.

The crisis of the sale of projects and their debt-producing effects forced the DMS to change gear. The next phase saw the sale of adjustment and stabilisation policies, with aid attached to these policies in the form of non-project aid with given advantages to the system: rapid disbursement of loans; an enlarged framework for the sale of projects; and the integration of economic policies in the aid process. The 1990s also witnessed the enlargement of the aid (or DMS) field of action to the political domain with the political reform and governance programmes.

During the past four decades, the aid evolutionary process has been from project aid to programme aid, from tied aid to aid with conditionalities, but the foundational philosophy has remained the same: push for the insertion of Africa into the global market and for its political integration into the Western fold.

This is why the conditionality for the first two decades was to belong to the Western ideological camp. It was real political corruption. The conditionality for assistance in the third decade was the adoption of the economic reform policies of the Bretton Woods institutions, proof of tying the country's economy to globalisation and the guarantee of debt repayment. The conditionality for the fourth decade is political reform based on the Western model to ensure that African political institutions will not be a constraint or obstacle to economic globalisation, in the interest of the DMS.

The evaluations of aid programmes, including those made by donors themselves – such as the OECD's Development Assistance Committee (DAC) –

are not positive. This is why aid reform programmes are envisaged, although unfortunately they remain encased in the initial ideology, addressing technical aid management questions and not fundamental issues.

It is very unlikely that the development of a country can be run on an external motor, especially if this is a financial motor. On the other hand, studies have shown how development aid has mortgaged the future of Africa, how it has siphoned off the vital fluid and injected a political anodyne, how it has capitalized knowledge to the detriment of Africa and to the advantage of the donors, and, finally, how it detracts from the real task of development. That is why it is high time that African countries started to think about how to get out of the DMS.

Conditionality of economic reforms

The second important instrument in the strategic arsenal of the DMS is the conditionality of economic reforms as prescribed by the Bretton Woods institutions. In spite of these policies, dark clouds persist in the sky of the continent: lack of sustained growth, debt crisis, low foreign direct investment, insignificant place in world trade, increase in poverty and other negative indicators. That all these actually got worse while Africa underwent the prescribed treatment suggests that these economic reforms were not meant to end the African crisis so much as to solve a specific problem for the DMS countries.

There are two possible logical responses to this situation: the logic of development, which remains the profound aspiration of African populations, and that of debt repayment and extraverted growth within a process of economic globalisation controlled by the DMS.

On the side of the DMS, however, the crisis of liberal economies is characterised mainly by the fact that profits from production were accumulating without sufficient profitable investment outlets to relaunch production within the national segments of the system. This accumulated floating capital increased more rapidly during the oil boom of the 1970s. Management of the crisis from the standpoint of the major DMS countries consists of looking for outlets for this floating capital to avoid a massive and brutal devaluation that would lead to the collapse of the system.

We can understand, therefore, the role the DMS assigned itself as grand marabout of the system in the management of the crisis: to push for (if not to impose) economic liberalisation in developing countries as well as those of Eastern Europe, and to subject these economies to the obligation of debt repayment while managing the flow of funds and discovering the programme and policy frameworks that will open up other investment perspectives. It is well known that the major strategic decisions of limited exceptions to these rules or to their functioning are made by the G7, or prepared in a doctrinal management framework like the World Economic Forum or other meetings of the OECD. Economic reforms in

Africa, therefore, are to be analysed in this perspective and not in that of the conventional literature on the subject. This is why these reforms are the conditionality on which assistance from the DMS depends.

The myth of growth through accessing foreign markets, attracting foreign direct investment, and, finally, debt reduction (or even possible cancellation) has been propagated as the expected result of the right application of these economic reform programmes. None of that has been proven. A word on Africa's debt: one should not forget that it was contracted on market terms. This may have benefited African leaders, but also, no doubt, the lenders. Further, the projects financed by the debt, which today are found to be hardly profitable, were technically conceived by or with the help of experts of the DMS. For its part, the DMS only financed projects in line with its interests − export sector, infrastructure, opening up of markets for its enterprises, etcetera − thus contributing to economic growth in DMS countries while employing their money with interest and putting African countries heavily into debt.

Seen from this point of view, economic reforms are meant not only to ensure that debt is repaid, but more especially to steer the adjustment of African economies so as to allow for their insertion in the process of globalisation, and to control the march and progress of these economies along the prescribed route. But, as earlier indicated, the theoretical benefits and opportunities that globalisation will open to African countries that come under the tutelage of the DMS are not evident. On the contrary, the risks and the menace to the prosperity of African countries in the sense of their sustainable human development (SHD) confirm that globalisation is actually a process of polarisation, marginalising and even excluding many (especially African) populations from its benefits.

Economic growth in the 1980s and 1990s − decades during which Africa has been undergoing economic reform programmes − shows clearly that these programmes failed to achieve their announced objectives, because growth fell sharply overall in the continent.

The globalisation of market fundamentalism and its paradigm is in reality nothing but a regime for keeping developing countries in step, addressing Africa as an object rather than as a partner. This is why I term it the *globalitarisation* of African economies. A controlled integration into globalisation, with the active role of the state, would position Africa better as a partner and subject, and make it less marginalised and polarised as it joins the globalisation process.

Conditionality of good governance and democratisation

The third important instrument in the DMS strategic arsenal is the good governance and democratisation conditionality. For decades, the DMS ignored the political dimension of development, seeing only the technical dimension in it. The ongoing crisis of African economic systems has continued to exclude and marginalise large segments of the population because the reform policies that were adopted had such a narrow social base. In various countries their political components were very similar, with strong single-party regimes and the crushing of civil society emerging as central features.

Structural adjustment programmes (SAPs) contributed to the exacerbation of the contradictions inherent in the economic and political systems, the adjustment burden being principally borne by the poor countries and masses, notably through significant budgetary cuts with negative effects on economic and social conditions. The debate over development models and structural adjustment solutions quickly turned into a critical focus on the political regimes responsible for applying and in many cases imposing SAPs. The necessity of political reforms now began to appear at the centre of the DMS approach.

The DMS now emphasised that economic reforms and the process of integration into the world economy should be accepted by the main economic and social forces in African countries, so removing any popular basis for contesting the implementation of adjustment. To this end, these forces should participate in adjustment policies and also have confidence in their political leaders, who in turn are required to be accountable to their populations and their economic and social stakeholders. In a nutshell, this is the origin of the good governance and democratisation ideas.

Good governance, of course, is understood to mean political regimes managing public affairs according to the world market creed and following the Western model. Any political regime able to carry out its economic and financial reforms effectively, to manage its incorporation into the world economy while controlling internal forces, is lauded to the sky even if it does not abide by all the rules of the democratic game. This is because it has met the core objective assigned to it by the system. The capacity of these regimes to resist or to remain adamant in the face of popular opposition to economic reform policies is part of 'good' governance. The state is thus instrumentalised in the service of market fundamentalism.

Let us recall that a preoccupation with good governance and democratisation appeared following the end of the Cold War and in the context of an acceleration of the globalisation process. By its very nature and functioning, the latter produces growing inequality between the rich countries of the North and the poor countries of the South, and between a few rich segments of the ruling class and the large poor segments of the population within the same country. The polarisation, marginalisation and exclusion that result create socio-political tension with a potential to cause social explosion known only too well. This suggests the prime function of the governance concept as a new DMS conditionality: to manage the contradictions within the globalisation process generated by economic reforms.

This so-called 'good' governance, with its democratisation of the adjustment process, is not the governance that Africa craves. The continent needs another development model in which the political component is the democratisation of the development process: development socialisation. This assigns priority to the national community's interests, implying a subjection of external relations to national priorities, collective and permanent social dialogue, true participation by the masses in choices and decisions concerning their likes, and the accountability and responsibility of ruling bodies and individuals at all levels. It is the democratisation of political, economic and social spheres.

Capacity-building policy in Africa

The fourth important instrument is the policy of capacity building in Africa. In the wake of the gaps theory, it is estimated that Africa suffers from a significant competence deficit, which could be remedied by the West through the provision of technical expertise or technical cooperation (TC). The declared objective is two-fold: on the one hand, aiding African countries to identify, define, implement, negotiate financing for and manage development projects, and, on the other hand, transferring knowledge and know-how to the African counterpart.

The evaluation of several decades of TC has shown that it has not achieved these objectives. The DMS thinks, therefore, that it is necessary to reform TC policies. But in reality, the unacknowledged DMS objectives of TC *have* been achieved: they are all about rendering service to the DMS through markets opening up, supervision of the spending of the loans and grants, tying down of African client countries, and so on. It is for this reason that, in the light of the aid system to which it belongs, TC has become an established system that lives, functions and reproduces itself as such, and not to fill any vacuum.

The capacity-building concept appeared in connection with two series of events: the failure of TC and that of SAPs. In fact, the capacity-building approach appeared within the resistance to and slowness in the implementation of economic reform policies. It is therefore also connected with slowness in the sale of projects tied to economic reform and, of course, with the African debt crisis.

The basic idea is that if the different technical and social forces that are contesting or resisting reform policies are involved in their formulation, they will internalise them and cease to resist their implementation. Indeed, they will become the real players and advocates of the DMS. African governments will then have fewer internal disputes. It is for this reason that they need to be trained and to build capacities related to the appropriation of reform policies in their diverse generations, allowing them to formulate and implement policies that comply with DMS strategies, for only these can be approved, financed and declared to be good economic policies. The capacity to elaborate other policies, particularly if they tend to extricate Africa from the lap of the DMS and to give it a large autonomy, are by the same token unacceptable.

It is for this reason that capacity building, as it is understood today by the DMS, involves all the major players that could contest economic reforms: the state and public institutions, the private sector, and important segments of civil society. In terms of operational instruments, the DMS advocates education and training in economic management or development management in general, redefined TC, exchange of experts or the pairing of African institutions with those in the North, the establishment of the African Capacity Building Foundation (ACBF) in Harare and the creation of centres of excellence.

In order to accelerate the implementation of its projects and reform programmes, and to that end the disbursement of funds, particularly when it comes to loans, the DMS has gone to the extent of paying salary components or incentives to civil servants involved in the implementation of these projects and reform programmes. By so doing, the system corrupts the administrative system of every African country. Even though African countries have trained many of their managing staff in all development domains, it should be recognised that on this count the DMS itself has contributed to the weakening of capacities in Africa.

To begin with, it has ended up transforming African administrations into local administrations in the given areas of projects and programmes that it is financing. These administrations are kept busy managing not their own development strategies, but rather the portfolios of projects financed by lenders. They also spend a lot of their time rendering account during periodic monitoring missions. When necessary, the DMS has created parallel structures for the management of its projects and programmes, excluding African administrations.

Africa's Challenge in the 21st Century

The 21st century should witness the historic writing of the development chapter for Africa. One may hope that this will take the form of a battle involving all African actors in extricating the continent from the impasse of the present paradigm, and embarking on the collective writing of a new development paradigm.

In this perspective, one should recall that human development concerns the future and what will become of people and countries. It involves the transformation of structures and socio-economic and political relationships, and is a field for the confrontation of groups, countries and interests. This confrontation manifests in the theoretical, ideological, economic, political, social and cultural dimensions of the whole process. Both the internal and external levels, notably as between Africa and the DMS, are also in play.

It is well known that we are not witnessing a united or unique world of growth and development transmission from the North towards the South, but rather two worlds resulting partially from the growth failure in more than a hundred countries in the world, where *per capita* income has gone below what it used to be 25 years ago! In 70 developing countries, income levels are below those of the 1960s and 1970s!

Let us recall that the proportion between the incomes of 20 per cent of the wealthiest households and those of the poorest households has widened from 30 : 1 in 1960, to 60 : 1 in 1990 and to 74 : 1 in 1997! Within the same periods, the 20 per cent of the poorest households witnessed a drop in their own share of global income from 2.3 per cent to 1.4 per cent. The developing countries account for 80 per cent of world population but only 20 per cent of global production.

Indeed, there is a *triple crisis* that characterises this situation: the *crisis of the state*, whose role as a dynamic and important development agent or actor is no longer recognised; the *crisis of the market* itself, which, even though considered the most appropriate institution to ensure continuous growth for the benefit of all, has not succeeded in this task; finally, the *crisis of science,* which, even though it has achieved remarkable progress, has not succeeded in steering the world away from disproportionate and deepening inequality. Yet we remain prisoners of the dominant, conventional strand of development theory, despite its failure to throw the needed light on development analysis and practice.

We need a common understanding of the content of the development concept. It can have an *explanatory* theoretical status, referring us to a thought concrete whose present and future functioning mechanisms and rules can be known and applied by imitation or adaptation. But the concept can also have a *normative* theoretical status: it then refers us to a norm or values, an ideal or an ethic that can be constructed. It defines the functioning rules and mechanisms as well as the required practices.

The conventional development theory and paradigm, which has been dominant during the last 50 years and continues to enjoy the support of numerous development analysts and practitioners, is based on the first apprehension of the concept. The alternative approaches which are based on the second apprehension, and which include the SHD paradigm, have remained marginalised for a long time, often without the support of practitioners, dismissed and ridiculed as utopian dreams or as theories in the pejorative sense of the term.

The conventional approach, in spite of some variants, could be characterised as linear: for it, there is only one way to salvation, which all countries should follow – *market fundamentalism* and the *liberal economy*. The stake for those who are late to set out or behind on this path is to catch up with the others or at least hang on to them. The appropriate strategy is to follow the route recommended by those who are ahead and in all things to imitate them, because it is on these conditions that the DMS will provide its aid. Africa has therefore taken it upon itself to follow the litany of recommended strategies and prescriptions from development marabouts. System merits were praised, economic take-off and growth miracles were said to be perceived or even achieved here and there. But the system started to run out of breath: projects were no longer selling well; indebtedness was becoming overwhelming; exports were no longer bringing in enough; the well-being of the masses was no longer being addressed. Perceived development miracles now appeared in their true reality: development appearances and trade were no longer deceiving anyone. The recriminations of humanists were beginning to be heard in the denunciation of the development model and the ruling paradigm.

It is in this movement that alternative approaches progressively began to be heard. They are characterised not only by their ethical vision and their analysis of the failure of the development path mapped by conventional theory, but also by their recognition of the diversity of development paths that countries could follow rather than adhering to the monorail of market fundamentalism. But most distinctive is their reversal of values: for them, the quality of human life is no longer secondary in the development paradigm, or rather is no longer considered as simply dependent on the maximization of wealth and economic growth. The human person, moreover, is no longer perceived as a mere factor of production in creating the nation's wealth. On the contrary, it is the quality of human lives that constitutes the central paradigm, while wealth maximization becomes a contributing factor. We look for riches to achieve an ideal: improving the lives of the masses, now and in the future.

Such an approach has a number of implications: the importance of investing in human resources and basic social services; the strategic role of the state in guaranteeing collective well-being; the availability of information, values and reference indicators for the formulation and implementation of SHD policies; and a general emphasis on the socio-cultural and socio-institutional dimensions of development. It is thus not only the overall perception of the aim of development that changes: so also do development priorities and strategies; the roles of different actors in the process (government, private sector, civil society, communities); and the chosen instruments and measurements of human development progress.

The Path for Africa in the 21st Century

If this is what constitutes the real meaning and reach of the development paradigm that Africa should build during this 21st century, how is it to be done? One should recall that the globalisation process occurs simultaneously with (and partly through) struggles and competitions between the DMS powers – over their market stakes, communication technologies, access to natural resources and the environment, electronics and space – in which Africa has almost no say. As the saying goes, when the elephants of the DMS fight –and they do fight – it is the African grass that suffers.

Would it be advisable for Africa to struggle towards the destruction of the DMS or simply to surrender to the functioning of its machine, under the pretext that it is the only way to salvation? The first option is mission impossible and suicidal. The DMS is simply too powerful for Africa, which is becoming progressively weaker and more dependent. The second option is also catastrophic for the continent, as the experience of 40 years of assisted development has shown. In spite of repeated DMS songs and sermons, sustainable development has proved elusive. Between these two extremes, there is, without doubt, another possible way: another development path, another kind of partnership and more significant coordinates of influence for the Africa of tomorrow on the global chessboard. As a matter of fact, is this not the outcome that China has been trying to achieve with the resources at its disposal?

Three principles can guide Africa in this direction. First, the principle of *internalisation of the accumulation base* means that the main economic function is realised at the level of the national or subregional market, and that basic sectors of economic accumulation engage in relationships not of the extortion type but rather of surplus exchange with the other sectors, with a view to ensuring sustained development.

Second, the *enlargement of the social base of development* signifies, on one hand, that relationships of surplus exchange are established between the different components of the population through the economic and social sectors that they represent. And on the other hand, it signifies that the people participate fully in the development process in its political, economic and social dimensions.

Third, the prerequisite and permanent principle is *the existence of peace and political stability*.

These principles should constitute the base of the three main development objectives of the continent in the 21st century:

- the building of peace and political and social stability;
- a sustained, endogenous and equitable economic growth;
- the improvement of the well-being of the population and the ending of human poverty.

To accomplish these, Africa will have to meet certain specific and daunting challenges:

- control of a population growth rate that remains high;
- good governance and democratisation in the idiom of development socialisation rather than structural adjustment;
- the development of an African tradition of excellence in science and technology;
- the successful management of environmental resources.

This requires, of course, another development strategy which includes both transversal and sectoral components. Amongst the transversal components, we can mention:

- controlled insertion in the globalisation process, grounding economic growth on domestic resources and investments and on internal and regional markets, and then accelerating sustainable and equitable economic growth on those foundations;
- effective and efficient public management;
- increasing economic integration at national and regional levels;

- international competitiveness based on African capacity to utilise the world economy in terms of the requirements of endogenised, sustainable and equitable growth;
- development of human and institutional capacities.

The sectoral components of the strategy will also be based on some important principles: which sectors have the greatest potential for sustainable economic growth and for accumulation, with capability for the development of other sectors in the model; the satisfaction of basic economic and social needs; and the amelioration of the human development index.

Managing this strategy for African countries means having the capacity to anticipate, plan for the future and outline the routes required by defined objectives; to mobilise available and potential resources; to guide, manage and monitor the implementation of the strategy; and to continuously manage the change through all its phases. Managing the development process is therefore about knowing how to mobilise the given resources and use them as factors and agents of change and transformation in an efficient and effective manner. But it also implies knowing how to define the respective roles of the major actors (government, the African private sector, civil society and external partners), and coordinating the dynamics of the whole so that each category of actors fulfils its role in a productive partnership.

Conclusion

The world is being globalised and Africa cannot afford to stay out of the process. But it cannot resign itself to entering this passage with both hands and legs bound. It has to be a player and handle its insertion into a dynamic process in the light of the self-defined development path that is best for the well-being of its people. Locating the African continent within the contemporary dynamic of human development means contributing to the building of a polycentrist and multipolar world in the interest of all, and contrary to the current unipolarisation of the globalisation process. The polycentric and multipolar approach, moreover, is not only economic and financial but also conceptual, including issues related to development thinking.

It has been my intention to share another reading of the African reality, and to discuss the management of an autonomous development strategy for Africa within the context of globalisation in the 21st century, bringing the economic and political liberalisation of a continent marginalised in the global chess game. I wish to participate in the discussion that African intellectuals, in a bid to serve the people of their continent, want to hold on its future in the wake of the 20th century. It is more than high time that such a debate should be reappropriated by Africans exercising that fundamental right – to reflect and decide on one's future – of which all other actions and efforts are only concrete manifestations.

But here lies a major risk. Whenever African intellectuals feel happy and satisfied in speaking out and relieving their consciences, convinced of their mission to tell world leaders what they believe the latter do not know, they run the risk of adding to the confusion of existing productions: all those studies, reports, predictions and prescriptions of the development prophets and marabouts.

African intellectuals continue to preach – and I do it with them – but the scope and effectiveness of their discourse is not quite evident. They have neither the political and social power, nor the economic weight that will enable them to communicate their message. There is, therefore, the issue of the conditions that frame a new discourse on an autonomous strategy for Africa and, in the same vein, the issue of identifying the enablers of such a discourse and the possibility of its implementation. When African intellectuals speak, who is their target audience? Is it political leaders who can effortlessly ignore them, claiming the clear day of political realism against the half-lit utopian dreamworld of intellectuals?

In any case, the implementation of an autonomous development strategy requires another African leadership. The continent has had leaders who struggled for her liberation from colonialism, who had a nationalist vision of their country's future, and who were able to mobilise their people around the ideals of this vision. It is for this reason that the first 15 to 20 years of independence were years of economic and social progress for Africa. In order to receive support and be sustained, this founding effort now needs to be followed by another type of leadership. Development leadership must succeed that of political liberation, whose historic mission can be considered terminated. This is the big challenge for Africa today and tomorrow: finding ways and means of bringing to political power development leaders who incarnate another development vision that can galvanise the continent to address the current and future challenges of development socialisation in a globalising world. Such development-oriented political leaders must be well and truly educated – educated enough to know the true meaning of holistic human development, and the imperative of putting their money where their mouth is.

Bibliography

Kankwenda, Mbaya (2000) *Marabouts ou Marchands du Développement en Afrique?*, Paris: L'Harmattan.

2

Mobilisation for the Implementation of Alternative Development Paradigms in 21st-Century Africa
Bade Onimode

After the lost decade of the 1980s, the deepening of the African crisis through the 1990s in spite of efforts to achieve Africa's second liberation, the massive adjustment of the African political economy to date and the search for alternative development during the last two decades, Africa must now grapple with new priorities. We cannot be seeking alternative development strategies and adjusting indefinitely while the region's development is held up (Adedeji, 1990).

This is why this Millennium Symposium must grapple with basic new priorities for Africa. These are the identification of existing alternative development paradigms that are feasible for African countries; urgent and systematic mobilisation of social forces for the practical implementation of these alternative development paradigms and strategies; the articulation and clarification of the African Agenda for the 21st century; and the crafting of the political programme for the realisation of this African Agenda in collaboration with the South Agenda for the 21st century (South Centre, 1999).

Unless Africa focuses on these priorities and mobilises seriously for their implementation, much of this new and highly competitive century of globalisation may be wasted needlessly in the pursuit of diversionary and counter-productive, foreign-dictated programmes for Africa and for partnership between Africa and the developed North. As a background to all these concerns, it is well to recapitulate the main issues in the African crisis and the main conclusions of the search for alternative development in the last two decades.

Africa's Crises and the Search for Alternative Development

Africa spent most of the 1980s and 1990s trying to cope with its composite crisis, implementing foreign-imposed adjustment programmes and searching for alternative development paradigms and strategies. The main conclusions of the different analyses of the African crisis are first, that the crisis has been a composite

socio-economic set of crises with significant economic, political, social, environmental and other components (Onimode, 1989).

Second, that the region's excessive external dependence and the increasing
hostility of the international economic environment from the late 1970s triggered
the crises. This was mainly through the collapse of the world commodity trade
from about 1978, the failure of African integration and the consequent foreign
debt crisis into which the region was plunged (Adedeji, 1993). Poor governance,
involving pervasive lack of democracy, denial of human rights and the crisis of the
legitimacy of authority – which encouraged military dictatorships, political
instability and widespread conflicts – also featured (Anyang' Nyong'o, 1990;
Mamdani 1983).

There were problems of poor management of resources and the economy.
These involved stinking corruption, massive looting of the state by the élites
(political, military, bureaucratic and business) and widespread internal policy
failures (Onimode, 1989).

As the crises deepened into the 1990s, two other elements were added: the
disastrous failure of the SAPs or economic reforms for external debt relief imposed
by the IMF and the World Bank; and the unprecedented marginalisation of Africa
on all fronts (Adedeji, 1993).

With the persistence of the African crisis, the search for alternative development paradigms and strategies was intensified and it has yielded some important
results that bear itemising here.

- *Human or people-centred development*, an approach that has adopted the slogan
  'Putting the People First'. This was indeed the theme of the International
  Conference on Popular Participation in the Recovery and Development
  process in Africa, organised by the ECA at Arusha, Tanzania, in February 1990.
  Its historic outcome was the African Charter for Popular Participation in
  Development and Transformation, popularly known as 'Africa's Magna Carta'.
  This is a rejection of the 'commodity fetishism' and putrid economism of the
  Western developmentalist or modernisation ideology that has been foisted on
  Africa (Ake, 1984). The basic points of this alternative development paradigm
  are that people are the most crucial catalysts of the development process and its
  ultimate beneficiaries. Hence the need for new or alternative measures of
  development and progress such as the Human Development Index (HDI) and
  the Human Poverty Index (HPI) (UNDP, various years).

- *The African Alternative to SAP (AAF–SAP)*, produced by the ECA in 1989,
  adopted by the OAU and endorsed by the General Assembly of the United
  Nations as the most elaborate and most technically sophisticated alternative
  recovery-with-development paradigm for Africa (ECA, 1989). But as soon as
  it was produced, the World Bank, in its traditional parallelism of imposing

alternative blueprints to those prepared by Africa, launched its laborious Long-Term Perspective Study, (LTPS, World Bank, 1989). This has been a main cause of the avoidance of the AAF–SAP by African countries and their failure to implement it to date.

- *African Integration in the Lagos Plan of Action (LPA) and Abuja Treaty for the establishment of the African Economic Community.* The LPA had been formulated for 1980–2000 to promote African integration and cooperation in order to forestall a general collapse of regional trade (OAU, 1980). But the World Bank opposed it. Instead of the inward-looking strategy for collective regional and subregional self-reliance advocated in the LPA, the Bank produced its counter, Agenda for Action, which foisted an outward-looking strategy of external dependence on the region (World Bank, 1980). Again, the Bank won and Africa lost. In 1991, as part of the efforts at the Second Liberation of Africa in the 1990s, the Abuja Treaty for the creation of an African Economic Community was signed, but its pace of implementation has been slow.

- *Participatory development.* This is one of the best strategies of development to emerge from the ruins of the crises of the 1980s. The United Nations Development Programme (UNDP) and the world NGO community have been instrumental in propagating it, especially at sub-national levels. The basic ideas are to democratise the development process; involve all social forces, women and mass organisations in it; promote transparency and accountability; release more popular energies for development; improve development priorities and promote self-development. The impact has been tremendous and truly salutary.

- *Bottom-up development* emphasises the need to modify élitist and paternalistic approaches to development, which marginalised and alienated the majority of the population. Instead, it demands that the process should start with the legitimate aspirations and priorities of the grassroots and rural majority (Adedeji and Ayo, 2000).

- *Sustainable development.* The debates on alternative development in the last two decades also led to the articulation and promotion of sustainable development. After Davidson's *False Start in Africa* (1984) and the spread of the world environmental movement, sustainable development became a dominant pre-occupation of development. The concerns are to ensure that the development process should become self-sustaining rather than dependent on foreign aid; be environmentally friendly; and promote gender and inter-generational equity. The UNDP has also been a major global catalyst of the strategy (UNDP, various years).

- *South Africa's Reconstruction and Development Programme (RPD).* This is a solid new structure on the ruins of apartheid and the boldest practical project yet to be put forward for implementing alternative development in Africa. The disastrous failure of SAPs across Africa, on one hand, and the political courage and clear 'African Renaissance' vision of South Africa and Mandela on the other, have contributed to the design and sustained implementation of the RPD – in spite of South Africa's recent economic problems (South Africa, 1993; Adedeji 1996).

The evaluation of the SAP experience across African countries has revealed that as the dominant economic programme foisted on Africa in the 1980s and 1990s, SAPs have been a catastrophic failure. It has contributed to increasing mass poverty and the collapse of the real economy of production in various sectors across the region, and promoted deindustrialisation, rising inflation and the growing marginalisation of Africa (Corina *et al.*, 1987; Onimode, 1992). This manifest failure of a dominant paradigm in Africa makes the implementation of alternative development paradigms more imperative. Indeed, it is the dogmatic insistence of the IMF and World Bank as well as their creditors and sponsors that has been the main obstacle to the implementation of alternative development strategies and programmes across Africa. As we enter the 21st century, all this must change. African countries must rise collectively with the African Union (AU) to demand that enough is enough. This region cannot continue to be the guinea-pig for an unprecedented social experiment that has been such a sustained and colossal failure (Mihevc, 1995; Chossudovsky, 1998).

The Increasing Relevance of Alternative Development Paradigms

Several developments across Africa and the rest of the world have been demonstrating the increasing relevance of alternative development paradigms. These bear summarising, too.

One is the widely publicised propaganda about the breakdown of the Washington Consensus on structural adjustment and external debt management. Whether the news is true or not, we must ensure that the collapse of the Consensus is realised. There must be increased resistance and pressure against IMF–World Bank conditionalties and mismanagement of Africa and other Third World regions. The visible openings in the World Bank's position – on the need for the role of the state in development, the imperative of people-centred development and the need for countries to own and design their national recovery programmes – should be pursued and widened (Shutt, 1998).

The collapse of the Bretton Woods international economic and financial system, and the growing international clamour for its replacement, is another positive turn of events that should be utilised for the pursuit of alternative development options. The increasing failure of the strategies and unchanging prescription of the system is a clear signal that alternative paradigms and programmes must be implemented in Africa and the rest of the South. Indeed, there are now specific proposals for the restructuring of both the World Bank and the IMF. These include the exclusion of the mandate of both institutions from questions of structural adjustment and economic recovery in developing countries: the demand that the Bank should concentrate mainly on mobilising development finance for poor countries, while the Fund focuses on being a World central bank and expanding international liquidity as a global lender of last resort (Killick, 1995; Amin, 1998).

The deterioration of the African political economy provides an equally compelling case for implementing alternative development paradigm strategies. If a medium-term adjustment programme has not worked in some 20 years, it must be fatally flawed, socially irrelevant and overdue for replacement. Far from achieving stated objectives such as sustained high growth rates, increasing exports and promotion of foreign investment, SAPs have aggravated the crises in African countries.

Given these extremely discouraging results, it is hard not to conclude that even from the early 1990s alternative development programmes should have been taking root across Africa (Adedeji, 1993; Onimode, 1992). In far-away Russia, orthodox IMF–World Bank economic reforms have also been a catastrophic failure. Indeed, the Russian disaster has been so embarrassing that additional funding has been poured into the country to stave off a major regional collapse. This is one of the reasons why Chossudovsky has argued quite persuasively that orthodox adjustment has been a programme for the 'globalisation of poverty' across the Third World (Chossudovsky, 1998).

The performance and result of South Africa's Reconstruction and Development Programme (RDP) – in spite of Western hostility and recent economic problems – have also been very impressive. This is one major reason why the SADC subregion, for example, has performed so much better than the rest of sub-Sahara Africa. The political imperative of mass pressures from below – from social organisations, NGOs, trade unions and other progressive mass movements – for alternative development is equally very clear and becoming more compelling. There are increasing signs that some of these pressures from below have a revolutionary potential and that impatience is growing amongst the majority of the population of African countries with rising poverty, chronic mass unemployment and the abusive neglect by the social minority of parasites and predators across Africa. With increasing popular participation in development, these angry and impatient social forces are the energies to be mobilised for demanding the urgent implementation of alternative development strategies across Africa.

The Implementation of Alternative Development and the African Agenda for the 21st Century

The implementation of alternative development paradigms and strategies in Africa should be carefully integrated into the global and South contexts. This requires some interrelated regional projects. These are:

- appreciation of the megatrends of the new millennium and the new century;
- the crafting of the African Agenda for meeting the challenges and opportunities for Africa in this 21st century;
- the role of the African intelligentsia in all these;
- the elaboration of specific anti-debt and anti-SAP programmes for the region;
- the formulation of the political programme for implementing the African Agenda;
- collaborative linkage of the African Agenda with the South Agenda;
- strategic engagement between the South and the North to be resumed, for example over the new World Trade Organisation (WTO) and its trade-related aspects of intellectual property rights (TRIPs) and Multilateral Agreement on Investment (MAI), regulation of the world economy, augmentation of development finance for the South, restructuring of the Bank and Fund, and reform of the UN system (Onimode, 2000).

At the global level, some of the megatrends of the world in transition to the 21st century include the new information technology; the prospects of winners and losers in biotech agriculture; the new world trading system (Lang and Hines, 1993); increasing global inequalities and the threat of the world democratic revolution; declining high quality world leadership and the need for the re-education of the public on these issues (Kennedy, 1993; Naisbitt and Aburdene, 1990).

This is the global context that defines the major challenges and opportunities that will confront Africa in this century. The major challenges include the termination of conflicts across the region in order to secure peace and stability for development; achievement of national food security and regional food self-sufficiency; accelerated establishment of regional and subregional cooperation; efforts to ensure popular governance and public accountability; women's liberation and environmental protection; control of AIDS/HIV together with an effective population policy; and the ending of illiteracy, mass poverty and the marginalisation of Africa.

These significant opportunities for Africa in this new century include the achievement of peace and security in the region through the activities of sub-regional and regional peacekeeping forces like ECOMOG in West Africa; the continuing democratisation of African political economies for effective popular participation in governance and development; the beginning of an anti-corruption campaign in African countries to ensure accountability and transparency in governance and national economic management; the pursuit of new approaches to regional and subregional cooperation such as the use of taxes for financing integration, the new Free Trade Area in the Southern African Development Community (SADC) and the continuing focus on the realisation of the African Economic Community; and the awakening of African interest in the global telecommunications revolution in the new competitive world economy of globalisation.

The African Agenda for the 21st century has to be crafted carefully to deal with these main challenges and opportunities. This is a collaboration effort for national, subregional and regional cooperation and coordination. The African intelligentsia has a very critical role to play.

- The mobilisation of social forces for the implementation of alternative development paradigms and the elaboration of the African Agenda for tackling the region's challenges and opportunities is partly the task of the African intelligentsia. More than ever before, its members must rise to their historic challenge of leading, charting and promoting the liberation of the African region. They played this role marvellously during the anti-colonial liberation struggles. The African intelligentsia in this new phase of regional development and transition must assist in articulating a vision for Africa.

- It has to inspire political leaders and the general public with this vision. The African intelligentsia should also participate actively in mass organisations by providing leadership, training and networking mechanisms among NGOs and other social movements. The defence of the interests and aspirations of African countries, especially at the international level, should be the consistent pre-occupation of the African intelligentsia. Correspondingly, they should withdraw their support and cooperation from counterproductive repressive regimes, social groups and ideologies (Amin, 1998). Then, there are programmes for economic reconstruction to be prepared. The intelligentsia must also systematically critique economic, political and social praxis in African countries. They should also assist in linking African countries systematically with the rest of the South and the rest of the world in this new phase of globalisation. More than ever before, the African intelligentsia must rise to their historic challenge of leading, charting and promoting the second (economic) liberation of Africa. They played this role marvellously during the anti-colonial (first) liberation struggles.

- The African intelligentsia can also assist in preparing appropriate and efficient national external debt management strategies and in the implementation of alternative programmes to failed SAPs. The starting point in the resolution of the external debt crisis is the realisation that it is also – and fundamentally – a political question. This means that African countries must act collectively through the OAU to press for: (1) debt cancellation – the Heavily Indebted Poor Country (HIPC) Initiatives are mainly delaying tactics; (2) debt–loot swap – Africa's stolen billions in Western countries should be used partly for repaying the region's debts. Western retaliatory measures against debt repudiation can be countered successfully by African counter-retaliatory measures (Payer, 1992; George, 1993).

As for anti-SAP measures, Africa must now demand that (1) foreign debt relief should be separated from economic reforms or structural adjustment imposed by the IMF–World Bank, because these reforms have failed disastrously; (2) as part of the exercise of national sovereignty, each country must design and own its recovery-with-transformation programme; (3) such national reconstruction programmes can be based on the AAF–SAP and other alternative development paradigms (Mihevc, 1995; Chossudovsky, 1998).

For obvious reasons, Africa alone cannot engage the rest of the world in the 21st century. So the African agenda has to be linked strategically to the South Agenda. This is to ensure effective strategic engagement between Africa and the South, on one hand, and between the South and North, on the other hand. Some of the major issues in the Africa–South linkage for negotiation with the North are:

1 reform of the WTO – not another Uruguay Round, but through negotiation on the existing agreements;
2 review of the issues involved in TRIPs (technology), MAI (foreign investment) and trade-related investment measures (TRIMs) (trade in services);
3 expansion of development finance and liquidity to the South;
4 review of collapsed international trade agreements and the new protectionism in the North;
5 North–South collaboration on the protection of our commons – especially on Agenda 21;
6 reform of the IMF, the World Bank and the UN system (Onimode, 2000).

Conclusion – a Political Programme for the Realisation of the African Agenda

The implementation of alternative development paradigms and the realisation of the overall African socio-economic goals for the 21st century require a political programme. This programme involves some specific tasks at national, subregional and regional levels (Amin, 1998).

The first is the development of broad consensus around the elements of alternative development and the African Agenda. These have to be disseminated widely through the media and at mass meetings, seminars, conferences, symposia, etcetera. This is to create a broad awareness about the issues involved. Then the social forces in civil society that will implement these programmes have to be identified and targeted. These are the social groups that stand to benefit most from the implementation of alternative development and the realisation of the African Agenda: the excluded middle and lower rungs of society, the trade unions, NGOs, youth and women's organisations, peasants, patriotic professionals, progressive politicians and clergy. Networking among these social forces or branches of civil society is crucial. They need to coordinate their activities with periodic consultative meetings in order to share information, plan common strategies and pool their typically fragile resources, especially funds and technology.

These social forces must then mount economic, political and social pressures on the legislative bodies and other organs of the state. This is to create the will in the political leadership to implement alternative development and pursue the African Agenda. This lack of will and vision is one of the most serious weaknesses of the political leadership in Africa – they are mostly neocolonial and comprador elements with a crippling loyalty to foreign masters. Pressure from below is required to reorient them to focus on national, subregional and regional priorities.

All these require the reconstruction of the authoritarian post-colonial state and politics across the African continent. The radical and unrelenting democratisation of politics, the state, society and economy is central to all these. A powerful anti-militarisation programme is needed to topple cliques in power and end abusive and reactionary military dictatorship. Political space must be created at all levels of society to ensure popular participation in politics, governance and development. This is what is needed to root out pervasive corruption and ensure transparency and public accountability (ECA, 1990).

Through these initiatives, social forces can be mobilised for the implementation of alternative development paradigms and strategies, and the realisation of the African Agenda for the 21st century can proceed. These programmes should be linked systematically, however, to the South Agenda for Strategic Engagement between Africa and the rest of the South, with the North. Africa must unite, but it should not try to go it alone – in spite of differentiation within the South (South Centre, 1999). *The factors and issues that unite Africa and the South are greater than those that divide them.*

Bibliography

Adedeji, Adebayo (1990) *Preparing Africa for the 21st Century – Agenda for the 1990s*, Addis Ababa: ECA.
——— (1993) *Africa and the World: Beyond Dispossession and Dependence*, London: Zed Books.
Adedeji, Adebayo (ed.) (1996) *South Africa and Africa: Within or Apart?* London: Zed Books;

Cape Town: SADRI Books; Ijebu Ode: ACDESS.

Adedeji, Adebayo and B. Ayo (eds.) (2000) *People-Centred Democracy in Nigeria?* Ibadan: Heinemann and ACDESS.

Ake, Claude (1984) *Revolutionary Pressures from Africa*, London: Zed Books.

Amin, S. (1998) *Capitalism in the Age of Globalisation*, London: Zed Books.

Anyang' Nyong'o, P. (1990) *Popular Struggles for Democracy in Africa*, London: Zed Books.

Chossudovsky, M. (1998) *The Globalisation of Poverty – Impacts of IMF and World Bank Reforms*, London: Zed Books.

Corina, G. A. *et al.* (1987*) Adjustment with a Human Face*, Vol. 1, New York: Oxford University Press and UN Children's Fund (UNICEF).

ECA (1989) *The African Alternative Framework to SAP* (AAF–SAP), Addis Ababa: ECA.

—— (1990) *African Charter for Popular Participation in Development*, Addis Ababa: Economic Commission for Africa.

George, S. (1993) 'The Uses and Abuses of the African Debt', in A. Adedeji (ed.), *Africa and the World*.

Kennedy, P. (1993) *Preparing for the 21st Century*, New Delhi: Indus.

Killick, T. (1995) 'Can the IMF Help Low-Income Countries – Experience with Its Structural Adjustment Facilities', *World Economy,* 18 (June).

Lang, T. and C. Hines (1993) *The New Protectionism – Protecting the Future Against Free Trade*, London: Earthscan.

Mamdani, Mahmoud (1983) *Imperialism and Fascism in Uganda*, London: Africa World Press.

Mihevc, J. (1995) *The Market Tells Us So – World Bank and Economic Fundamentalism in Africa*, Penang and Accra: Third World Network; London and New York: Zed Books.

Naisbitt, J. and P. Aburdene (1990) *Mega Trends 2000*, London: Pan Books.

OAU (1980) *The Lagos Plan of Action for the Economic Development of Africa from 1980 to 2000 (LPA)*, Addis Ababa: Organisation of African Unity.

Onimode, Bade (1989) *A Political Economy of the African Crisis*, London: Zed Books.

—— (1992) *A Future for Africa – Beyond the Politics of Adjustment*, London: Earthscan.

—— (2000) *Africa in the World of the 21st Century*, Ibadan: Ibadan University Press.

Payer, C. (1992) *Lent and Lost*, London: Zed Books.

Republic of South Africa (1993) *The Reconstruction and Development Programme (RPD)*, Cape Town: RSA.

Shutt, H. (1998) *The Trouble with Capitalism – an Enquiry into the Causes of Global Economic Failure*, London: Zed Books.

South Centre (1999*) Elements of an Agenda for the South*, Geneva: South Centre.

UNDP (various years) *Human Development Report*, New York: Oxford University Press.

World Bank (1980) *Accelerated Development in Sub-Saharan Africa – an Agenda for Action*, Washington, DC: World Bank.

—— (1989) *Sub-Saharan Africa: from Crisis to Sustainable Development – a Long-term Perspective Study (LTPS)*, Washington, DC: World Bank.

3

Revisiting the African Alternative Framework to Structural Adjustment Programmes for Socio-economic Recovery and Transformation (AAF–SAP) in Contemporary Nigeria
S. O. Tomori and O. W. Tomori

Since independence in 1960, Nigeria has been transformed from a subsistent agrarian economy into a largely monetized economy fuelled by the discovery and exploration of oil fields from the early 1960s. The transformation later coincided with an oil boom under military rule from the early 1970s. The boom has had a pervasive effect on the growth and development of the economy. Petroleum quickly became the dominant sector, accounting for about 90 per cent of export earnings and the main source of government revenue. Between 1972 and 1974, federal revenue from oil increased fivefold, constituting 80 per cent of total revenue (World Bank, 1994a). Nigeria's new wealth radically affected the scope and content of investment and production as well as consumption patterns and the government's approach to macro-economic management, and the policies and programmes implemented. Federal expenditures increased rapidly, doubling between 1973 and 1974, and again between 1974 and 1975. Much of this increase in government expenditures went to investment. Measured at 1984 prices, the share of investment in GDP increased from less than 12 per cent in 1971 to more than 25 per cent by 1977 (World Bank, 1994b).

The growth in oil revenue was absorbed largely by public sector spending, particularly on infrastructure. The increase in public expenditure went largely to improving transportation and social services, so as to ameliorate the effects of the Civil War (1967–70). The rapid growth of the public sector and the construction boom that followed the massive investment programme altered the prevailing patterns of relative prices and wages. Wage and price increases depressed the non-oil traded goods sector. The exchange rate appreciation with rising oil revenues was responsible for the sharp deterioration in international competitiveness of Nigeria's products.

Despite the rapid increase in public expenditures, the simultaneous growth in oil revenues was sufficient to maintain a federal budgetary surplus. In 1975, however, expenditures nevertheless began to exceed revenue. State budgets also began to show deficits. Moreover, in the construction and services sectors, wages were inflated to keep pace with the wages offered in the other sectors of the economy.

Economic problem began to surface in 1978. In 1980–1, the terms of trade, which had remained relatively constant, deteriorated considerably. The growth rate of GDP averaged only 4.2 per cent. The agricultural component of GDP grew by 6.4 per cent while the industrial sector rose by 7.3 per cent. Exports fell by 9.5 percent while imports grew by 27.2 per cent (World Bank, 1994b).

Thus severe terms of trade variations led to extra-large fluctuations in real income. Whereas real income had increased by 200 per cent between 1972 and 1980, it had declined by almost 60 per cent by 1983 from its 1980 peak. As the oil boom could not generate enough revenue to keep pace with public expenditures, real income further declined. Government was forced to run a budget deficit and increase its borrowing. By 1983 the federal budget deficit amounted to 12 per cent of GDP.

The Buhari military government which seized power in January 1984 continued the 1982 austerity measures of the Shagari government which it had overthrown. It sought to control public expenditures by imposing a wage freeze on public sector employees, declaring a large number of civil servants redundant, and by introducing user fees in the educational and health sectors. These measures made a dent in Nigeria's budget deficit, which moved from 13 per cent of GDP in 1983 to about 3 per cent in 1984. But the administration continued to fund inefficient parastatals, while cutting funds for maintaining infrastructure and equipment.

The decline in public expenditures had its severest impact on the construction and service sectors. Employment and production declined sharply in most other sectors. Capacity utilisation declined and plant closures were widespread as the access of the import-dependent industrial sector to imported inputs was sharply curtailed. Imports declined by 22.7 per cent in 1984 while non-oil exports declined by 44.2 per cent. Also accompanying the decline in imports and exports was a significant rise in domestic prices and an increase in the rate of inflation to 40 per cent. Domestic savings and investment also declined; investment fell to 12 per cent of GDP, down from 24 per cent of total investment in 1985, compared to 50 per cent in the 1970s. External debt service requirements on private debt and rescheduled arrears reached 34 per cent of exports of goods and non-factor services in 1985.

It is against this background that the structural adjustment programme (SAP) was introduced in 1986. It was supposed to rectify these anomalies and put the economy back on the rails. Its fate explains why this chapter attempts to revisit the African alternative to SAPs – the AAF–SAP – in the context of contemporary Nigerian experience.

Nigeria's Economy during the Structural Adjustment Programme

The Babangida government that came to power in mid-1985 declared its intention to move from 'austerity alone to austerity with structural adjustment'. With a further collapse in oil prices adding urgency, the government adopted a far-reaching reform programme in 1986 aimed at revitalising the non-oil economy, with stabilisation policies designed to restore balance of payments equilibrium and improve the efficiency of public management. Import licences and the agricultural marketing boards were eliminated, price controls were scrapped and the deregulation of the banking system initiated. The restructuring of domestic production and the liberalisation of the incentive regime led to the resurgence of agriculture and manufacturing.

But the resurgence was both uneven and short-lived as all sectors suffered from the vagaries of an increasingly erratic macro-economic environment. Successive cycles of contractionary and expansionary policies – with their attendant effects on prices and activity levels – rocked the economy. From late 1986 to the end of 1987, macro-economic policy was reasonably tight. But responding to criticisms that the adjustment programme was too harsh, it turned expansionary in 1988, only to reverse itself a year later when the inflationary consequences of more liberal policies became painful. In 1990, increased international oil prices associated with the Gulf crisis fuelled higher spending, which continued when world oil prices subsequently collapsed. Mirroring earlier periods, Nigeria built up large fiscal deficits over 1990–2, which by 1992 amounted to 10 per cent of GDP. The 1992 GDP *per capita* had fallen from over $1,000 in 1985 to $320. This trend continued in 1993, when the fiscal deficit increased to 11.4 per cent. Money supply increased by 57 per cent during 1992 and by 68 per cent in 1993.

Exchange rate reform was at the core of the structural adjustment programme. Although the specific modalities and the effectiveness of implementation varied over the adjustment period, the foreign exchange reform facilitated a cumulative depreciation in the real effective exchange rate of about 80 per cent between September 1986 and the end of 1992. The resort to large monetary financing of the fiscal deficit led to the rapid depreciation of the Naira. With foreign exchange reserves nearly depleted by early 1993, the government switched back to a non-price system for determining the official exchange rate. The 1994 budget formalised this approach to foreign exchange allocation and prohibited free-market transactions. Although initial trade reforms reduced the protection that had encouraged assembly operations based on imported inputs, some of the programme's first-round reduction and the pruning of the import prohibition list were later rolled back.

The government encouraged private sector development by removing impediments on foreign investment, reducing corporate tax rates, and introducing a debt–equity conversion programme. Yet private development still faced cumbersome regulations and approval processes that raised the cost of doing business in Nigeria. Difficulties with the management of public utilities marked the provision of critical infrastructure services, such as power and telecommunications, which hindered private sector development. Most critical, Nigeria's unstable macroeconomic and exchange rate policies and political uncertainty increasingly discouraged investors.

Much-needed financial sector and monetary policy reform began under the adjustment programme. Financial sector reforms included new legislation that embraced international standards for evaluating the health of the banking system. Within the banking system, new entrants aiming to secure foreign exchange allocation mushroomed, and serious financial distress emerged in established financial institutions; classified loans accounted for one-third of total bank credit. While the Central Bank and the National Deposit Insurance Corporation (NDIC) began to address the difficult task of restructuring banks with non-performing loans, the eventual disposition of some of these banks and sources of financing for the restructuring remained unclear. Meanwhile, the federal government started to divest its equity participation in most commercial and merchant banks through public offers. There was a proliferation of sectoral banks and other non-bank financial institutions that fall outside the control of the Central Bank of Nigeria's supervision.

The adjustment also included public enterprise reforms. Some 58 small public enterprises were privatised, mostly through public offers on the Nigerian Stock Exchange. Although this was an achievement, the privatisation of several large enterprises was delayed. Even less success was achieved with the commercialisation programme. Eleven parastatals were slated for full commercialisation, with performing contracts (including a ten-year corporate plan) having been signed. But only limited progress was made. Institution-building efforts and the creation of appropriate regulatory framework were stalled, while service delivery remained intermittent, raising operating costs to public and private sector users.

In order to improve the procedures for public expenditure and budgetary planning, the adjustment programme instituted a rolling plan process that could not compensate for deep-rooted weakness in public expenditure management. For example, the temporary revenue windfall accruing from the hiking of oil prices in 1990 led to the re-emergence of large-scale government spending through 'dedication accounts' and other devices outside the control of the statutory budgetary and accounting framework. Increased off-budget spending undermined fiscal and monetary discipline. Also these expenditures were not directed toward the provision of basic social services, or infrastructure projects designed to build human physical capacity and to meet the needs of a majority of the people.

Despite difficulties in implementation and over spending, the policies incorporated in the SAP, particularly the large depreciation of the real effective exchange rate produced results. In contrast to an average decline of 2 to 3 per cent a year between 1980 and 1986, Nigeria's real GDP grew by about 5 per cent a year between 1986 and 1990, primarily reflecting recovery in agriculture and manu-facturing. In response to the general worsening in the economic and financial situation after 1991, however, economic growth slowed for three consecutive years, falling below 3 per cent in 1993. Consistent with Nigeria's comparative advantage, the agricultural sector experienced a long-awaited recovery. Some of Nigeria's earlier anti-export bias in manufacturing disappeared under the adjust-ment programme, and producers switched from the use of imported to local inputs. Particularly in agro-processing and textile manufacturing, there was greater use of locally produced materials. The assembly-based manufacturing sector, which depends on imported inputs and had been shielded from competition and market signals, contracted during the programme period. Following a shift in relative prices in favour of the rural sector, the production of traditional food and cash crops increased, and agricultural output grew at a yearly average rate of 4 per cent. By 1994, Nigeria spent one-fifth of what it spent in 1986 on food imports.

From 1986 onward, the rate of inflation fluctuated widely, reflecting variation in the stance of macro-economic policy. In 1986, despite a 70 per cent deprecia-tion of the exchange rate, satisfactory monetary performance kept inflation at 16 per cent. And while inflation decelerated in 1987, the expansionary 1988 budget boosted prices by 55 per cent. Inflation rates moderated once again, as tight fiscal and monetary policies were implemented in 1989, with inflation actually falling below 7 per cent in 1990. However, subsequent expansionary fiscal and monetary policies caused inflation to rebound. By the end of 1992, it was approaching 50 per cent and exceeded that level in 1993 and 1994.

Although the adjustment programme revived Nigeria's economic growth, shifting that growth could not compensate for the huge drop in purchasing power associated with the collapse of international oil prices. With GDP growing at 5 per cent per year and population at 3 per cent, *per capita* income grew at 2 per cent. At that rate it would have taken about 30 years for Nigeria to recover its peak living standard of 1981. But the slack in the resurgence, particularly from 1990 onwards, and the extremely high rates of inflation which led to the fall in GDP growth rate also led to negative *per capita* growth. The urban middle class – primarily civil servants and workers in import-substituting industries – bore the cost of adjusting. Small farmers were the primary beneficiaries of the adjustment before the period of hyper-inflation.

Evaluation of Nigeria's Structural Adjustment Programme

The quality of economic management improved between 1987 and 1989, but progressively deteriorated from 1990, resulting in a slowdown in growth. Fiscal and balance of payment deficits had increased and inflation had accelerated. Trade and price distortions that had been partially rectified in the late 1980s had re-emerged. Exchange rates and interest rates were set administratively; they bore no relation to their market rates.

Poverty and social indicators

The impact of economic mismanagement and negative external shocks reduced *per capita* income from $1,000 in 1980 to $320 in 1992, significantly increasing the incidence of poverty. In real *per capita* terms, consumption and income were not higher than they were in the early 1970s, prior to the onset of the oil boom. Basic social indicators placed Nigeria among the 20 poorest countries world-wide. Infant mortality rates were around 85 per 1,000 live births; half of all children aged two to five years showed signs of persistent malnutrition, and only about two-thirds of the relevant age group were enrolled in primary schools, down from 90 per cent in the early 1980s.

Comprehensive and far-sighted policies for education, health and population had been adopted. These policies accorded preference to the promotion of health and education services at the primary over the tertiary level; provided access to universal primary education free of charge; encouraged adoption of cost-recovery measures in health care; and aimed to improve the health of women and children through birth spacing. Without a commensurate increase in budgetary provisions, notably for recurrent over capital expenditures, and within recurrent budgets for supplies and maintenance, funding had remained a critical constraint for reversing the decline in enrolments, quality of services, and utilisation rates.

While some women played a dynamic role in political and economic life in parts of the country, women generally tended to be seriously disadvantaged, particularly in rural areas. Legal, cultural, and social barriers had limited their access to land, credit, farming inputs, technology and support services, and constrained their earning capacity. They spent long hours in low-output, physically demanding activities such as fetching water and fuelwood, transport, manual crop processing, and headloading of farm produce, in addition to their responsibilities for house-hold and family maintenance tasks. They were more illiterate and poorly nourished than men, and they faced extreme health risks because of frequent pregnancies starting at a young age.

Environment

Like most of sub-Sahara Africa, Nigeria's key environmental problems are soil degradation, water contamination and deforestation. Unaddressed, these and other environmental problems could cost the economy an estimated $5 billion a year in the long term (World Bank, 1994a). Traditional bush-fallow farming systems were land-intensive but sustainable and compatible with the environment as long as the population remained in check. But with a rising population, farmers cultivated exhausted soils, and their incomes declined. The worsening of poverty engendered demand for more children to help the family survive on the land, which in turn puts more pressure on the environment and so on, in a vicious circle.

The government of Nigeria had taken several none-too-successful steps towards redressing the country's many environmental problems. A national environmental agency had been set up to coordinate environmental activities. Legislation had been enacted regulating effluent limitation and industrial wastes and requiring environmental impact assessments. Government has also taken steps to implement a broad sectoral programme for environmental management, including forestry, water and sanitation, gas flaring reduction (Nigeria was the world's largest flarer of natural gas), industrial and hazardous waste management, and coastal zone management.

The external environment

The pressure on the external balance had been exacerbated by the downturn in world oil prices. Meanwhile, Nigeria's regional competitiveness for non-oil exports was declining, reflecting domestic price increase in excess of those of its trading partners, the impact of the CFA devaluation in neighbouring countries. Another key parameter with domestic and external implications for Nigeria's economic development in the medium term was its external debt overhang. The Nigerian economy was highly exposed to price fluctuation in world oil markets. Each $1 per barrel change in oil price was worth $650 million at current export volumes. The market outlook was for oil prices to decline slightly in real terms in 1994 and to remain unchanged over the medium term, with any increase in global demand being more than offset by increases in supplies from the Organisation of Petroleum Exporting Countries (OPEC) and non-OPEC sources, Nigeria's efforts to increase its productive capacity to 2.5 million barrels a day by the middle of 1994 was unattainable even though favourable new terms had been negotiated with joint venture companies. However, government budgetary cuts restricted the level of new investments. Direct foreign investment, most of which is related to the oil sector, was expected to remain stable over the medium term. Government efforts to diversify Nigeria's energy exports, notably through a liquefied natural gas project, remained under active discussion with potential foreign investors but had not been actualised at the end of 1994.

Balance of payments and external debt

Throughout the adjustment period, Nigeria ran a large trade surplus, except in 1990 when there was a current account deficit, reflecting large payments for interest and other services. Nigeria's net transfer position was persistently negative throughout this period, averaging 5 per cent of GDP in 1986–92. Nigeria's stock of public and public guaranteed long-term external debt increased from $19.2 billion at the end of 1985 to around $29.8 billion by the end of 1993. This 50 per cent increase occurred mostly between 1985 and 1987 and was principally due to cross-currency revaluations, which boosted the value of non-dollar-denominated debt of a large stock of trade arrears from the 1982–3 period (World Bank, 1994a). In the post-1986 period, Nigeria signed and honoured three rescheduling agreements with the Paris Club creditors.

Overall evaluation of the SAP

An evaluation of the SAP makes it glaringly obvious that the programme failed to address Nigeria's long-term development objectives and the fundamental structural bottleneck of its economy. This led the ECA, with the financial support of the UNDP, to embark on a search for an African alternative framework to SAPs, a process that reached its final stage in April 1989 when African development and finance ministries adopted the African Alternative Framework to Structural Adjustment Programmes for Socio-Economic Recovery and Transformation (AAF–SAP). The features and policy directions of the AAF–SAP are addressed below.

Features of the AAF–SAP

The AAF–SAP is based on three sets of macro-entities: namely, operative forces, available resources and needs to be catered for. The operative forces are political, economic, scientific and technological, environmental, cultural and sociological. These together act on the general pattern and rate of development. With respect to resources, the main categories taken into account in the framework include human resources, especially in terms of quality and skill mixes; natural resources, especially land, water and forests; domestic savings; and external financial resources (ECA, 1989). In line with the thrust of human-centred adjustment and transformation, the needs elaborated in the context of the proposed framework include vital goods and services and the ability to acquire them.

The alternative framework is expressed in three modules. The first module specifies the interaction of certain forces with the level and pattern of allocation of resources to determine the type and quantity of different categories of output. It was in this module that the different sets of relationships in the process of producing goods and services and generating factor incomes – including aspects such as the efficiency and productivity of resources – were defined. The second module explains the forces that characterise the distribution of output and determine the level and pattern of allocation of factor income. In this module, the different sets of relationships dealing with income distribution were specified. The third module identifies the set of operative forces that interact with the level of income and pattern of income distribution. This determines the degree of domestic satisfaction of the needs and the external transactions. It was in this module that the sets of relationships dealing with the elements of domestic demand and transactions with the rest of the world were specified for each country. In the framework it is emphasised that all the macro-entities – operative forces, available resources and needs to catered for – are individually and collectively dynamic over time and space. Over time, the operating forces will change in composition and the interactive importance of the different components will shift. Also, the resources available will change with time in terms of composition and relative importance. Similarly, the needs of society are not static since, with development, the resultant changes in society's total needs will generate a new set of normative or perceived needs. All the forces, resources and needs in the framework will also change over space.

Also, the entire system, consisting of the three modules, is seen as dynamically interactive. The existence of gaps between the needs that have to be catered for and the actual product mixes will necessitate adjustments in the parameters and values of variables relating to the factor income generation and allocation. This will ensure the closing of the gaps.

Moreover, the framework is designed to enable African countries to identify the major components of the forces at play, the needs of society, the resources required and the principal interactions and relationships among these. Even though the framework does not constitute a standard model for generating standard policy prescriptions irrespective of the peculiar circumstance of a given country, it is broad and flexible enough to be used along with selected policy directions, taking into account the specificity of social and economic structures of the country adopting it.

Policy Directions in the AAF–SAP

Conceptually and operationally, the policy directions provide the broad guidelines for overcoming the structural bottlenecks of the African economies and then attaining the region's development objectives. The policy directions also serve as general bounds for determining, within the context of the proposed macro-economic framework, the models for individual African countries and for the subsequent choice of policy instruments and measures specific to a given country (ECA, 1989).

To strengthen and diversify Africa's production capacity and the productivity of investment, the following major policy directions have been put forward (ECA, 1989):

- Enhanced production and efficient resources use which ensures resistance to the logic of always having to balance the budget at the expense of growth and production. Such productive and efficient use of resources would involve a policy change to bring about significant shifts towards the production possibility curve and increasing returns to investment.

- Greater and more efficient domestic resource mobilisation, given the uncertainties surrounding the quantum of external resource flow to Africa, and increasingly stiff conditionalities attached to such inflows.

- Improving human resources capacity in education, health and other social infrastructure areas, including the maintenance of law and order, which are prerequisites of an enabling environment. In the AAF–SAP, it was recommended that an annual average of at least 30 per cent of total government outlays should be devoted to the social sector and that the annual rate of growth of social investment should be significantly higher than the population growth rate.

- Strengthening the scientific and technological base which is essential for transforming national raw materials in the form of agricultural products, minerals, and forest and aquatic resources into consumable goods and services, for both local and export markets. This can be achieved by focusing on the national socio-economic needs of the people; enhancing endogenous infrastructural capacity to deal with the development and application of science and technology; establishing a technologically focused educational system; finding alternatives to the export of raw materials by the development of new products and processes; and ensuring the competitiveness of African products in the world market. (ECA, 1989).

- Vertical and horizontal diversification through the production of essential goods and services to meet the needs of the majority of the population in all sectors; and the need to lessen monocultural export dependence and its associated instability in terms of earnings.

- Establishing a pragmatic balance between the public and private sector through the building of the physical, human and institutional infrastructure, environmental protection and conservation, and the provision of essential services by the public sector.

- Creating an enabling environment for sustainable development through a broad participation in decision making, consensus building, maintenance of equity and justice, elimination of civil strife and instability, facilitation of access to opportunities for all and creating a favourable investment climate. This could also be achieved by encouraging entrepreneurship and the effective contribution of the private sector and appropriate grassroots initiatives to the development process through consistent policy incentives.

- Shifting of resources by minimising non-productive expenditure and excessive military spending.

- Improving the pattern of income distribution among different socio-economic categories of households by ensuring that, in the generation of output, the poor and the disadvantaged have increased access to the means of production, especially land.

• Striving for food self-sufficiency by achieving a proper balance between the food subsector and the production of agricultural export commodities.

• Lessening import dependence by moving away from a situation whereby most of the essential needs, intermediate inputs and capital goods in African countries are satisfied from imports.

• Realignment of consumption patterns with production patterns by consuming more of what is domestically produced, especially in the areas of food, clothing, housing and other essential necessities.

• Managing debt and debt servicing by establishing strong debt management systems through a continuous assessment of payment capacity in the short and long terms.

The question one needs to ask is: have all these objectives been achieved in Africa in general and in Nigeria in particular since the formulation of the AAF–SAP? The answer to this question is addressed in the following section.

Assessment of the AAF–SAP in Nigeria Using Socio-economic Indications

Electricity

Electricity is so vital to development that the rate of energy utilisation is often used as a developmental index. This is due to the fact that the effect of electricity usage reverberates through the economy, serving as a source of energy for industrial and commercial outfits as well as domestic use. Moreover, the process of electricity generation serves as an outlet for the development of other industries like coal, oil and natural gas. Electricity, therefore has both a demand and supply effect.

Electricity generation in Nigeria is almost the exclusive preserve of the Nigerian Electric Power Authority (NEPA), a public corporation accounting for 99.5 per cent of the total electricity generated, while purchases from private firms account for the balance. Thermal energy sources account for about 68.8 per cent of the total electricity generated, while hydroelectricity sources supply 37.7 per cent.

Table 3.1 gives the electricity generated between May 1999 and May 2000: from it we can observe that electricity generation has not been stable. Uneven performance has been attributed to the breakdown of power transformers due to overloading, the poor condition of power stations and lack of materials for maintenance, among others.

Table 3.1 Electricity Generation in Nigeria, May 1999–May 2000

Months	Year	Megawatts	% of installed capacity
May	1999	1600	27.3
June	1999	1500	25.6
September	1999	2129	36.3
December	1999	2500	42.7
March	2000	1183	20.2
May	2000	2400	40.0

Note: Installed capacity as at May 2000 is 5,860 megawatts.
Source: The Guardian, 17 and 19 March 2000; 12, 15 and 22 May 2000.

A further analysis of the structure of electricity generation in Nigeria is shown in Tables 3.2a and 3.2b, which reveal that while the combined capacity of the hydroelectricity power plants and thermal stations amounted to 5,957.4 MW, the actual power generation during the first quarter of 2000 was 1,716 MW, or 28.8 per cent of the rated capacity. In addition to the inadequate electricity generation capacity, there are problems in transmission leading to power losses estimated at over 40 per cent. Thus only an average of 1,800 MW actually reaches consumers (NESG, 2000).

Table 3.2a Hydroelectric Power Stations in Nigeria

Station	Date commissioned	Rated capacity	Actual capacity	% of the actual
Kanji	1968	760 MW	217 MW	28.6
Jebba	1985	578.4 MW	382.0 MW	66.0
Shiroro	1990	600 MW	298 MW	49.7
Total		1938.4 MW	897 MW	144.3

Table 3.2b Thermal Power Stations in Nigeria

Station	Date commissioned	Rated capacity	Actual capacity	% of the actual
Afam (PH)	1963	969 MW	—	—
Egbin (Ikorodu)	—	1320 MW	652 MW	49.4
Delta in Ugheli	1991	600 MW	12 MW	2.0
Sapele(Delta)	1980	1020 MW	12 MW	15.2
Ijora (Lagos)	—	110.6 MW	—	—
Total		4090.6 MW	819 MW	20.0
Overall total		5957.4 MW	1718 MW	28.8

Source: This Day, Tuesday, 21 March 2000.

The poor supply of electricity has far-reaching implications for the environment. For instance, fuelwood is one of the major sources of household energy in Nigeria today. The growing inadequacy of electricity generation and transmission has accelerated deforestation. This in turn has exposed many fragile ecosystems, such as watersheds and hillsides, to severe soil erosion. As rural fuelwood supplies decline, wood is being collected faster than it can grow. In the course of 1997, for example, 400,000 hectares were reforested, while 9.1 million hectares were cut down. In that year, the protected forest area as a percentage of total land area was just 10 per cent (CBN, 1997). It should be noted that some interior parts of the country still rely predominantly on biomass – wood, charcoal, dung and crop residues – for cooking, heating and even for lighting. At the same time, the rapid growth of agriculture, the pace of migration to cities, and the growing number of people entering the market economy place unprecedented pressure on the biomass base (WCED, 1987). Regrettably, the search for alternative sources of energy in Nigeria has not gone beyond the research stage and action for the improvement of energy-use efficiency is so far limited to the introduction of efficient woodfuel stoves.

Transportation

It is hard to overemphasise the role played by the process of conveying goods and people from place to place in a country's commercial life, industry and overall economic development. Development leads to an enormous increase in the volume of trade and makes it possible for a concentrated population to survive in terms of food provision. In Nigeria – apart from road, air and water routes – transportation through pipelines has been important. However, these and other modes of transport have far-reaching implications for the environment. The frequent crude oil spillage and perennial gas flaring in the oil-producing areas, and the attendant adverse effects on all forms of life, have rendered most of these areas so barren that they are now abandoned. Oil spill incidence in Nigeria has been on the increase in recent times. The most devastating episode was the oil spill offshore in Akwa Ibom State, in which about 40,000 barrels of crude oil from a damaged pipeline affected vast areas of Akwa Ibom, Rivers, Bayelsa, Delta, Ondo and Lagos State (Adewoye, 1998). A total number of 2,908 spillage incidents were estimated between 1970 and 1995 (Adenuga, 1999).

In Nigeria, the transport sector is responsible for 30 per cent of fossil fuel consumption annually. World-wide, motor vehicles cause more air pollution than any other single human activity. They are a major source of emissions for a variety of atmospheric pollutants, contributing nearly one-half of the human-induced oxides of nitrogen, two-thirds of carbon monoxide, and about one half of the hydrocarbons in industrialised countries as well as 95 per cent of the air-borne lead in developing countries (Adewoye, 1998). Lead stands out among heavy metals that pose localised health risk because of its prevalence at a high level. Unlike some other pollutants, lead can affect health through several pathways, including ingestion and inhalation. Lead is believed to cause blood enzyme changes, anaemia, hyperactivity and other neuro-behavioural effects. High levels in children are linked with hindered neurological development, including lower intelligent quotient (IQ) and agility. In adults, the consequences include risks of higher blood pressure, particularly in men, and higher risks of heart attacks, strokes and death.

Education

In economic development, the role of education is pervasive. Education is both a goal of development and a means of achieving the associated goals of health, higher labour productivity and more rapid GDP growth, as well as the broader goal of social integration, including participation in cultural and political affairs. The nationalists saw education as 'the instrument to lift the nation out of its primitive morass, to enlighten the masses for democratic participation in national politics, and to enable the nation to participate in international affairs' (Yesufu, 1996: 137). Table 3.3 reveals that the adult literacy rate in Nigeria rose from 55 per cent in 1994 to 57 per cent in 1997, and has been stable at that rate since.

Table 3.3 Adult Literacy Rate (%) in Nigeria

Year	Total adults literacy rate (%)
1994	55
1997	57
1998	57
1999	57

Sources: CBN, Annual Report and Statement of Accounts, various years.

The glaring fact about Nigeria's education is that Nigeria spends an almost insignificant proportion of her financial resources on education. It was a mere 0.55 per cent of the total expenditure in 1970, with the highest proportion of 10.29 per cent in 1995 (Anyanwu *et al.*, 1997: 604). The neglect of this sector by past administrations has negative implications for the environment. The high level of illiteracy in the country means that only a few are aware of the importance of environment to sustainable development. As a result, deforestation for firewood, bush burning for farming and hunting, and the use of chemicals and explosives for fishing in streams and ponds are still widespread. For example, while the annual rate of tropical deforestation world-wide is 0.6 per cent, the total area of moist tropical forests cleared annually in Nigeria and Côte d'Ivoire stands at 5.2 per cent. This trend, if continued, will result in total deforestation of both countries by the year 2017. Forest resources, therefore, are subjected to a ruinous competition between conservation to maintain genetic resources and biological diversity and the livelihoods of the people living in or on those forests. As a way of addressing the problem of environmental degradation arising from illiteracy, the Federal Environmental Protection Agency (FEPA) Decree (No. 58) was promulgated in December 1998 by the Federal government of Nigeria to enlighten the public about the importance of environmental sustainability. Even before this, it should be pointed out, FEPA had intensified and improved on its various activities to ensure environmental protection of the country. Through the National Hazardous Chemical Tracking Programme, for example, FEPA inspected and analysed 477,188 tonnes of chemical and pesticides in 1997 (CBN, 1997).

Housing

The housing situation in Nigeria differs between the urban and rural areas. In the urban areas, the major problem is the shortage of housing, with its associated overcrowding and squalid environmental conditions. In the rural areas, however, the problem is largely that of poorly ventilated structures that lack services like potable water and electricity supply, among others. In both areas, housing problems are exacerbated by the predominance of the poor and low-income group, (about 70 per cent of the populace) in the country as a whole. The housing problems are manifested not only in the quantitative and the qualitative shortages, but also in the uneven distribution of accommodation, high rents relative to incomes, high building costs, and bottlenecks in the land tenure system and land use administration.

In Nigeria, few households have refuse disposal facilities. As of 1994, only 13 per cent disposed of their refuse through their own or government-supplied bins; the remaining 87 per cent disposed of their refuse in the vicinity of their homes, where it constituted a health hazard through air and water pollution (FOS, 1996). FEPA has not been able to coordinate the activities of town planning authorities in Nigeria successfully regarding the siting of building development to prevent overcrowding, poor ventilation and the adjacence of residential and industrial/commercial areas. Environmental impact assessment is not a requirement for approval of schemes and projects by planning and health authorities. All over the country, refuse is dumped into drains and this has become a major cause of flooding. Factories are still sited in or near residential areas, producing uncontrolled and unbearable noise levels, especially in the urban areas.

Water

Water is an important national resource, and one that is taken far too lightly in government circles. Admittedly a number of schemes aimed at developing the nation's water resources, with the aim of making water freely available to all citizens, have been hatched at various times in Nigeria. Available statistics show that between 1992 and 1995 a total number of 13 dams were constructed and 264 boreholes were sunk (Anyanwu et al., 1997). Table 3.4 shows the allocation by the Federal Government.

Table 3.4 Nigerian Federal Government Budget Allocation to Water Supply

	1994	1998	1999	2000
Allocation to water supply (billions of Naira)	0.2	3.5	3.6	0.8
Percentage of annual Federal budget	0.6	0.01	0.01	0.0

Sources: CBN Annual Report and Statement of Accounts, various years.

As can be seen, the percentage of the annual federal budget allocated to water resources has been declining. A high percentage of Nigerians have no access to safe drinking water: only 18.5 per cent of households in 1982, rising slowly to 24.7 per cent in 1990. Access to safe drinking water is a social indicator of development everywhere. Without it, Nigeria has known a high rate of morbidity and low productivity.

Other macro-economic variables

A further examination of the impact of the financial sector on key macro-economic variables like savings, investment, industrial growth, capacity utilisation, and bank credit to the private sector is presented in Table 3.5. We compare the behaviour of financial and related real variables over the three sub-periods 1986–9, 1989–93 and 1994–8. According to the table, the average rate of growth in money supply (M_1) between 1986 and 1998 is higher than the average growth rate of real GDP. The decline in the average growth rate of the money supply in the period 1990–8 is associated with a decline in the growth rate of output. Inflation has an effect on both the real and the nominal interest rates. While inflation and the nominal interest rate move in the same direction, inflation and the real interest rate move in opposite directions. Naturally, as a higher inflation rate increases the nominal (or reduces the real) interest rate, the higher interest rate has reduced the real growth rate of manufacturing output. A decline in manufacturing output arises from under-capacity utilisation in the subsector. This low capacity utilisation is a result of 'high cost of production owing to high cost of foreign exchange; low demand for manufactures resulting from dwindling consumers' purchasing power as well as influx of smuggled and cheaper finished products; lack of working capital; and poor performing and inadequate infrastructures' (CBN, 1997: 112).

Nigeria's small and medium enterprises find it difficult to borrow from financial institutions because they (the former) are considered highly risky. Besides, they find it difficult to provide the collateral securities required by the banks. As an alternative to borrowing, therefore, the manufacturers turn to the informal sector, where the cost of borrowing is relatively high.

It is worth noting (Table 3.5) that credit extended to the private sector, as a percentage of GDP, declined between 1986 and 1998: from 14.2 per cent in the period 1986–9 to 2.6 per cent in the period 1994–8. The effect of this is reflected

Table 3.5 Financial Development, Savings, Investment and Growth in Nigeria, 1986–98

Indicators	1986–9	1990–3	1994–8
Financial development indicators			
Real M_1 average growth rate	18.8	46.2	22.7
M_2/GNP ratio	30.8	32.8	19.0
Real GDP average growth rate	5.2	5.0	2.5
Gross domestic savings (5 GDP)	12.2	15.6	11.7
Gross domestic investment (% GDP)	9.1	11.2	8.4
Fiscal deficit (ration of GDP)	–8.2	–10.5	–0.2
Inflation rate	23.7	30.6	35.5
Interest rates			
Nominal lending rate	17.9	29.5	21.5
Real lending rate	–5.8	–1.1	–14.0
Nominal deposit rate	12.7	16.4	12.6
Real deposit rate	–11.0	–14.2	–22.9
Exchange rate (Naira/$)	4.2	14.3	21.9
Growth rate manufacturing (%)	9.2	6.7	5.0
Share of manufacturing in GDP (%)	8.3	8.0	6.9
Manufacturing capacity utilisation (%)	40.2	39.5	33.4
Bank credit to the private sector (% GDP)	14.2	8.8	2.6

Note: The figures are computed.

Sources: International Financial Statistics, various years; CBN *Statistical Bulletin*, 9, 2 (1998) and CBN Annual Report and Statement of Accounts, various years.

in manufacturing capacity utilisation, which declined from 40.2 per cent in the period 1986–9 to 33.4 per cent in the period 1994–8.

The growth rate of manufacturing in the period 1986–9 was 9.2 per cent. This fell sharply to 5 per cent in the period 1994–8. This poor performance is attributable to the high cost of borrowing, the depreciation of the Naira, which made the importation of raw materials and spare parts expensive, and macro-economic instability.

Policy Recommendations and Conclusion

No adjustment and transformation programmes, however sound and innovative in their blueprints, can achieve the objectives of development if they are not properly implemented. Half-hearted commitment to programmes often leads to policy discontinuity, and this is true of the AAF–SAP in Africa, and in Nigeria in particular.

This chapter has revisited the AAF–SAP in the context of the Nigerian experience by tracing the Nigerian economy prior to and during the SAP. An assessment of the SAP has been undertaken. Its weakness to address the long-term development objectives and the fundamental structural bottlenecks of African economies necessitated the adoption of the AAF–SAP. Features and policy directions of the AAF–SAP have been reviewed and assessed using Nigerian socio-economic indicators.

The diversity of experiences with reform in Nigeria provides an ideal framework from which to draw some broad lessons for future reformers and to identify challenges that countries already in the reform process must address. A key component for successful reform is effective macro-economic stabilisation through prudent monetary policy. Monetary policy should aim at maintaining prudent monetary targets, mitigating inflationary pressures, and facilitating liquidity for financial intermediation.

The success of reform also depends on a clear commitment to change on the part of the government, thus sending a message of policy certainty to the private sector. Government must show commitment to industrialisation by providing an appropriate enabling environment in which the private sector can thrive.

Previous governments have damaged the Nigerian economy, and the present civilian government under President Olusegun Obasanjo recently indicated that the dividends of democracy have not trickled down to the grassroots because of the severity of damage that the economy has experienced. For the policy to achieve its desired objectives, our leaders must be ready to lead by example through transparent governance and accountability. The anti-corruption crusade of the present administration is a move in the right direction but its practicalisation lacks lustre. Indeed, if the Nigerian media are to be believed, corruption has escalated since 1999. Certainly, only a government that steers clear of the SAP can ever hope to achieve sustainable growth, and win the war against corruption.

Bibliography

Adenuga, A. O. (1999) 'Petroleum Industry and Environmental Protection: the Nigerian Experience', *CBN Bulletin*, 23, 4: 95–103.

Adewoye R. O. (1998) 'Environmental Hazard of Energy Production and Use in Nigeria' *CBN Bulletin*, 22, 4: 50–3.

Anyanwu, J. C. *et al.* (1997) *The Structure of the Nigerian Economy (1960–1997)*, Onitsha, Nigeria: Joanee Educational Publishers Ltd, chapters 18, 19 and 20.

CBN (1997) *Annual Report and Statement of Accounts*, 31 December, pp. 148 and 152.

ECA (1989) *African Alternative Framework to Structural Adjustment Programmes for Socio-Economic Recovery and Transformation*, Addis Ababa: Economic Commission for Africa.

Federal Office of Statistics (FOS) (1996) *Socio-Economic Profile of Nigeria*, Ibadan: Federal Office of Statistics, chapters 3–7.

Nigerian Economic Summit Group (NESG) (2000) *Economic Indicators*, 6, 2 (June): 25.

World Bank (1994a) *World Development Report 1994: Infrastructure for Development*, Oxford and New York: Oxford University Press for the World Bank.

—— (1994b) *Trends in Developing Economies*, Washington, DC: World Bank, pp. 370–4.

—— (1995) *Restructuring Urban Nigeria: a Strategy for Restoring Urban Infrastructure and Services in Nigeria*, Washington, DC: World Bank, pp. 9–10.

WCED (World Commission on Environment and Development) (1987), *Our Common Future*, Oxford: Oxford University Press, pp. 28–31.

Yesufu, T. M. (1996) *The Nigerian Economy: Growth Without Development*. Benin: Benin Social Science Series for Africa, University of Benin.

4

The AAF–SAP: First Step on the African Path to Sustainable Human Development
Mbaya Kankwenda

Revisiting the AAF–SAP

The African Alternative Framework to Structural Adjustment Programmes for Socio-Economic Recovery and Transformation (AAF–SAP) was launched in 1989. I personally participated in the discussion of its draft version in January of the same year with a number of other African economists at the ECA. Let me quickly look at it almost a decade and a half later.

The AAF–SAP is a 60-page document structured into six chapters: (1) an analysis of the politico-economic structure of African countries; (2) a definition of development objectives for Africa; (3) an evaluation of orthodox SAPs; (4) a definition of the reference framework itself; (5) instruments and policy directions; and (6) strategy and implementation. Each chapter deserves detailed discussion in terms of the relevance of the analysis carried out, the operationality or practicability of its conclusions and recommendations, and, finally, in terms of impact on the ground. But the African and global environment today, the emergence of civil society as a long-forgotten actor, perennial crises and political conflicts, and the increasing scourge of poverty are among important features of the current development environment in Africa that were nascent in the 1980s.

In terms of political scope, the AAF–SAP was a response to the IMF/World Bank SAPs. The justification and intention are still valid. Facing the negative social effects of SAPs on African populations, their doubtful promise and the false hope of sustained economic growth that is yet to occur, and having regard to Africa's overwhelming submission to SAP blackmail by the Bretton Woods institutions, it was the ECA's task to awake, warn and sensitise African governments and other decision makers as well as regional organisations and research centres. The AAF–SAP was therefore another approach and another strategy for addressing the African crisis. It was also a reassertion of the right of Africa to forge its future and define the development path and the appropriate strategy for achieving its objectives. African development policies and programmes should not be designed by outsiders or under their direction, even if they are the development partners and major funding agencies. This political stand is still valid.

Theoretical analysis of the AAF–SAP

The contents of the AAF–SAP document and its theoretical analysis need close re-examination. In this perspective, the AAF–SAP:

1   Recognises the relevance of SAP policy instruments in orthodox liberal economics, but insists on their limitations and pervasive negative effect in the context of African economies. This is demonstrated through a thorough analysis of policy objectives and implications of the IMF/World Bank stabilisation and adjustment programmes, and an evaluation of their basic principles and socio-economic results on the ground during the first seven years of the adoption and implementation of SAPs in Africa. The AAF–SAP calls instead for a paradigm which takes into account the economic structure of African countries and the imperative of its transformation.

2   Addresses the African crisis in terms of structural transformation, including production, consumption, and external economic relations. Accordingly, the AAF–SAP does not limit the policy horizon to short-term solutions. Because the African socio-economic crisis is basically the consequence of a persistent lack of socio-economic and political transformation, the AAF–SAP postulates that any meaningful and sustainable solution should have a long-tem perspective of socio-economic development in Africa. This perspective is still valid and relevant. However, the theoretical analysis seems partial in my view in the sense that it does not raise the important issue of the nature of the accumulation model, neither the one in place nor the alternative to build.

3   Proposes to address the African problem not only in terms of crisis management – one of the major objectives of SAPs – but with a much greater emphasis on African development. It gives direction by defining development objectives for the continent that go far beyond the classic goals of macro-economic equilibria, debt payments and export-oriented growth preached and prescribed by SAPs. The document defines three major development objectives for Africa: putting the human being at the centre stage of development efforts for poverty eradication and improvement of the standards of living; setting-up a development process through sustained and sustainable economic growth; and the integration of African economies for national and regional self-reliance. These objectives have a number of sub-objectives. I must say that they are more than valid today. As globalisation yanks African economic canoes along in the rough wake of giant Western economic vessels,

the scourge of rapidly accelerating human poverty makes it high time for Africa to commit and mobilise its political, social and economic forces towards the fundamental transformation of the polity, the society and the economy.

4   Suggests a new framework which focuses on three major components – production, consumption and external economic relations – in a dynamic and flexible approach, rather than the classic static SAP with its one-size-fits-all prescription. Consequently, instruments and policy directions for the new framework of SAP with structural transformation include the strengthening and diversification of African production and investment, substantial and fundamental revision of the resources allocation model and structure, with a view to satisfying basic human needs first and foremost. In addition, putting in place appropriate institutional measures is part and parcel of the model. The AAF–SAP also discusses the respective roles of government and the private sector as well as regional institutions and the donor community.

Even when it was launched, AAF–SAP policy instruments and directions were seriously questioned by donors, particularly by international financial institutions, in terms of coherence, consistency and practicability. However, these instruments and policy directions are mainly economistic. They venture nothing in terms of political role and direction, nothing substantial enough in terms of democratisation or socialisation of the whole transformation process. What this means is that in spite of the AAF–SAP's broad and valid development objectives, its policy instruments and directions are caught in the same trap as SAPs are. They claim to be alternatives to SAP policies, but remain within the narrow, economistic approach of the classic SAP. In 21st-century Africa, these limitations have to be surpassed.

5   Proposes an implementation strategy that insists on the role and responsibility of African governments in driving the development process, including the AAF–SAP itself. General indications are given for the resource mobilisation, covering both domestic and foreign financial resources. But the indications are too broad and only one paragraph is devoted to programme popularisation. This is obviously another demonstration of the unbalanced economistic perspective of the AAF–SAP. This defect was ameliorated by the ECA in February 1990, however, when the African Charter for Popular Participation in Development and Transformation ('Africa's Magna Carta') was adopted.

Although the AAF-SAP was officially adopted by African governments through the ECA governing bodies, and subsequently by the OAU heads of state and government and the United Nations General Assembly, it did not enjoy the financial support of the IMF and the World Bank. It could not therefore be implemented in a meaningful way in Africa. It was vehemently opposed by the forces behind the orthodox SAPs – the development merchant system. At the experts' meeting on the draft of the AAF–SAP, I remember that I raised the issue: while SAPs have their funding institutions, what would be the funding institutions for the AAF–SAP? I was told that these would be the African governments with the support of their development partners. But Professor Adebayo Adedeji remarked to me at the same time how difficult it is for poor countries to keep their dignity!

The bottom line for the AAF–SAP is that while designing a sound development policy is a good exercise, it becomes a waste of effort if there is no political will and mobilisation to back it. It is ineffective if it does not properly take into account the interests of established, powerful actors. That was another weakness of the AAF–SAP; it was almost still-born because it revealed publicly that SAPs were fundamentally flawed, a message the Bretton Woods institutions were loath to hear.

Impact of the AAF–SAP

But the AAF–SAP has had a tremendous political outreach in Africa and outside:

1   As a precursor of the sustainable human development and human-focused development strategy, the AAF–SAP has contributed to a shift in the development paradigm in Africa and world-wide as well. In defining development objectives for Africa, it has demonstrated that what was needed was not short-term, so-called structural adjustment mechanics under the orthodox classical system, but rather an African alternative that endeavoured to address simultaneously management crisis measures and the long-term structural transformation of African economies, putting human beings at the centre stage of the process.

2   It contributed to position the ECA as a development-oriented organisation in Africa, challenging the ambitious monopoly of the Bretton Woods institutions in this area, but also as an African development-oriented compass.

3   By its success, at least in terms of the political sensitisation of researchers, decision makers and other development actors, it undermined the smooth selling of SAPs in Africa. It then provoked the convening of the Maastricht meeting in early 1990 to explore commonalities between the approach of the Bretton Woods institutions and the AAF–SAP. One result was the creation of the Global Coalition for Africa (GCA) and the African Capacity Building Foundation (ACBF).

Conclusion – the AAF–SAP today

Revisiting AAF-SAP today, it is my opinion that:

1 One should not separate it from the African Charter for Popular Participation in Development and Transformation, which the ECA under Professor Adedeji's leadership crafted six months after the AAF–SAP was launched to redress the economism of the alternative paradigm. Put together, they complement each other and constitute the African version of the sustainable human development (SHD) paradigm.

2 The main message of the AAF–SAP is still valid.

3 The current overwhelming globalisation environment and its challenge to Africa have to be taken into account.

4 Any development paradigm has both technical and political dimensions. The political dimension has to be properly defined, therefore, and not merely understood as a Western-type democratic system of governance. Moreover, a new development paradigm needs a new development leadership to operationalise it.

5 The socialisation of the development process is part of the human development paradigm in terms of democratisation not only of the political arena, but also of the economic, social and cultural domains.

5

The Centrality of Planning to Alternative Development Paradigms in Africa
Olu Ajakaiye

At independence, during the late 1950s and 1960s, virtually all African countries inherited a mixed economy in which there were at least three groups of actors: government, indigenous private investors and private foreign investors. The overwhelming majority of the indigenous private investors were confined to primary production and petty trading (the traditional sector) while the foreign private investors dominated the modern sector which consisted essentially of modern trading outfits set up to collect and export raw materials and import manufactured goods. The government typically inherited public enterprises in railways, electricity, post and telecommunications services, and the marketing boards. Although the new nationalists inherited these essentially mixed economies, the bipolar world that prevailed during this period presented two ideological options to the newly independent states: socialism and capitalism.

An attribute of this era was that, regardless of ideological dispositions, it was expedient in the early stages of the development process to make extensive use of public enterprises, at least to get things started (Hassen, 1959). In other words, the prevailing wisdom was that government had to participate in directly productive activities in addition to investing in social overhead capital so as to launch the development process. It is reasonable to expect that where the dominant political motive is to build a socialist state, government participation in direct productive activities will tend to be permanent, because of the conviction that this is the sure way of achieving more equitable relations among the people. Where the dominant political motive is to build a capitalist economy, government participation in directly productive activities will necessarily be transitory, and, indeed, government will eventually give way to private providers even of social overhead capital.

It turned out that, in the early stage of independence, participation by African governments in the economy knew no boundaries. Between the late 1950s and early 1980s, virtually all African governments drew up comprehensive development plans in conjunction with visiting experts from the World Bank and elsewhere (UNRISD, 2000: 2). The overriding objective of these development plans was to improve the welfare of the people by sustained increase in *per capita* income. Available evidence in Rodrik (1999: 106), for example, suggests that between 1960 and 1973 the average *per capita* GDP of sub-Saharan African countries grew at 1.88 per cent, implying that during the decade of independence, when the planning approach to development was dominant, appreciable progress was made in improving the welfare of the people.

During the second decade of independence, however, the average *per capita* GDP growth rate had decelerated to 0.31 per cent (Rodrik, 1999: 106). This deceleration prompted the World Bank to prepare a report tagged *Accelerated Development in Sub-Saharan Africa: an Agenda for Action* in 1981 under the leadership of Eliot Berg. This report laid the blame for deceleration on internal structural problems and external factors as well as domestic policy inadequacies, especially:

- trade and exchange rate policies which over-protected industries, held back agriculture and absorbed much of the administrative capacity;
- administrative constraints in mobilising resources for development, given the widespread weakness of planning; and
- consistent bias against agriculture in price, tax and exchange rate policies (World Bank, 1981: 4).

This report provides the background for the official response to the crisis: SAPs, which were inspired and, in several cases, authored by experts from the World Bank. An attribute of SAPs is an aversion to planning and regional integration. Indeed, SAPs have lessened the capacity of African states and governments to create the conditions necessary for economic reforms, as they require indiscriminate universal expenditure reductions, including expenditures on health, education, water supply and infrastructure in an environment devoid of social safety nets. SAPs also encouraged the wholesale privatisation of public enterprises instead of liberalising entry and promoting the participation by indigenous entrepreneurs in partnership with their foreign counterparts. Reckless trade liberalisation, with high interest rates and exchange rate depreciation policies, also led to severe decay of the nascent industrial sector, decimated the purchasing power of the people and resulted in massive lay-offs to increase the army of unemployed, with the attendant escalation of crime. Little wonder, therefore, that average growth of real *per capita* GDP for sub-Sahara Africa between 1984 and 1994 was 0.31 per cent. Evidently, SAPs had not only failed to revive the African economy, but had actually worsened the situation.

Meanwhile, the world has changed dramatically since the commencement of SAPs in Africa. Perhaps the most fundamental changes are globalisation, liberalisation and regional integration, especially among the developed countries. At the institutional level, the establishment of the World Trade Organisation (WTO) to join the World Bank and the IMF means that virtually all instruments that can be manipulated by the authorities in developing countries now fall within the parameters of these organisations, leaving the African governments virtually no room in which to manoeuvre. In such circumstances, it is imperative for each of the African countries to articulate its own development paradigm, taking into account its individual socio-cultural realities as well as increased uncertainties in all spheres of human activity at the beginning of the 21st century (Brito, 1995).

Regardless of the specific course pursued in each country, the centrality of long-term planning to the development paradigm as a whole must be fully appreciated. In this chapter it is argued that long-term planning is necessary if African countries are going to exit from their socio-economic quagmire and catch up with the rest of the world. In other words, it is imperative for African governments to realise that short-term plans like SAPs, that do not draw on the longer-term perspective, are doomed to fail.

Long-term Planning and African Development

Economic planning has been defined in a number of ways, but for present purposes it is sufficient to conceive it as the conscious effort by a central authority to coordinate economic decision making over the long term in order to give direction to and accelerate the pace of development of the economy (Blitzer, 1977). The central authority in the case of a nation is the government, defined as a political organisation composed of individuals and institutions authorised to formulate public policies and conduct the affairs of the state. A state is a political organisation exercising authority over a defined territory. Government, therefore, can be conceived as the groups and persons who form the supreme administrative body of a country; in other words, it is the practical representation of the state.

The primary function of a state, and hence a government, is to secure the maximum welfare of members of the social aggregate over which it exercises control. According to Aristotle, a good government is one which best serves the welfare of the generality of the people, while a bad government is one that subordinates the general good to the good of the individuals or groups of individuals in power or having power. It can, therefore, be presumed that a major strategy of government in maximising the welfare of the people is planning as defined above.

As well as governments, it is best to be clear about what markets are if we aim to establish the centrality of planning to the development paradigm. Again, a market has been defined in several ways. One definition is that a market is a place set apart where people attempt to outwit one another. Mainstream economists generally take the market for granted, but the author of one of the popular textbooks has defined it as an area over which buyers and sellers negotiate and exchange a well-defined commodity (Lipsey, 1983: 69). For present purposes, it is more appropriate to define the market as a set of social institutions in which a large number of commodity exchanges of a specific type regularly take place and, to some extent, are facilitated and structured by those institutions (Hodgson, 1996: 173–94).

Hodgson (1996) points out that this institutional definition of a market has a number of theoretical consequences. Perhaps the most pertinent of them here is that a market, as a social institution, has its own enabling and constraining functions. In particular, the market structures the process of cognition of the agents and can actually affect their preferences and beliefs: in a subtle way, the individual in the market is, to some extent, coerced into specific types of behaviour. As such, the market cannot be entirely free in the classic liberal sense and does not necessarily guarantee maximum freedom for the individual. A related observation is that markets are social institutions created and regulated by an authority because doing so minimises transaction costs, including the cost of policing and enforcing contracts.

Against this background, it can be seen that a market, as a social institution, is really a part of the interwoven institutions that can be manipulated by governments in order to satisfy the central goal of maximising social welfare, as argued by Timbergen (1972). The other institutions are the firms (public and private) and socio–economic associations (labour unions, employers' associations and civil society organisations). The instruments with which government can manipulate these institutions include prices, bargaining, money, credit, taxes and a wide range of regulatory controls over prices (commodity prices, interest rates, exchange rates, tariffs and other forms of taxes/subsidies), production and consumption activities, investment, export, import and employment of inputs (Ajakaiye, 1990).

It is obvious, therefore, that the primary function of a good government as suggested by Aristotle is really to plan (as defined earlier) the combination of these institutions (markets, inclusive) and instruments with the sole aim of maximising the welfare of the overwhelming majority of the people. It follows, therefore, that the attempt by the World Bank to reconceptualise the role of the state (government) by defining good governance in terms of supporting the develop- ment of a market economy on the assumption that the promotion of markets will universally promote the achievement of the goal of maximising the welfare of the people is hopelessly flawed (World Bank, 1997: 4). Specifically, the attempt by the World Bank to define the form of state intervention which it considers essential for the proper functioning and continuing stability of the neoclassical model of development amounts to elevating an instrument to the status of an objective. Put differently, the objective of any reasonable state is not to promote and support the development and functioning of a market economy, but to secure and sustain the maximum welfare for the majority of the people through a judicious combination of the institutions and instruments listed earlier. Accordingly, the combination of institutions and the manipulation of instruments so as to achieve this overriding objective in any country should depend on the historical and socio–cultural contexts, the political structure and process, and the level of development in the various sectors of the socio-economic system, and not on any ideologically fixed idea about the best institutional arrangement for an economy.

Planning in Contemporary African Mixed Economies

During the first two decades of independence, therefore, African government planning combined existing institutions and utilised available instruments with a view to improving the welfare of the people and also to altering the structure of their economies. Specifically, given the level of development and the historical context, African governments emphasised the use of public enterprises to increase the size, scope and depth of the modern sector and reduce the dominance of foreigners in the sector. They used other policies to enhance the participation of private indigenous entrepreneurs while using public enterprises, again, to expand the scope and coverage of economic and social infrastructure.

The dismal performance of African economies during the second decade of political independence was blamed on domestic policy inadequacies and the imposition of policies inspired by the neoliberal development paradigm, which elevated an instrument (the market) to the level of an objective. Consequently, the centrality of planning to the success of the neoliberal development paradigm was ignored, and this mistake has contributed in a major way to the abysmal failure of SAPs on the African continent.

With the emergence of the unipolar world, African governments are being coerced once again to adopt the so-called private-sector-led development strategy, which may amount to no more than a repackaging of SAPs with the risk of a continued absence of planning. Needless to say, any development paradigm which ignores planning in developing countries, is bound to fail. Meanwhile, African governments should insist on furthering the development of their mixed economies, which would generate sufficient income and saving with less dependence on external sources of capital and manpower, beyond that which is usual through the natural incentives of international commerce. Moreover, African governments, while recognising the inevitability of reliance on foreign private investment to supplement domestic savings in the short term, should continue to insist on the fullest participation of their citizens in the ownership, direction and management of the private sector of their economies.

Against this background, planning that is aimed at coordinating economic decision making in order to give direction to and accelerate the pace of development of a mixed economy should have the following three major components. The first is government's deliberate utilisation of domestic savings and foreign finance to execute public investment projects. This implies that African governments should take the responsibility of mobilising and channelling scarce resources into areas that can be expected to make the greatest impact, and thus contribute towards the achievement of long-term economic progress. Such areas will include the construction of roads, especially in the rural areas, the establishment of schools and health facilities, the provision of potable water, etcetera. All these will improve the standard of living and productivity of the people, and, hence, overall economic growth. In other words, African governments' investments in economic infrastructure should create the enabling environment for firms to maximise output, profits, employment and income; simultaneously, the provision of social infrastructure should create the enabling environment for households to maximise their utility, improve the quality of labour services and, hence, their earnings from the labour services supplied to private and public sectors of the economy.

The second major component of planning is in the form of designing appropriate policy packages to facilitate, stimulate, and direct private economic activities in order to promote a harmonious relationship between the desires of private business and households, on one hand, and the economic plans of the government on the other. This type of planning usually takes the form of government's conscious effort to attain rapid economic growth, high employment, stable prices and a favourable balance of payments through appropriate fiscal and monetary policies. In recognition of the fact that the unfettered operation of the market mechanism can engender highly unstable situations that may be reflected in severe fluctuations of income and employment over the course of business cycles, African governments should make a conscious effort to create conditions that will prevent economic instability, while at the same time stimulating economic growth. For instance, increased employment and higher incomes for a growing population may be induced by expansionary monetary policy, increased government expenditure and the adjustment of tax rates. Similarly, inflation and deflation may be controlled by counter-cyclical fiscal polices, interest rate adjustment and wage–price guidelines, otherwise known as incomes policies. Also, balance of payments fluctuations can be managed by several policy mixes, critical among which are tariff adjustments and exchange rate adjustments, import quotas and tax incentives. Typically, these active policy instruments should be managed in indirect ways to create favourable conditions that will influence decision makers in households and firms in a manner that is conducive to the continuous realisation of stable economic growth. In other words, African governments, through judicious and pragmatic manipulation of their policy instruments, should become veritable enablers.

Finally, African governments should be and remain free to participate in directly productive activities, at least to get things started, while taking steps to actively seek indigenous private sector participation and eventual takeover of such activities at the earliest possible opportunity. There should be no doubt that the development of Africa is and should be, the responsibility primarily of Africans. Foreign investment should be essentially supplementary, therefore, and not the primary source of development impetus. After a time, African governments should sell their interests in such activities and use the proceeds to get things started on new frontiers and at higher levels. In other words, in the process of developing the African mixed economy, government investments in directly productive activities should be aimed at shifting the frontiers of development opportunities by getting things started in such areas, while taking steps to encourage the indigenous private sector to take over such activities at the earliest possible time.

Implications for the Planning Process in Contemporary Africa

Clearly, the three major aspects of planning in a mixed economy where the private sector will be the main engine of growth have implications for the planning process in the contemporary African situation. A major element of the contemporary African situation is the restoration of democratic governance with the associated improvement in budgetary discipline and better commitment to plans. Another major element is the continuing dependence of virtually all African governments on volatile and unpredictable fiscal resources necessary to support production, employment and income as well as consumption, investment, and export and import activities.

Against this background, the first implication is that the planning process should be robust enough to cope with the uncertainties surrounding the resources profiles of the African countries. In this regard, it is recommended that a rolling plan system should be adopted. Put simply, a rolling plan is the capital budget of that year. At the end of the year, the rolling plan is reviewed and, based on experience during the year, the plan may be extended by another year and all uncompleted capital projects may be rolled over. In this way, the integrity of the plan is maintained despite the uncertainties surrounding the resource profile. In a democracy, the process must be streamlined in such a way that the integrity of the rolling plan is not thwarted by the capital expenditure programmes of the annual budget.

With respect to policies, all arms of government should ensure that the thrusts of the policies are compatible with the necessity to create an enabling environment for economic growth. In doing so, necessary consultation should be held with the relevant stakeholders with a view to ensuring that these operators are satisfied that the implementation of such policies will be conducive to their activities, and to obtain assurances that they will respond appropriately to the policies.

In terms of the exit programme for government involvement in productive activities, consultations should be held constantly with the relevant agencies of government and other stakeholders, with a view to obtaining updates on the actions being taken to increase indigenous private sector participation and the eventual takeover of such ventures at the earliest possible time. This will avoid the usual practice whereby the bureaucrats are quick to enter a sector but reluctant to quit – for several reasons, including the lust for power and influence over the activities of public enterprises.

Conclusion

If Africa is to make a success of the policy of developing a private-sector-led economy in a globalising world, planning should not be taken as 'business as usual'. All stakeholders – especially the government and credible members of the indigenous private sector, the civil society organisations and the labour unions – should secure a rolling consensus, which has played a major, but seldom stated, role in the newly industrialising countries of East Asia. The instrumentality of the rolling plan system supported by a rolling consensus should put African countries in a good position to catch up with the Asian Tigers, with whom they started the development race at about the same point some four decades ago.

Bibliography

Aboyade, O. (1983) *Integration Economics: a Study of Developing Economics*, Boston, MA: Addison-Wesley Publishers.

Ajakaiye, D. O. (1984) 'Impact of Policy on Public Enterprise Performance in Nigeria', *Nigerian Journal of Economic and Social Studies*, 26, 3: 371–401.

—— (1988) 'Motive and Consequences of Privatisation Under SAP' in *Privatisation of Public Enterprises in Nigeria: Processing of the 1988 One Seminar*, Ibadan: Nigerian Economic Society.

—— (1990) 'Balance between Public and Private Investment Programmes', in O. A. Adeyemo and E. C. Ndekwu (eds.), *Readings in Public Expenditure Programming in Nigeria*, Ibadan: National Centre for Economic Management and Administration (NCEMA).

—— (1994) 'Sectional Planning Process in Nigeria', in M. I. Obadan and G. O. Ogiogio (eds.), *Planning and Budgeting in Nigeria: Institutional and Policy Reforms*, Ibadan: NCEMA.

Anyanwu, J. C. (2000) 'The State in Nigerian Economic Development', paper presented to NISER as part of a review of Nigerian development.

Anyanwu, J. C. et al. (1997), *The Structure of the Nigerian Economy (1960–1997)*, Onitsha: JOANEE Educational Publishers Ltd.

Aron, J. (1996) 'The Institutional Functions of Growth', in S. Ellis (ed.), *Africa Now: People, Policies and Institutions*, The Hague: Ministry of Foreign Affairs.

Blitzer, C. R. (1977) 'The Status of Planning: an Overview', in C. R. Blitzer, P. B. Clark and L. Taylor (eds.), *Economy-Wide Models and Development Planning*, Washington, DC: World Bank.

Brito, J. (1995) 'Africa's Future Is at Stake', *Africa Recovery*, 9, 3 (November): 1.

Brown, M. B. and P. Tiffen (1992) *Short Changed: Africa and World Trade*, London: Pluto Press.

Chowdhury, A and C. Kirkpatrick (1994) *Development Policy and Planning*, London and New York: Routledge.

Federal Republic of Nigeria (1962) *Nigerian National Development Plan, 1962–68*, Lagos: Federal Government Printers.

—— (1970) *Second National Development Plan, 1970–74*, Lagos: Federal Government Printers.

—— (1975) *Third National Development Plan, 1975–80*, Lagos: Federal Government Printers.

—— (1981) *Fourth National Development Plan, 1981–85*, Lagos: Federal Government Printers.

—— (1986) *The Structural Adjustment Programme for Nigeria, 1986–88*, Lagos: Federal Government Printers.

—— (various issues) *National Rolling Plan of Nigeria*, Lagos and Abuja: National Planning Commission.

Hassen, A. H. (1959) *Public Enterprises and Economic Development* (London: Routledge and Kegan Paul).

Hodgson, G. M. (1996) *Economic and Institutions: a Manifesto of Modern Institutional Economics*, Cambridge: Polity Press.

Kaplan, E. J. (1972) *Japan: the Government–Business Relationship*, Washington, DC: US Department of Commerce.

Lewis, W. A. (1966) *Development Planning: the Essentials of Economic Policy*, London: Longman, George Allen and Unwin Limited.

Lipsey, R. (1983) *Positive Economics*, London:Weidenfield and Nicolson, 6th edition.

Obadan, M. I. (1996) 'Development Planning in Nigeria: Retrospect and Prospects', paper delivered at the Development Policy Planning Centre, University of Bradford.

Rodrik, D. (1999) *The New Global Economy and Developing Countries: Making Openness Work*, Policy Essay No. 24, Washington, DC: Overseas Development Council.

Spoor, M. (1994) 'Issues of State and Market: from Interventionism to Deregulation of Food Markets in Nicaragua', *World Development*, 22, 4 (April): 517–34.

Stiglitz, J. (1997) *The State and Development: Some New Thinking*, Washington, DC: World Bank.

Thorbecke, Erik (1998) 'The Institutional Foundations of Macroeconomic Stability: Indonesia versus Nigeria', in Yujiro Hayami and Masahiko Aoki (eds.), *The Institutional Foundation of East Asian Economic Development*, New York: St Martin's Press, in assocation with the International Economic Association (IEA).

Timbergen, J. (1972) *Mathematical Models of Economic Growth*, New York: McGraw-Hill.

Todaro, M. P. (1986) *Economics for a Developing World: an Introduction to the Principles, Problems and Policies of Development*, London: Longman.

Waterston, A. (1965) *Development Planning: Lesson of Experience*, Baltimore: Johns Hopkins Press.

World Bank (1981) *Accelerated Development in Sub-Saharan Africa: an Agenda for Action*, Washington, DC: World Bank.

—— (1997), *World Development Report: the State in a Changing World*, Washington, DC: World Bank.

UNRISD (2000) *Visible Hands: Taking Responsibility for Social Development*, Geneva: UN Research Institute for Social Development.

6

Implementation of Africa's Development Paradigms: Solution to Africa's Socio-economic Problems

Hassan A. Sunmonu

If people are deceiving you, don't deceive yourself. (An African proverb.)

Africa's numerous socio-economic problems have mostly been identified, analysed and provided with optional solutions by Africans themselves. During the colonial period, and up until the independence of most African countries, European scholars often wrote that Africa had no history! It took years of research and erudite scholarship for African historians to prove not only that Africans do have an abundant and rich history, but also that Africa is the very cradle of humanity and ·civilization!

You cannot shave somebody's head in his/her absence. (Another African proverb.)

Continuously since the era of slavery, through the time of colonialism, up to the present, the heads of Africans have been shaved in their absence by the colonial and former colonial masters, who have now become our development partners. We, the African peoples, have not been allowed to decide for ourselves whether we want to have our hair cut, nor have we been allowed to decide the style of our haircut, nor the barber! So, when our development partners talk about human rights, we in Africa will be excused for wondering whether these human rights apply to us in our relations with them or are reserved only for Euro-Americans and the developed countries.

In the traditional African culture, *group rights* supersede *individual rights*. That is why land used to be owned by the community, but individual members of the community were allocated communal land according to their needs. The Chief or King held the land in trust for the entire community. He had to be transparent and impartial in the allocation of the land to his community. Egocentrism, greed and cheating were not tolerated by the African society. Every African was his brother's/sister's keeper.

After the independence of most African countries in the early 1960s, and the founding of the Organisation of African Unity (OAU) on 25 May 1963, the struggle for the complete decolonisation of Africa was fought ferociously, in tandem with the fight against apartheid in South Africa. The last colonial battle and victory were fought and won against Portuguese colonialism in Africa, with the independence of Angola, Mozambique, Cape Verde and Guinea–Bissau in 1975. Then there was the independence of Zimbabwe in 1980, and another 14 years before the end of apartheid in South Africa in April 1994, with the election of the first democratic, non-racial government led by President Nelson Mandela.

It is to the eternal credit of African leaders, through the support and collaboration of the OAU and the United Nations Economic Commission for Africa (UNECA), that the Lagos Plan of Action (LPA) for the Economic Development of Africa (1980–2000) and the Final Act of Lagos (FAL), were adopted by the African Heads of State and Government at the special summit of the OAU in Lagos in April 1980.

The main objectives of the Lagos Plan of Action and the Final Act of Lagos were:

- food self-sufficiency;
- the satisfaction of the basic needs of the African peoples;
- creation of employment opportunities;
- internal mass production of essential consumer goods;
- establishment of the African Economic Community by the year 2000.

These were the objectives set for Africa by African leaders some 20 years ago. Where is Africa today with respect to these objectives? Where did it go wrong? The African Centre for Development and Strategic Studies (ACDESS), and its founder, Professor Adebayo Adedeji, should be congratulated for this Millennium Symposium, which, I hope, will provide answers to the above questions.

This chapter will focus on three of Africa's development initiatives:

1 the African Alternative Framework to Structural Adjustment Programmes for Socio-Economic Recovery and Transformation (AAF–SAP);
2 the African Charter for Popular Participation in Development and Transformation (Arusha 1990); and,
3 the treaty establishing the African Economic Community (Abuja 1991).

The African Alternative Framework to Structural Adjustment Programmes for Socio-economic Recovery and Transformation (AAF–SAP)

The economic crisis experienced by many African countries from the late 1970s up to the present forced most of them to turn to the International Monetary Fund

(IMF) and the World Bank for financial assistance. The Fund and the Bank obliged, but set their conditions. Principally, SAPs – intended to reorient African economic policies to the market economy model – were forced upon governments in spite of the structural rigidities of African political economies.

The main features of the orthodox SAPs of the IMF and the World Bank include:

1 Withdrawal of government subsidies on social services such as education, health, housing, water, electricity and transport. The Bank and the Fund insist on the payment of 'user fees' for these services, putting them out of the reach of the poor who constitute the majority of African population.

2 Massive devaluation of currencies was a *sine qua non* of SAPs. In a number of cases, the devaluations are 50 per cent and more, and on a continuing basis. These devaluations are arbitrary and without any consideration for the purchasing power parity of the currencies. For example, in 1980, the Nigerian Naira was worth US$1.1. By 2000 and 2002 respectively it had fallen as low as 117 and 135 Naira to US$1, and it is still on the downward slope. In December 1981 the Ghanaian currency was exchanged at 2.5 Cedis to $1. When I assumed duty in Accra in November 1986 as Secretary-General of the Organisation of African Trade Union Unity (OATUU), US$1 was worth 90 Cedis. Today, it is worth 77,000. The effect of these arbitrary devaluations of national currencies include:

   • an astronomical increase in the debts of African countries;
   • increased poverty of the majority of the African population;
   • increased cost of production of locally manufactured goods, making them too expensive and uncompetitive. Many factories were closed down, with the attendant loss of millions of jobs throughout Africa;
   • excessive inflation in African countries.

3 High interest rates, (of the magnitude of 30–50 per cent) were a great disincentive for local entrepreneurship. The highest profit rate that most businesses can make is about 25 per cent, which is less than the interest rates of 30 to 50 per cent. Therefore, the claim by the IMF and the World Bank that their orthodox SAPs encourage and strengthen the private sector is false. Rather, the local private sector is weakened and left at the mercy of the foreign private sector, mostly transnational corporations.

4 Privatisation of state-owned enterprises (SOEs), irrespective of whether they are profitable or not, and utilisation of the proceeds not for productive purposes but for consumption. The objective of this neoliberal economic ideology of the Fund and Bank is to make poor African countries sell their 'family silver' so as to pay mounting external debts – further aggravating poverty.

5   Massive retrenchment of public service workers of between 35 and 40 per cent of the workforce. These retrenchments are arbitrary, without due regard for trade union rights, and without adequate and prompt compensation of the affected workers. Many workers and their families die of hunger while waiting to receive their gratuities and end-of-service payments, while pensioners are consumed by deprivation due to non-payment of their pensions.

6   Trade liberalisation, imposed by orthodox SAPs on weak African economies, has contributed greatly to the de-industrialisation of many African countries. There is no country in the developed world that has fully liberalised its economy. What even the strongest economies do not practise, is what the IMF and the World Bank have been imposing on failing African economies since the early 1980s.

The above features of the orthodox SAPs of the IMF and the World Bank are the pillars of their ideological dogma, to which they arrogantly claim that there is no alternative (the TINA syndrome). The OATUU was among the first to challenge this fallacy, because it was not the text of the Holy Quran or the Bible, in which even a comma cannot be changed. The contention of the OATUU is that any human conception or blueprint is subject to change.

Fortunately for Africa, the ECA and the OAU rose to the challenge. The AAF–SAP was produced and submitted by the ECA to the African Heads of State and Government at the OAU Summit of July 1989, and to the General Assembly of the United Nations in September 1989.

The orthodox SAPs of the IMF/World Bank – Success or Failure?

The OATUU's criticism of the orthodox SAPs started in late 1986, and our criticism was considered as heresy at the time. In 1987, organisations like the United Nations Children's Fund (UNICEF) also criticised the orthodox SAPs. In its publication on *The State of the World's Children*, UNICEF highlighted the damaging impact of the orthodox SAPs on children in the developing countries and called for 'Adjustment with a Human Face'.

At the 15th Annual Meeting of the Economic and Social Interest Groups of the African, Caribbean and Pacific countries (ACP) and the European Union, held in Brussels on 2–4 December 1991, Dr Steven Webb, a Senior Economist with the World Bank, admitted that the Bank made seven mistakes in its structural adjustment policies. In his address at the African-American Institute's Conference in Reston, Virginia, in May 1993, Edward V. K. Jaycox, former Vice-President for Africa in the World Bank, announced broad policy measures to correct the failure.

Instead of correcting the failures of their orthodox SAPs, however, the Fund and the Bank made Africa the guinea-pig for right-wing economic theories that have completely destroyed the African middle class and triggered endemic poverty and mounting debts. The end result is that 33 African countries had joined the league of Least Developed Countries, out of 48 world-wide by the end of the 1990s.

The AAF–SAP was written on the basis of African-authored objectives in the Lagos Plan of Action and the Final Act of Lagos. While the orthodox SAPs take the short-term view that Africa should be adjusting to the financial crisis – domestic or external – the AAF–SAP insists that African economies really require structural transformation, diversification and a response to the problem of under-development and pervasive poverty. While balancing budgets is the obsession of orthodox SAPs, the AAF–SAP believes that balancing of budgets on its own can never make the African peoples richer, and can also never bring about real development. The AAF–SAP believes that any adjustment programme must not compromise the long-term development objectives of the African countries.

The AAF–SAP insists that any adjustment carried out in any country should be done in such a way that:

- it does not make the life of the people impossible;
- it does not postpone the process of transformation.

In short, the only adjustment that should ever be undertaken is that which is both humane and developmental. On the question of who is to adjust and for whom, the AAF–SAP answer is that adjustment must be for the benefit of the majority of the people, and that adjustment programmes must therefore be initiated from within. Adjustment with transformation must include:

- access of the poor to factors of production (economic empowerment);
- creation of employment opportunities (to ensure the creation of wealth and eradication of poverty);
- improvement of the way national wealth is shared among the population in order to ensure equity.

As to who should implement the alternative framework, it is necessary to emphasise the role of popular participation and the empowerment of the people.

Another superior feature of the AAF–SAP is its advocacy of expenditure switching by government from the military to the social sectors, such as education, health and housing, so as to satisfy the basic needs of the people. The AAF–SAP also stresses the importance of regional cooperation in the design, choice and implementation of programmes of adjustment with transformation. Coordination between countries and the pooling of financial resources are needed to put a number of projects into action. The exploration of African rivers and gas resources to produce electric power is one example. Rail and highway links that run from the interior to the ports – a legacy of colonial times – need to be extended into a network connecting African countries. Improved transportation and communication links will encourage intra-African trade and ease dependence on overseas markets.

By whatever criteria one compares the AAF–SAP with the orthodox SAPs of the IMF and the World Bank, it will be found that the AAF–SAP is superior because it addresses the fundamental problems of development and transformation in a holistic manner. The AAF–SAP is people-friendly and participatory, not a uniform one-size-fits-all; it creates employment and wealth; it integrates and is not divisive; it transforms both people's lives and economies for better and not for worse. Until African countries discard the orthodox SAPs, there will be no end to the poverty, indebtedness, misery and social instability that plague African peoples and the continent. We should remember the African proverb – 'If somebody is deceiving you, don't deceive yourself.'

African Charter for Popular Participation in Development and Transformation (Arusha 1990)

When our development partners talk about the need for democracy in Africa nowadays, some of us laugh. Why? Because Africa decided on its democratic option with the adoption of the African Charter for Popular Participation in Development and Transformation (Arusha 1990) by the African Heads of States and Government at the Addis Ababa Summit of the OAU in July 1990. Paragraph 7 of the Charter reads:

> We affirm that nations cannot be built without the popular support and full participation of the people, nor can the economic crisis be resolved and the human and economic conditions improved without the full and effective contribution, creativity and popular enthusiasm of the vast majority of the people. After all, it is to the people that the very benefits of development should and must accrue. We are convinced that neither can Africa's perpetual economic crisis be overcome, nor can a bright future for Africa and its people see the light of the day unless the structures, patterns and political contexts of the process of socio-economic development are appropriately altered!

Democracy is defined as 'government of the people by the people for the people'. It is, however, easy for democracy to be hijacked from the people by the élites, as we have seen in many African countries. The élites may be the few rich or the officer corps of the military. In that case, democracy becomes, 'government of the people by the élite, for the élite, on behalf of the people'. That is why the African Charter gave a new concept to democracy in Africa, encapsulated in:

- popular participation;
- employment of the people;
- accountability;

- social and economic justice;
- respect for human and trade union rights and the rule of law.

These *five pillars of African democracy*, enunciated by the Charter, will ensure that governance is of the people, for the people, and by the people, without the usurpation of the people's empowerment by the rich, the military or any powerful élite in the society.

All that we need to do in Africa, when talking about democracy and good governance, is to put into practice the African Charter. It is the African Bible and Quran for democracy in our continent. But Africans should be on guard, as some of the language in the Charter has been used to hoodwink us. Two to three years after its adoption in 1990, some international institutions and donors started to talk about popular participation of the African peoples in the development process. Deliberately, however, they forgot to add any reference to empowerment of the people, as contained in the Charter. The five pillars of the Charter are the answer to democracy and good governance in Africa, or anywhere else in the world for that matter. Africa should not throw away diamonds in exchange for silver, because diamonds are forever. The current mobilisation and empowerment of the African civil society, which we have now witnessed in many African countries, gives living effect to the Charter's ideals.

For our part in the OATUU, the AAF-SAP and the African Economic Community have become textbooks in our Workers' Education Programmes throughout Africa. Other African civil society organisations should do likewise, so as to speed up participation and empowerment in Africa.

The Treaty Establishing the African Economic Community (Abuja, 1991)

In some other regions of the world, the process of globalisation has spurred countries to bury their differences in order to integrate their economies so that they can have bigger markets and be more competitive. The European Union started the process some four decades ago with the Treaty of Rome. Beginning with six members it expanded to nine, then to 12 and now to 15 European countries. Within the next five years, the membership of the EU might extend to 28 countries.

The North American Free Trade Agreement (NAFTA) has the United States, Canada and Mexico as members. In Asia, the Association of South-East Asian Nations (ASEAN) is also working for economic integration. *When the son of the rich is warned, the son of the poor must open his ears to listen*, says the African proverb. When economically powerful countries see the necessity to integrate their economies, poor African countries should hurry to integrate theirs. This is the context in which we discuss the treaty for establishing the African Economic Community.

Formation of economic blocs is the order of the day. Most of the national economies in Africa are classified as micro-economies: individually, in the context of globalisation, they cannot rid their populations of poverty and under-development, because of their small markets, and inability to generate national development.

The treaty establishing the African Economic Community was adopted by the African Heads of State and Government at the Abuja Summit of the OAU in June 1991. It took another three years for the treaty to be ratified by two thirds (35) of the OAU member countries on 12 May 1994. It is supposed to be built on the pillars of five regional economic communities (RECs), from the five subregions of Africa, three of which were established by the ECA under the leadership of Professor Adedeji:

- the Economic Community of West African States (ECOWAS);
- the Economic Community of Central African States (ECCAS);
- the Southern African Development Community (SADC);
- the Arab Maghreb Union (AMU);
- the Preferential Trade Area of Eastern and Southern Africa (PTA COMESA).

The six stages during which the African Community will be established, as envisaged in the treaty, will take 34 years. And if the time between the adoption of the treaty and its ratification was approximately three years, then even 34 years may turn out be optimistic!

Can the whole world wait for 34 years for Africa's economic integration? Is it in the best interests of Africa and African peoples to wait that long? Why has the economic integration process in Africa been so slow? Will the new Africa Union make much of a difference by accelerating the integration process?

In answering these questions, it is important to reflect on the fact that *most socio-economic initiatives in Africa are taken by African governments alone, without the active support of African peoples*. Unlike the African Charter for Popular Participation in Development and Transformation and the AAF–SAP, in which African civil society organisations participated effectively during both conceptualisation and implementation stages, the other socio-economic initiatives, including the much acclaimed New Partnership for Africa's Development (NEPAD), have not enjoyed the wide participation and support of African civil society.

This has been the major reason for the slow progress of Africa's economic integration. This reminds us of the late President Julius Nyerere's speech at the first ACDESS International Conference in Dakar in November 1992, when he said that the only thing he regretted about the Organisation of African Unity (OAU), was that it was created for Africa's governments, not for its peoples.

In order, therefore, to redress the slow pace of Africa's economic integration, we have to seize the opportunity created by the Constitutive Act of the African Union, which the OAU Heads of State and Government adopted at the 36th summit of the OAU in Lome on 12 July 2000 and which became operational two years later in July 2002. It is the sure way in which we can fast-track Africa's economic integration; otherwise, Africa will be left behind for centuries to come.

Conclusion

The solution to Africa's socio-economic problems lies in the hands of the African governments and peoples. The three African-authored socio-economic initiatives discussed in this chapter contain all the ingredients of this solution.

Africa has to restructure its economy. The restructuring has to be endogenous and not imposed from outside by the international financial and trade institutions (the multilateral bureaucracy). The restructuring should also be carried out by Africa's socio-economic actors, including governments, the private and informal sectors, workers, farmers, women and young people, and should be based upon the AAF–SAP.

Africa has to acquire and nurture a democratic culture based on the five pillars of the African Charter. African peoples should never again allow their heads to be shaved in their absence!

Africa's economic integration should be speeded up, with the active participation and empowerment of the African peoples in the process. The Constitutive Act of the African Union should fast-track the realisation of the African Economic Community.

Bibliography

ECA (1989) *African Alternative Framework to Structural Adjustment Programmes for Socio-Economic Recovery and Transformation (AAF–SAP)*, Addis Ababa: Economic Commission for Africa.

—— (1990). *African Charter for Popular Participation in Development and Transformation*, Addis Ababa: Economic Commission for Africa.

OAU (1991) *Treaty Establishing The African Economic Community*, Addis Ababa: Organisation of African Unity.

UNICEF (1987) *The State of the World's Children*, Oxford: Oxford University Press.

7

Modernisation, Globalisation and Africa's Political Economy: the Case of Nigeria

Elsie Onubogu

There is little doubt that Nigeria has experienced and continues to experience severe and devastating socio-economic, political and developmental crises. An evaluation of Nigeria's development framework is laden with components such as consumerism, corruption, ten per cent contract kickbacks, human rights abuses, incessant military coups/regimes, gender inequality, and failed socio-economic and political policies. Plagued by such factors, rather than achieving sustainable development, Nigeria has been faced with what Dr Elise Boulding defines as 'mal-development'.

Other less glaring but very dangerous factors are the effects of modernisation and globalisation, and their relationship to the developmental approaches adopted by Nigeria since independence. Modernisation, economic growth and economic development have often been used synonymously in discussing the problems facing less developed countries; actually, they refer to clearly distinct phenomena. All countries, for instance, experience fluctuations in their economic growth, but not all countries are economically developed. Economic development seems to refer to a process whereby an economy becomes larger, more complex, and more diverse. This gives rise, quite naturally, to an economistic understanding of economic development. The tendency to think that the problems of economic development are primarily economic has a certain intuitive plausibility. Lack of development is most often an economic issue: lack of access to economic resources, poor growth rates, lack of industrialisation, inflation, high interest rates, lack of savings, low levels of investment, and so on are the main impeding factors.

Until quite recently, this is how the problem of economic development was understood and considered. This understanding stemmed from the pioneering works in growth economics of John Maynard Keynes and others of his school of thought who were concerned with the problems of economic growth in the developed countries in the wake of the recession of the 1930s. This economistic understanding of development became the genesis of growth theories and models that were developed and designed to show how an economy can be induced to grow out of a slump. Subsequently, one of the most persistent ways of explaining the differences between developed and less developed economies was to track certain key variables familiar to economic theory.

However, the post-war experience of many developing countries (as well as developed countries), has caused a rethinking of the economistic understanding of economic development. These experiences have revealed that periods of economic growth do not necessarily lead to economic development. Conversely, assisting the development of a complex and diverse economy is not the same thing as stimulating or ensuring economic growth. What is true, however, is that economies with more stable growth usually do sustain economic development. Growth, then, has become only a variable in the overall determination of economic development.

Modernisation, on the other hand, seems to relocate the fundamental assumption linking growth and economic development. I believe that this assumption is rooted in the ubiquitous dominance of the forces of globalisation, which posits that economic growth is best achieved in a world of free markets and competitive advantage. Modernisation and globalisation, therefore, seem to be two sides of the same coin. Modernisation theorists lean more towards the neoclassical school of thought in advocating that developing countries allow markets to allocate resources free from government intervention. This would, of course, mean removing structural impediments in the economy, getting prices right, privatisation, banking sector reforms, tax reforms, and many other measures: in other words, linking one's economy to the global economy. The implication of this thinking was that the economic development of developing countries such as Nigeria would result from changes in certain economic fundamentals, such as the level of investment and/or, most importantly, the operation of market forces.

This frenzy was heightened in the second half of the 1980s and accelerated in the early 1990s, but it remains difficult to pinpoint the origin, causes and metamorphoses of modernisation in developing countries. It seems more plausible to locate the evolution of this trend to at least five major global episodes:

1   decolonisation;
2   the demise of the Bretton Woods System;
3   globalisation of the world economy;
4   the fall of communism;
5   awareness that structural adjustment programmes were not leading to sustained economic growth.

Suffice it to say that these global changes have had tremendous impact on the economies of developing countries. For instance, the impact of globalising the world economy could be seen in Asia with the 'Asian 'Flu' and in Europe with the 'Russian crisis'. On the other hand, within the African continent, most countries could hardly be described as having survived the 'colonial contraptions', those rickety economies with which they started out at independence. This is not to suggest that the problems of African economies rest solely on the effects of colonialism. Rather, there is need for a radical reversal of colonial contraptions, and the inescapable question is: what have successive leaders and regimes in Africa done to obtain that reversal?

Incidentally, since these African economies have only played peripheral roles in the overall global economic architecture, (though the foreign accounts of some leaders, such as the late Mobutu and Abacha, would affirm otherwise), prescriptions offered for their emancipation from stagnation and decay have often been ethnocentric and arrogant: ethnocentric because they are always based on abstract theories, which fail to take into account the socio-historical paths trodden by these developing economies; arrogant because they are imposed. Several economists, led by Professor Adebayo Adedeji, expressed grave concerns about the effectiveness of SAPs in Africa as prescribed by the Bretton Woods institutions. Despite this, however, it would be fallacious to suggest that Nigeria's economic problems were caused entirely by these changes and prescribed programmes. Internally, poor management of resources (especially oil and related products), corruption, incessant military coups, bad leadership, sentimental creation of non-revenue-generating states, consumerism, importation and dependent policies, lack of and non-execution of prudent policies, and intolerance of ethnic differences are the factors that undoubtedly have had a marked impact on the path of development in Nigeria.

Prescribed Economic Programmes

Despite the deeper, more structural reasons, it has frequently been assumed that the failure of SAPs in Africa has more to do with the issues of poor management conceded in the preceding paragraph. It is pertinent to mention that Nigeria is not alone in this quagmire. At the end of 1970s, African Ministers of Finance and Economic Planning had collectively appealed to the World Bank and the International Monetary Fund (IMF) to intervene. The Berg Report was the outcome of the study that sought to identify the African problem and prescribe solutions. This was the origin of the 'structural adjustment' capsule. By 1986, 35 countries in sub-Sahara Africa had been obliged to adopt SAPs. Among them was Nigeria. The Babangida military regime introduced the SAP with a view to correcting the distortions at the root of the economic malaise, and to reverse the adverse effects of the economic crisis on the welfare of his country's citizenry. However, after six years, the SAP had aggravated rather than solved the crisis. This situation forced Babangida to abandon the SAP (as prescribed by the Paris Club). Needless to say, Babangida's 'militocratic macro-economic' strategy failed woefully. A frustrated Ernest Shonekan, appointed by Babangida to head a transition government which he set up after annulling the 1993 Presidential elections, had this to say in his 1993 budget speech:

> In spite of the gains recorded under SAP, certain macro-economic problems had defied solutions. These include the continuing depreciation of the Naira; high and volatile interest rates; the depressing activities in the real sectors of the economy and skyrocketing inflation. Other problems causing concern are the burgeoning fiscal deficit, coupled with excessive money supply; increasing unemployment, especially of young school leavers; and the erosion of the standard of living of most Nigerians. (Okagbue and Ayua, 1996: 152)

Contrary to Shonekan's brief compliment, several commentators (and indeed most Nigerians) have described the SAP as a failure, a venture in which no gains were visible. Sarcastically, Professor Ihonvbere of the Ford Foundation stated:

> such gains are evident not only in the increased profit margins of multinational corporations and merchant banks, and in the bank accounts of top military and civilian politicians, but also in the kickbacks of sycophantic speculators, contractors and consultants who have increased their takes from 10 to 15 per cent. (Ihonvbere, 1991)

Subsequently, in a rather harsh but objective assessment of structural adjustment programmes, a joint task force of the International Labour Organisation (ILO) and the United Nations Development Programme (UNDP) posited that

> structural adjustment in sub-Saharan Africa had been purchased at the high price of economic contraction, high unemployment and massive poverty. This report mandated by the World Summit on Social Development in Copenhagen 1995, noted that unemployment rates have increased from 15 per cent to over 20 per cent, with an alarming projected increase to 30 per cent by the years 2000. (Lobe, 1998: 16)

The impact of these prescriptions is much felt throughout the developing world. Yet, attention still seems to be focused on economic variables as determinants of sustainable development or building a strong economy. Many more countries are being urged to wear their modernisation straitjackets. The unfortunate result is a moribund ferment of policy documents that are obviously too grandiose to be effectively and successfully implemented.

Nigeria thus presents an eloquent testimony to the vagaries of the market; it also presents a suitable site for research into the socio-economic, socio-cultural and socio-political problems that usually accompany such programmes of modernisation, but are usually not factored in as variables in designing the programmes.

The Economic Climate

It is obvious that the socio-economic climate in Nigeria within the past three or four decades has not promoted the kind of social and economic welfare that would insulate children and other vulnerable family members from the vagaries of the market. The Vision 2010 programme handed to the late Sanni Abacha's regime on 20 September 1997 (and adopted by the government of Abdulsalami) was a master plan anchored on free market principles and aimed at transforming Nigeria into a developed country in 12 years. It recommended a movement from guided deregulation to complete deregulation – that is, total privatisation.

There is nothing wrong with privatisation *per se*. However, the impossibility of reconciling the incongruent nature of such programmes with reality has been the source of a whirlpool of socio-economic problems in Nigeria. There is the possibility that these programmes may bring some positive results from the perspective of their designers. One wonders, however, how an economy estimated to have nearly 70 per cent of its population still living in rural villages with no basic amenities, an economy fraught with marginalised groups (both across regions and between sexes), a nation functioning on exclusionary policies at all levels and sectors, laden with inequalities and inequitable distribution of resources, including appointments to federal offices, could be transformed in 12 years – or even in a century – into a developed economy. As one Nigerian proverb captures it, 'you cannot dig a hole without creating a mound'.

The intrinsic element in SAPs is their advocacy of the primacy of the market in the determination of socio-economic development. Within the confines of such postulates, no room is left for safety nets. Against this background, therefore, the ripple effects of SAPs cannot be contained. The social implications of the 'fast-track' alignment of economies to the imperatives of modernisation and globali-sation are gruesome and need to be addressed. In our effort to build a strong and viable economy, we must balance the effects of prescribed programmes and globalisation against antecedent and consequent socio-economic, political or, indeed, ethnic and religious problems.

The path of nation building in Nigeria cannot therefore afford the luxury of modernisation and globalisation in its entirety without creating a future generation of socio-economic problems. Also, it cannot afford to ignore lessons learned in order to avoid past mistakes. Fast-track decisions such as the last increase of civil servants' salaries (under Abdulsalami, and more recently by Obasanjo), though laudable and long overdue, must be realistic and aligned to the nation's budget. The path to nation building may depend on an open economy, and it is ideal to have an open economy. It is equally ideal to have growth targets, structural adjustments and free trade. A developmental imperative, however, is the balance between such economic reform programmes and the socio-economic, cultural and political reform cost. Our inability to create such a balance has resulted in lopsided development in Nigeria. Such lopsidedness reinforces the woes of marginalisation, servitude, and the widening gaps between the 'haves' and the 'have nots'. With such gaps, Nigeria cannot honestly claim to be on the path to nation building. With such gaps, the administration is only reinforcing the achievements of the affluent few and history will judge it harshly. As the former Secretary-General of the United Nations Perez de Cuellar cautioned, a society is judged not so much by the achievements of its most affluent members as by the provision which it is able to assure its weakest citizens.

In our bid to globalise our economy, we must strive to bridge the existing gaps. A blind adoption of global theories and trends may widen further negative rifts among Nigerians. In this light, history has shown that the universalisation of most socio-economic theories stands condemned by cultural and socio-historical relativity. To avoid such condemnation, Nigeria must critically evaluate existing theories and programmes and balance such programmes against its own socio-cultural realities.

Existing Paradigms

Against this background, Nigeria should not attempt development through existing paradigms, but through paths that take into account their own socio-historical realities. One such reality, which has been avoided by past leaders, is genuine conciliation among the different ethnic groups, especially after the civil war. We can no longer attempt to distort our past, or wish it never happened. Our past definitely has a link to our present, and may well indeed impact on our future. For a country awash in ethnic sentiments, it may be impossible to contain violent impulses.

The deadweight of our past must be lifted. True healing, genuine conciliation and forgiveness, will assist us to respect individualism, diversity and human dignity. Though Obasanjo may be right in his fast-track attempt to promote alignment to the world economy as the 'buzz way', beneath this veneer of globalisation and alignment, 'in-house arrangement' should be given the utmost priority – after all, charity begins at home. Understood in another fashion by a Nigerian proverb, 'a fleeing rat cannot be the priority of a man whose house is under fire'. While the President of Nigeria may find delight with the West in his global embrace, he must not lose sight of the fact that, on the scale of priorities, he should first seek to hold his country's approbation in his arms.

For too long our developmental strategy has been afflicted with endless hiccups brought on by the persistent drain on its human resources. No government has made concerted efforts to create a stable environment for our professionals and other valued citizens. Rather, our globetrotting leaders have appeared to give approval to the exodus of Nigerians by basking in the wasteful receptions organised by Nigerian expatriates around the world to herald their visits. Recently, Solomon Lar offered justification for the globetrotting as being favourable to Nigeria's international standing. In his explanation he stated that it was an honour for Nigeria that the incessant overseas visits by the Nigerian President were helping other countries. One wonders who really needs whose assistance. While the drain on our manpower remains at its present level, one is at a loss to know how our economy can be sustained. The so-called experts argue that foreign investments solve our economic problems; hence the banner of privatisation is frequently flashed. While acknowledging the importance of foreign direct investment, a word of caution is apposite because it is a trite rule of business that charity has no business in a boardroom, whether at a national or international level. The prevalence of foreign business in a country tends to promote corruption both because the foreigners have fewer scruples in violating the norms of the society and because their control of important avenues to economic well-being forces potential native entrepreneurs to attempt to make their fortunes through politics.

As the administration strives to mimic and align our economy to global theories and trends, let us be mindful that the new paradigm of development has created and will continue to create avenues for corruption, destitution, pollution and prostitution. The new paradigm of development, therefore, must include more than economic variables. Indeed, recent studies and approaches have emphasised the importance of factors such as good governance, accountability, transparency, democracy, respect for human rights, gender equality and gender mainstreaming in all policies and programmes, as fundamental to sustainable development and long-lasting democracy. All these will no doubt create an enabling environment which is not only essential for foreign direct investment but also for equitable distribution and optional utilisation of resources.

The development paradigm should also call for a shift in the definition of development from a purely economistic perspective to cultural, historical, social, political and environmental components. By so doing, development will adopt a holistic perspective, becoming inclusive and not exclusive in nature. It does not marginalise, neither does it favour any one group on grounds of sex, religion, race or gender. It is built on the principles of equality, fairness, equity and justice, which also creates an environment to lure back drained human resources – an important theme in our drive for sustainable development.

Equity, Fairness, Gender Equality and Justice

I am quite sure that the government of Nigeria needs no reminding that the new paradigm of sustainable development is one that respects every individual and his or her rights, including the rights enshrined in the Nigerian constitution and the various international conventions that Nigeria has ratified. It encompasses the right to education, health, food, shelter and access to resources for all citizens. Nigeria must also align its domestic laws with such treaty provisions as the 30 per cent critical mass for women in governance adopted by the Beijing Platform for Action in 1995, and the ban on early marriages and traditional customs and practices that are not pro-female. Nigeria must also be proactive in the domain of affirmative policies and actions. From the gender perspective, it was an African philosopher,

Ibn Rashid, who cautioned that 'a society, which enslaves women' – or indeed anyone, we might add – 'is a society doomed to decay'.

Against this background, therefore, our nation-building efforts must meet the challenges of reducing poverty, promoting sustainable development and redressing existing inequalities. Such inequalities underscore the need to understand the synergy between decision making and policy making, between legislative and judicial processes, and between policy and implementation in the development process. The present administration has not only exhibited insensitivity with regard to commitments to engender its policies and programmes, but also failed at both the policy and implementation levels.

Ethnicity, Religion, Crime and Violence

The provision of resources and equitable representation is imperative, because history has shown that there is a causal link between the lack of basic needs and ethnic sentiments. The combined effects of these two factors are poverty, corruption and violence. The Ogoni, Modakeke, Ijaw Youth, OPC, Bakassi and other vigilante groups around the country are the consequence of pervasive poverty. Their existence and the growing call for a new Biafra are symptomatic. With hindsight, it can be said that the causal link between ethnicity and violence in Nigeria lies in our non-acknowledgement of our past. The resultant effect is enduring marginalisation of the citizenry, whose collective frustrations are manifested through communal, ethnic and religious clashes.

This assertion holds true because it is human nature that once the state, the expected provider, fails to fulfil its obligations, individuals are left with no choice other than to look inwards to immediate family or kinship ties. In other words, alternative coping strategies are explored that may heighten ethnic sentiments. The balkanisation theory has supported the hypothesis that any society plagued by ethnicity and violence is bound to collapse. With continued violence in different parts of the country, Nigeria may well be on the brink of collapse. From policy, democracy, and good governance perspectives, the federal government must engage in the equitable distribution of resources. By its present policies and appointments, the administration seems to reinforce what Peter Uvin terms 'structural conditions' that make violence inevitable. Uvin describes structural violence as

> exerted against the majority of the poor; it manifests itself in a deep and widening inequality of life chances; corruption, arbitrariness and impunity; the permanence of social and economic exclusion; lack of access to information, education, health and minimal basic needs; and an authoritarian and condescending state. (Uvin, 1998)

This reveals how exclusion policies may reinforce individual vulnerability to the extent of leading to violence. The government must therefore adopt a participatory approach to development. No one should be made to feel marginal-ised. Finally, from religious and customary perspectives, all discriminatory laws such as limited inheritance laws, early marriages, female genital mutilation and the *osu* caste system must be annulled and prohibited. These laws and customs belong to the Stone Age, and are indeed contrary to natural law, equity and good conscience. They perpetuate servitude and marginalisation. As a former Justice of Nigeria's own Supreme Court stated,

> Servitude, whether limited, whereby one's chattels are temporarily controlled by another, or absolute, whereby one's chattels are permanently put at another's disposal, is contrary to natural law, for God created all men free and equal in their humanity. (Oputa, 1990)

In our developmental efforts, we must not limit any potential. Every individual must be allowed his or her God-given right to contribute and enjoy resources. As Africa endeavours to claim the 21st century, its agenda must be sustainable development and not mal- or lopsided development.

An Agenda for Nation Building

Over forty years after the shackles of the colonial contraption that perpetuated servitude were loosened, Nigeria must adopt a sustainable, participatory agenda for development. Four decades after Nigeria joined the rest of the world to keep the peace in the Congo, we, especially our men, must fight and resolve to keep the peace in our own country. Three decades after we fought the senseless civil war that left many with lifelong scars, the succeeding generation must be spared from any new grief. All our children must be part of the national agenda for peace and not violence or war. Ten years after the shackles of apartheid released one of Africa's legendary leaders – Nelson Mandela – and the principle of reconciliation and *ubuntu* was enshrined in the South African constitution, we must reconcile our differences in Nigeria and proclaim *ubuntu* – our common humanity. Remembering the Beijing Conference and its Platform for Action, Nigerian women must be part of the national agenda for peace. The theme of the special session of the UN General Assembly in 2000, 'Women 2000, Gender Equality, Development and Peace for the 21st Century', was apt. Obasanjo should now align our national gender agenda to the global agenda, which is holistic. Such an agenda can be transformed into reality only if in the oneness of our shared humanity we resolve never to fight again. In the spirit of 'never again', Nigeria must adopt a faceless, sexless, and holistic human development agenda, and create an enabling environ-ment for sustainable development in Nigeria.

Finally, the Nigerian ship has the potential and wherewithal to navigate through the stormy seas of sustainable development. However, such potential can only be actualised through the following:

- political will and commitment;
- genuine reconciliation, forgiveness and the positive affirmation of 'never again';
- equitable distribution and representation of resources at all levels;
- gender equality and mainstreaming in all policies and programmes;
- gender-sensitive federal and state budgets;
- enabling environment to attract essential expatriate human and material resources currently in the diaspora and foreign direct investment;
- prudent socio-economic and political policies and programmes;
- affirmative policies where necessary to redress existing inequalities;
- balance between global theories and trends and national realities.

The path to nation building may indeed be daunting, but is achievable. Several nations with lesser resources and even greater diversities and idiosyncrasies have recorded success stories. Nigeria can also present just such an eloquent success story to the world. To accomplish this, however, our developmental path must be one which aligns our diversities and idiosyncrasies at all levels. Our ethnic, religious, biological, gender, and professional diversities need to be aligned. President Obasanjo must therefore begin his 'fast-track' alignment with an 'in-house' alignment – otherwise, he may be in pursuit of the proverbial rat, while his house is on fire.

Bibliography

Ihonvbere, J. O. (1991) 'Structural Adjustment in Nigeria', quoted in B. Turok (ed.), *Debt and Democracy*, London: Institute for African Alternatives.

Lobe, Jim (1998), 'Joint Task Report', quoted in *Peace and Freedom*, magazine of the Women's International League for Peace and Freedom, 58, 2 (March–April).

Okagbue, I. and I. A. Ayua (eds.) (1996) 'The Rights of the Child in Nigeria', Institute of Advanced Legal Studies, *Budget 93*, Lagos: Federal Government Printer.

Oputa, Chukwudifu (1990) Justice of the Supreme Court of Nigeria.

Uvin, P. (1998) *Aiding Violence: The Development Enterprise in Rwanda*, West Hartford, CT: Kumarian Press.

PART II
Governance and Development

8

Governance, Security and Conflict Resolution
Peter Anyang' Nyong'o

In *Arms and Daggers in the Heart of Africa* (Olisa, 1993), Michael Olisa noted that external intervention in an internal conflict could be problematic, even if carried out on humanitarian grounds. All sides of the conflict must see the intervening force as indeed neutral for it to succeed in its mission. The conflicting forces must also accept, separately and individually, that intervention is in their interest. In turn, the act of intervention must be precise and clear in objective, with the capability to be implemented in accordance with a programme endorsed by all parties.

There are many conflicts in Africa where external intervention has failed because the conditions that Olisa spelt out were not met. Soon after independence, the Congo faced a major internal conflict in which the United Nations Organisation intervened with disastrous consequences. Patrice Lumumba, the then Prime Minister of the Congo, was arrested by his opponents and assassinated – an action which did more to enhance the conflict than create conditions for its solution. Not long after that, the UN Secretary-General perished in the jungles of Northern Rhodesia (now Zambia) after a plane crash. It was never known whether the plane was shot down or came down accidentally. The end result, however, was that it left the UN rudderless in charting its way through the Congo crisis. The Congo never actually recovered, in spite of more than three decades of military dictatorship under Mobutu. The current conflict in the country could be traced to those years of failed external intervention followed by a long period of bad governance.

The recent conflicts in Somalia that saw the intervention of the United Nations – with strong backing from the US government – failed for very similar reasons. Following the collapse of the Siad Barre dictatorship and the disintegration of the Somali state, the warring factions had little appreciation for external intervention. Whatever military force came from outside could neither shake nor subdue the guerrilla fighters' determination to carve territory for themselves at the cost of thousands of human lives. The external intervention came at a time when there was no central power in Mogadishu, almost in the same way that there was no central power in Leopoldville (now Kinshasa) at the time of the Congo crisis. The end result in the case of Somalia has been continued disintegration, while in the Congo at least a military dictatorship emerged to impose some kind of order on society for a time.

In the case of Liberia and the ECOMOG intervention, Olisa noted that the objective was that of peacekeeping: to try to re-establish order and peace in Liberia at the end of an internal conflict that included the assassination of the former President, Samuel Kenyon Doe. The intervention was immediately contested on the grounds that the Organisation of African Unity, and not ECOMOG, had a legitimate mandate in attempting to solve the crisis; and that ECOMOG was thus contravening the OAU Charter by moving into Liberia without the sanction of the OAU. Further, it was argued that ECOMOG had no justification to go into Liberia without being invited by an internal and legitimate authority. Even the ECOWAS members themselves were not unanimous regarding ECOMOG's intervention; the intervention has thus been construed by some as opportunism, bordering on imperialist expansionism, taking advantage of internal weaknesses in a neighbouring state.

All that notwithstanding, as in the case of Somalia, Olisa observed, there was no legitimate authority to invite anybody into Liberia after Doe had rigged the election. The OAU, for its part, had hardly demonstrated the capacity to intervene successfully in such situations. Its earlier attempt to do so in Chad had ended in fiasco. ECOMOG, whatever controversy surrounded its initial move, was merely filling a vacuum and doing a job that had to be done. It was a choice between putting an end to a bloodbath or dithering among the legal niceties, dots and commas of international law.

Although ECOMOG managed to put an interim government in place soon after its intervention, this government never managed to establish authority over the whole of the Liberian territory. The existence of three different seats of power was to be the basis of an extended and protracted internal conflict in Liberia that ECOMOG's intervention could neither manage nor settle. Much later, with some internal accord that led the conflicting parties to a general election, the parties to the conflict agreed to put down arms and let the choice of the people determine who had the authority to exercise political power in Liberia. Whatever the shortcomings of the Liberian elections, the fact that the parties to the conflict agreed to participate in elections, as a peaceful mechanism for conflict resolution and the means to forming a legitimate government, is important.

Having carefully documented the genesis and evolution of the external conflict in Rwanda, Dixon Kamukama concluded that there was a need for regional, continental and international organisations to assist Rwanda in addressing the conflict (Kamukama, 1993). Well before the genocide of 1994 and the civil war that followed, he noted that the conflicts in Rwanda had assumed an international character when rebellious forces invaded the Congo with the backing of Rwanda and Uganda. Kamukama observed that neighbouring countries – all members of the OAU – would inevitably be drawn into the Rwandan conflict and that eventually they would have to formulate a solution, necessarily regional in character.

Internal Conflicts and Regional Intervention in Africa

The assumption was that parties to the Rwandan conflict would finally accept external intervention as a legitimate way of settling internal conflicts. External intervention of a humanitarian nature was, of course, largely accepted. But when intervention involves cessation of hostilities and determination as to who is to exercise legitimate authority, parties to the conflict are often more than cautiously reluctant to engage in a process of negotiation under the aegis of external forces.

Conflicts within African states can no longer be regarded as purely internal affairs. This is the situation in which the region of the Great Lakes finds itself, as the epicentre of political instability in the whole of the Horn and Central and Eastern African regions. Certain so-called external forces do not really regard themselves as external. Both Rwanda and Uganda, for example, see the internal conflict in the Congo as not so internal. Any government in Kinshasa that antagonises the Tutsi population in the Congo will send refugees fleeing into Rwanda. This, obviously, would destabilise Rwanda. Further, following the plight of Rwanda Hutu refugees in the Congo after the genocide, the present Rwandan government looks with suspicion at any regime in Kinshasa that is likely to be partial to these refugees and to support their ambition of waging an armed struggle against the Kigali government. Uganda, having hosted many Rwandan refugees over the last three decades, is also interested in political stability in Rwanda and in stemming the outflow of Rwandans into Uganda.

Tanzania, with regard to Burundi, is in the same position as Uganda *vis-à-vis* Rwanda. Burundi is one of the poorest nations in Africa, and one of the most densely populated. The landlocked population of 5.5 million people depends almost exclusively on subsistence agriculture. The two export crops, coffee and tea, earn Burundi just enough money to keep the small economy interacting with the modern world. The ethnic composition – 80 per cent Hutu and 20 per cent Tutsi – has been the source of historical problems: since independence, the Tutsi minority have almost always dominated political and economic life. The unexpected change in 1986, with the election of the first Hutu president, M. Ndadaye, led the Tutsi into a panic, fearing Hutu revenge after many years of being under minority domination. The fact that the Tutsi still dominated the army was a great risk and threat to the Ndadaye government. It was no surprise, therefore, that on 21 October 1993 Tutsi soldiers mounted a coup in which Ndadaye was assassinated and about 700,000 Hutus driven into exile, mainly into Tanzania.

The Burundi crisis is a typical case of internal conflict arising from bad governance based on ethnic minority rule and fear. The occupation of governmental institutions through ethnic demarcation itself leads to the inherent instability of such governments, with political insecurity and fear leading to violent conflicts. When neighbours are subsequently affected by such conflicts, leading to refugee outflows, it is not realistic for such neighbours to be indifferent to the conflicts. They must seek not only to be involved in stopping the conflicts when they occur, but also in creating political and economic conditions that would prevent such conflicts.

Governance and Conflict Resolution

We therefore want to advance the thesis that in order to have effective mechanisms for conflict prevention as well as resolution, parties to conflicts should accept the need to discuss and agree on issues of governance as fundamental to conflict resolution. These issues of governance cannot be settled as if they are 'purely internal matters'. The so-called 'no interference in the internal affairs of the state' cannot serve as a viable principle in international relations in Africa, where the construction of the state has itself created conflicts that cannot, by their very nature, be settled purely within the borders of the state.

The issue of Tutsi–Hutu relationship in Uganda, Rwanda, Burundi and the Congo goes beyond the borders of each of these states. The presence of Hutu refugees in Tanzania is a product of internal conflicts in Burundi. The presence of Hutu refugees in the Congo is the outcome of conflicts in Rwanda. Neither the Congo nor Tanzania can deal with the refugee problem within their borders without addressing the issues of governance in the neighbouring countries from where the Hutus are forced to emigrate. Further, were these countries to insist that they cannot accept refugees from their neighbours, the same neighbours would complain that their peoples are not being given the proper humanitarian treatment they need when they are faced with human rights issues within their own states. It is therefore necessary to recognise that all issues of governance, security and conflict resolution, in such contexts, need to be conceived and dealt with regionally.

The regionalisation of conflict resolution, promotion of security and good governance has been recognised in the Draft Treaty for the Establishment of the East African Community (Secretariat, 1998). In the Draft Treaty the partner states agree that peace and security are prerequisites to social and economic development within the Community and vital to the achievement of its objectives. In this regard, the partner states enjoin themselves to foster and maintain an atmosphere conducive to peace and security through cooperation and consultation on issues pertaining to the peace and security of the partner states, with a view to preventing, managing and resolving disputes and conflicts between them. Further, they undertake to promote and maintain good neighbourliness as a basis for promoting peace and security within the community; this includes such issues as refugees and disaster management (*ibid.*: Article 122).

The Draft Treaty further envisages a rapid progression towards a political federation by the three founding member states in East Africa: Kenya, Uganda and Tanzania. There is, however, provision that other neighbouring states can join the Community or the Federation, provided they adhere to the articles of accession, which establish, among other things, respect for good governance and peaceful resolution of conflicts. The essence of this is that, while the nation state is being superseded as a viable framework for further social progress, it is also being seen as inadequate for preventing and managing conflicts.

Lenin once argued that in nation states comprising several nationalities, each nationality has the democratic right of self-determination, whose exercise may include secession when necessary (Lenin, 1967). Lenin qualified this statement by adding that the class character of self-determination must be clearly determined. In so far as the bourgeoisie is the dominant and ruling class in the nation state, it may seek to use self-determination to pursue purely selfish and chauvinistic ends, or it may use it to fight against a progressive cause. Thus the proletariat must always give the bourgeoisie only conditional support on the national question.

What every bourgeoisie is out for, in terms of the national question, is privilege or exceptional advantages for its own nation; this is called being 'practical'. The proletariat is opposed to all privileges, to all exclusiveness. To demand that it should be 'practical' means following the lead of the bourgeoisie, falling into opportunism (*ibid.*: 613–14).

It was therefore not a question of supporting all calls for self-determination all the time, but of supporting them in terms of their social and political context. In general, bourgeois nationalism would always be nationalism to protect the class privilege of the bourgeoisie, and not nationalism to promote universal principles of social and economic justice and equality. In the anti-colonial struggles, however, bourgeois and proletarian nationalisms coincide, the oppressor being the common enemy. In so far as the bourgeoisie of the oppressed nation fights the oppressor, the proletariat and all other oppressed classes will support the bourgeoisie almost unconditionally. But in so far as the bourgeoisie of the oppressed nation stands for its own bourgeois nationalism to protect, for example, its economic privileges in the world capitalist system, the proletariat and other subordinate classes need to stand against such nationalism in support for proletarian internationalism (*ibid.*: 615).

Nationality and Class Questions in Africa Conflict

Lenin's arguments may sound outdated in an era where there is a growing assumption that class divisions within nation states are not that sharp, and that the economies of nation states tend to draw the bourgeoisie and the proletariat towards a common front. This turns out to be very far from the truth when one examines the character of internal conflicts in Africa, which arise from both nationality questions and controversies over class privileges.

If we take, for example, the problems in Rwanda, Lenin's thesis would be soundly vindicated. Just before the takeover of state power by the Rwandese Patriotic Front (RPF) led by Paul Kagame and his team, the Hutu-dominated government of President Juvenal Habyarimana embarked on a chauvinistic campaign fuelled by an ideology based on hatred for the Tutsi. The administration resuscitated the caste issue in a bid to rally the Hutu emotionally against a traditionally oppressive superior caste. They presented the RPF as a force intent on restoring the old monarchical structure that favoured the Tutsi. The RPF, on the other hand, was advancing a class campaign: it was pointing to the existence in Rwandan society of classes that were oppressed regardless of nationality. As Kamukama noted,

> Their problem is not the Bahutu, but a corrupt, oppressive and discriminative state. They hope that with time they will coexist amicably with the people, prove to them that contrary to the state propaganda, they are good people with the sole motive of liberating Rwanda. (Kamukama, 1993: 155)

To demonstrate that the RPF stand was a threat to the Hutu ruling class in Rwanda, it is to be noted that the regime murdered in cold blood any Hutu who was found to be sympathising with or supporting the sentiments of the RPF. Thus a good number of the Hutu middle class, regarded as liberals by the regime, were eliminated under the suspicion that they were likely to be sympathetic to the RPF. It is in this context that the Hutu Prime Minister, having called for reforms which would avert further internal conflicts, was herself assassinated by her own government on the eve of the RPF takeover.

Uganda's support for the RPF incursions into, and eventual takeover of the state in Rwanda was also interpreted in a contradictory manner within the region. There are those who saw support for the RPF as Museveni's expansionist policies in the region. On the other hand, there are those who saw it as legitimate support for a force that could liberate the Rwandese from oppression. The social and political programme that the RPF has pursued since taking power has demonstrated that it is more interested in democratising society than in imposing yet another oppressive and chauvinistic regime on the Rwandan people. The manner in which the regime has treated its political prisoners and the perpetrators of the genocide demonstrates its civility and commitment to the rule of law. Indeed, the fact that the trial of those accused of genocide is being conducted in Arusha under the authority of the United Nations underlines the importance of the regionalisation of internal conflicts and their resolution in Africa.

It is perhaps too early to assess the successes or failure of the RPF in Rwanda. But the manner in which the crisis in the Congo is resolved may depend very much on how persuasive the case of the RPF is to the warring factions within the region. The Rassemblement Démocratique Congolais (RDC), the insurgent movement led by Wamba dia Wamba and challenging the Kabila regime, has made an argument similar to the RPF's, presenting itself as a liberation movement seeking to establish democracy in the Congo. The National Resistance Movement (NRM) in Uganda, the RPF in Rwanda and the African National Congress (ANC) in South Africa have recognised it. In its pronouncements from Goma, it commits itself to the social transformation of society based on the rule of law, promotion of human rights, eradication of all forms of authoritarianism in society and the end of social bigotry of all sorts. Kabila's short stint in government reveals very little difference from the Mobutuism he sought to eliminate.

Good intentions, by themselves, are not enough to persuade the Congolese people that the RDC is the only alternative to Kabila. Indeed, the propaganda from Kinshasa that the RDC wants to impose a Tutsi-dominated regime on the other Congolese acts as a strong deterrent against the political advancement of the RDC as it campaigns to win the hearts and minds of the people. Further, in a context where both forces are relying more on arms to advance and defend their cause, the Congolese people may find it difficult to tell the difference between the two. Who is using arms to advance a noble cause and who is using them to oppress the people? Should the armed conflict continue for too long, the destruction caused might leave the people so demoralised that travelling in that country would be very hazardous.

Negotiation, Democracy and Conflict Resolution in Africa

It is for this reason that recent attempts to bring the parties in the conflict to participate in round-table negotiations are important. It is recognised that, however noble their intentions are, the RDC may find it very difficult to dislodge Kabila from power, even in the long run. Given the underdevelopment of Congo, even were they to dislodge him, creating political order where too many groups have had access to guns will be a daunting task. The longer the war lasts the more likely it will be for more routes to be mined, and more bridges and towns destroyed. The recent and ongoing histories of Angola and Southern Sudan are staring Africa full in the face.

One of the major problems in trying to create any viable administrative mechanism in Angola is the landmine menace. After over three decades of civil war, Angola is so landmined that construction, forestation and many other productive activities are threatened by this monster. The same could be true of certain parts of Southern Sudan. In both countries, many innocent people have been maimed as a result of tripping over landmines left undetonated after several years of civil war. To remove the landmines requires financial investment and technical assistance that will, of course, mean yet another diversion of scarce resources needed for social and economic reconstruction.

It is with the above in mind that what is currently stipulated in the Treaty for the Establishment of the East African Community is important. While attempts to promote regional integration and regional conflict resolution are laudable, they need to be assessed with regard to the principles under which they will be implemented. Conflicts arise as a result of unresolved grievances. Such grievances need not necessarily be resolved to the satisfaction of the contending parties simply because they are regionalised. That is why Lenin laid so much emphasis on the political and social content of any programme and the class character of nationalism: faith in the latter as a road towards better ways of conflict resolution, social and economic transformation and good governance need to be seen in terms of the interests it will defend and promote. Professionals, workers and peasants, organised in civil society, need to find avenues of expressions that will put their interests on the agenda of projects and programmes in regional initiatives.

The problem of 'creating political order' is important. The benchmark for deciding whether or not certain political claims within the nation or region are to be regarded as legitimate must be related to the kind of political order that we think will be created for resolving conflicts that arise out of such claims. History suggests that democracy offers the most appropriate political order known to humanity. The long-term strategy in reforms of conflict in Africa must therefore be predicted upon the regionalisation of democracy as well as conflict resolution (Zolberg, 1967).

Conclusion

The purpose of this chapter has been a reflection on creating political order in Eastern Africa under the aegis of the many regional initiatives being undertaken. The leading ones here are the East African Community and the Intergovernmental Agreement on Desertification and Development (IGADD). Both organisations have tried to deal with problems of conflict within the Great Lakes area as well as the Horn of Africa. But the initiatives have been at the level of trying to resolve the conflicts after they have erupted, as opposed to taking preventive measures that would allay future conflicts.

There is a possibility, for example, that the East African Community could lay down rules for belonging to the Community that are predicated upon governance issues. If belonging was attractive to a state, it would seek to satisfy such rules before applying for membership. Perhaps such a pull effect would create a regional environment in which governments would strive to create a political order less prone to conflict and more conducive to good governance.

That, however, assumes that the founding members of the community move rapidly towards institutionalising good governance domestically and are able to assert it at the Community level. The research question here is: what are the possibilities for the institutionalisation of democratic governance that can be reasonably cushioned from internal conflicts in Kenya, Uganda and Tanzania? To what extent would the creation of the East African Community, as presently envisaged, help reduce internal conflicts in Uganda, and thereby create an East African enabling environment for conflict prevention within the region?

Bibliography

Kamukama, Dixon (1993) 'Pride and Prejudice in Ethnic Relations: Rwanda,' in P. Anyang' Nyong'o (ed.), *Arms and Daggers in the Heart of Africa*, Nairobi: Academy Science Publishers.

Olisa, Michael (1993) chapter in P. Anyang' Nyong'o, (ed.), *Arms and Daggers in the Heart of Africa*, Nairobi: Academy Science Publishers.

Secretariat of the Permanent Tripartite Commission of East African Cooperation (1998) *Draft Treaty for the Establishment of the East African Community*, Arusha: International Conference Centre.

Lenin, V. I. (1967) 'The Right of Nations to Self-Determination', *Selected Works*, Vol. 1, Moscow: Progress Publishers, pp. 599–654.

Zolberg, A. (1967) *Creating Political Order*, Princeton: Princeton University Press.

9

Achieving Good Governance: the Role of Women in Policy Making

Khadija Yaya Mansaray

The symposium initiative is timely, its theme especially relevant today. I have long harboured the feeling that the African development experience was in danger of getting too little attention, because too many fundamental issues of political and social development were simply not getting debated and addressed with sufficient intellectual rigour. Issues such as gender equality and governance, peace building and the role of civil society are among them. The issue of gender equality and governance deserves to be addressed especially rigorously because it raises the whole matter of women's leadership and participation in policy making.

In this presentation, I propose to discuss – engaging the debate and practice, as well as the issues they pose – gender equality and governance; the legal barriers to the participation of women in power structures and decision making; and the implementation of the Beijing Platform for Action. Then, I would like to address myself to the main concern of the symposium: making Africa face the challenges of the 21st century through mobilisation for the implementation of alternative development paradigms.

Good governance requires an effective separation of powers between the legislature, the judiciary and the executive organs of government. While good governance is difficult to define, it requires the state to be responsible, to take into account the interests of the people, combat illiteracy, and seek to achieve gender balance. It also requires the participation of women in public life. In this connection, women have a key role to play in ensuring good governance because they could bring new and different perspectives into politics. The issue is the conceptualisation of women's role in relation to all governments and communities where decisions crucial to good governance are made.

While good governance remains elusive in most countries of Africa, it is not enough that women and men participate in governance; the policies and decisions must also be responsive to the gender imperative. The possible impact on women and men must be taken into account before policy decisions are made. In this instance, for example, when a decision to cut spending on education is made, it is likely that more girls than boys would drop out of school. Swayed by cultural attitudes, parents faced with the burden of paying fees often choose to pay for boys, who are seen as an investment by the family. The negative impact on girls might not be intended but such a decision would be gender-insensitive if its potential impact on girls was not assessed in advance.

Decision making takes place at all levels, including the community level, but women who are not used to power and leadership cannot be expected to become national leaders overnight. Although training has helped, there is a need to encourage and mobilise women to participate in demanding accountability within their local structures. As they succeed, they will begin to see and appreciate the power and usefulness of participation. It is a hands-on empowerment learning process. There is the legendary fact that no ruling group willingly shares power unless such sharing is in its interest. The objective of participation by women has to be seen as a process of identifying and articulating the various advantages of such participation for women and society, and for advancing the interests of the ruling group.

Barriers to Women's Participation

It is often believed that low education levels and lack of skills are the impediments to women's participation in decision making. While this might be true to a certain extent, women must not feel powerless since men in power are often equally handicapped and have to learn on the job. The challenge is for women's NGOs and other organisations to support women candidates, while the women them-selves have to be motivated to learn.

Good governance requires that governments should be politically and financially accountable. Globalisation and its institutions have ignored issues of equality and participation in government and civil society. All political systems have the potential to be corrupted. The challenge is for women and men to ensure that the law and related mechanisms make it very difficult for anybody to be corrupted and easy for the corrupt to be apprehended. Political accountability includes politicians and governments delivering on programmes and election promises, and making decisions that take into account the concerns of their constituents. Civic education programmes should thus go beyond preparing people for elections. They should also equip them with the analytical skills for making the connections between their right to vote and their right to demand accountability from those for whom they voted.

In Africa today, we are witnessing a significant number of countries emerging from periods of strife and armed conflicts. These countries are concerned with the rehabilitation of both people and systems, including political and economic systems. In countries where both men and women had been engaged in armed struggle, there is often a new respect and understanding of the capabilities of women. There is, therefore, both need and opportunity to re-examine economic, social, legal and political systems of governance and development, based on the new socio-political realities. Post-conflict and rehabilitation periods provide opportunities for structural transformation towards gender equality and women's enhanced participation in decision making and public life. In this connection, the best strategies and partnership for a gender-sensitive culture of peace should be institutionalised. Concrete mechanisms and resources are needed for obstructing the use of anti-personnel landmines, banned by the 1997 Ottawa Convention but still claiming lives daily.

Women's role in peace making does not emanate only from their generally compassionate nature, but also from their proven aptitude and resourcefulness in organising communities for survival. They have demonstrated their capacity to develop specific tools to handle crises: consultation; informal codes of behaviour; communication and pledging; the use of music; lobbying for government action; and civil society activism. In Sierra Leone, Liberia and Rwanda, for instance, women have demonstrated their ability to organise self-help projects, small-scale trading and other business ventures so as to assist others in the community through the social values of caring, nurturing and sharing. They called for an end to violence through demonstrations and rallies, petitions, visits to the President and other high-ranking government officials, and use of the media. In picking up the pieces after crisis, especially at the local municipality level, women developed local solidarity and income-generating groups, and initiated action for stimulating government efforts.

A second area of concern is the legal barriers to the participation of women in government on the grounds of sex, race, age, culture, religion or other status. Many women in Africa encounter specific obstacles related to their family status, including their living conditions in rural, isolated or impoverished areas. Additional barriers also exist for refugee women.

International Conventions and Support for Women's Participation

Women's legal and human rights, especially in Africa, should be evaluated and reformed against the background of the 1993 Vienna Conference on Human Rights. The conference took historic new steps to promote and protect the rights of women and children. Paragraph 18 of the Vienna Declaration stated explicitly that 'the human rights of women and the girl child are an inalienable, integral and indivisible part of human rights' (World Conference on Human Rights, 1993: 33–4).

It called for full and equal participation of women in political, civic, economic, social and cultural life at the national, regional and international levels, and the eradication of all forms of discrimination on grounds of sex. Paragraph 36 of the Vienna Declaration (*ibid*.: 42) underlined the importance of the integration and full participation of women as both agents and beneficiaries in the development process, and established a global action for women towards sustainable development in the Rio Declaration on the Environment and also in Chapter 24 of Agenda 21 (*ibid*.: 43).

Articles 7 and 8 of the Convention on the Elimination of All Forms of Discrimination Against Women (CEDAW) also refer to the subject of political decision making (Commission on the Status of Women, 1995: paragraph 17). Article 7 'requires state parties to the convention to take all appropriate measures to eliminate discrimination against women in political and public life, and to participate in the formulation of government policy and the implementation thereof ...'.

The struggle by women, therefore, gave support to the United Nations Decade for Women (1976–85) as well as the 1975 International Women's Year, proclaimed and covered by the UN. The period covered by the International Year and the following Decade for Women saw three United Nations-sponsored global conferences. These conferences (the 1975 World Conference of the International Women's Year in Mexico, the 1980 World Conference of the United Nations Decade for Women in Copenhagen and the Nairobi World Conference which reviewed and appraised the UN Decade for Women in 1985) made important contributions to the international effort to eliminate discrimination against women (UN Fourth World Conference on Women, 1995: 19–20).

Over a 10-day period in September 1995, Beijing hosted a watershed event in the history of women's rights. More than 40,000 participants from 189 countries attended one of the largest global conferences ever held – the Fourth World Conference on Women. The Conference sought to galvanise women's movements world-wide and to forge partnerships with governments in their struggle for gender equality. The result was a Platform for Action that includes 12 critical areas of concern for achieving equality (UN General Assembly, 2000: 7).

The main plank of the Platform for Action established that women share common concerns that can be addressed only by working together, and in partnership with men, towards the goal of gender equality around the world.

The Platform of Action for Women's Participation

Since its adoption, the Platform for Action has yielded added value in a number of areas. First, it focused attention on the human rights of women, thus leading to a marked paradigm shift towards a rights-based approach to gender equality. It advanced a major step beyond the 1985 Nairobi Forward-Looking Strategies in its approach to reproductive rights and sexual and reproductive health, reflecting agreements reached at the 1994 International Conference on Population and

Development and reconfirmed recently at the 1999 Special Session of the General Assembly (*ibid*.: 6).

Second, it underscored the role of men and their important contribution to achieving gender equality, based on the understanding that the dynamics of gender roles and relationship have a significant, if not defining, impact on development outcomes.

Third, the Platform for Action reinforced a life-cycle approach that calls for action to address the needs of women from infancy to old age; in this context, special attention is given to the girl-child, one of the critical areas of concern.

Fourth, the Beijing Platform for Action assigned primary responsibility for implementation to governments, but also included recommendations for the UN system, NGOs, political parties, the private sector and other institutions. It called for action to ensure the eradication of gender-based discrimination, and for measures to achieve gender equality through institutional reform, commitment of resources and fundamental changes in attitudes and behaviour.

Fifth, the Platform for Action strongly endorsed gender mainstreaming as the principal global strategy for promoting gender equality. It required a commitment to the use of gender analysis as an integral tool in policy and programme development, as well as in decision making on resource allocation, management and institutional development.

Sixth, it called for universal ratification of CEDAW. The unanimous adoption of CEDAW's Optional Protocol by the General Assembly in October 1999 (resolution 54/4) is clear testimony to the firm commitment of governments to provide women, not only with the necessary legal framework to protect and promote their human rights, but also with concrete procedures for translating those rights into reality.

Five years after the Fourth World Conference on Women met in Beijing in September 1995, the UN General Assembly held its 23rd Special Session in New York, 5–9 June 2000. Its purpose was to review and appraise progress throughout the world in implementing the recommendations of the Beijing Platform for Action, adopted in 1995, and the Forward-Looking Strategies adopted in 1985 at the Third World Conference on Women in Nairobi. With little apparent sense of urgency, preparations for the Special Session commonly referred to as Beijing + 5 began in 1999 under the aegis of the designated Preparatory Commission, the UN Commission on the Status of Women (CSW). The documents with which the Special Session dealt included a political Declaration (*ibid*.: 4), negotiated during the March 2000 Session of CSW, and an outcome document entitled 'Review and Appraisal of Progress Made in the Implementation of the 12 Areas of Concern in the Beijing Platform for Action, and Further Actions and Initiatives for Overcoming Obstacles to Implementation of the Beijing Platform for Action'. The consensus text which described it in greater detail was finally referred to the General Assembly (*ibid*.).

Responses to the Platform of Action on Women

Analysis of the country responses to Secretary General's questionnaire on the implementation of the Beijing Platform for Action indicates that significant progress has been achieved in creating an enabling environment for gender equality world-wide. The UN Decade for Women (1976–85) and especially the Fourth World Conference on Women in Beijing in 1995 have had a profound impact on bringing gender equality issues to the centre of public awareness and policy making. More importantly, over the past two decades the global gender agenda has systematically trickled down to all segments of societies around the world.

Safeguarding the gains made so far and further promoting the full implementation of the Beijing commitments remain central to the goals of the gender equality agenda at national, regional and international levels. The challenge, in the context of globalisation, is to advance gender equality, development and peace through establishing new and innovative modalities and alliances for building an inclusive global society, based on notions of social justice and equality.

The Beijing + 5 Beyond 2000 programme can be envisioned in the context of emerging global trends. First, globalisation brought greater economic opportunity and autonomy to some women, while others have become more vulnerable. Second, technological change brings new opportunities. But millions of the world's poorest women still do not have access to these facilities, thus becoming even further marginalised. Third, the progression of the HIV/AIDS epidemic in the developing world has had a strong impact on women. Particularly in Africa, the burden of care for people living with HIV, including orphans, falls on women, as state infrastructure is inadequate to respond to the challenges being posed (*ibid.*: 21).

In order to redirect development in general to correspond with women's views and aspirations, it is necessary that women should have access to power and participate in designing, planning and decision making on development, in all walks of life and at all levels of society, on an equal footing with men. Achieving a balance between male and female participation in decision making is the most important way in which to develop a better balance in life, and secure more humane progress of societies in general. It is not enough simply to have more women in the decision-making bodies; it is decisively important that they should develop their awareness and knowledge as women, in order to acquire growing competence in authentically representing the female half of humanity.

However, the final responsibility lies with the people. As U Thant said, 'the ultimate strength of the organisation and its capacity to promote and achieve the objectives for which it has been established lie in the degree to which its aims and activities are understood and supported by the peoples of the world' (quoted in UN, 1990).

The words of Secretary-General U Thant in 1996 are still valid and also relevant to the issues discussed in this chapter. In fact, they imply the principles of the people's responsibility to see to it that governments implement the resolutions and recommendations they have adopted within the United Nations system. The key actors in this case are, in particular, women and their organisations in each country. They have to study in depth the Beijing Platform and the convention (CEDAW), because these documents give leverage to their insistence that governments keep their promises.

Challenges of Governance in Africa

As Africa faces the herculean task of achieving good governance in the 21st century, the role of women in policy making has five fundamental challenges to address:

- *peace building,* since three decades of conflict have left many African countries in ruin and peace is a *sine qua non* for development;
- giving a greater role to *civil society*, through a fundamental transformation in the relationship between the state and civil society;
- *mainstreaming* women in politics and public administration;
- improving African institutions and people for *better governance and participation* – this includes traditional institutions such as the legislature, judiciary and political parties;
- *reforming the legal and institutional framework* so that both in theory and practice the rule of law is supreme. An independent judiciary to determine and resolve conflicts is of utmost importance. Achieving good governance can only come about if a country has a sound, just and effective legal system.

Bibliography

CSW (1995) United Nations Commission on the Status of Women, 39th Session (E/CN.6.1995/3/Add.6).

UN (1990) *The World's Women: 1970–1990*, UN Publications, No. E, 90 XVII, 3, New York: Praeger.

UN Fourth World Conference on Women (1995) A/Conf.177/20, 17 October.

UN General Assembly (2000) Report of the Ad Hoc Committee of the whole of the 23rd Special Session of the General Assembly (A/S-23/10/Rev.1).

World Conference on Human Rights (1993) *The Vienna Declaration and Programme of Action*, Vienna, June.

10

Contemporary External Influences on Corporate Governance: Coping with the Challenges in Africa
Ejeviome Eloho Otobo

Governance has been at the centre stage of the development discourse, and equally prominent on Africa's development agenda. This reflects the recognition that, over the past two decades, Africa's dismal economic performance has been partially attributable to weak or ineffective governance. Improving governance thus currently ranks high among policy priorities for African governments as well as for the continent's bilateral and multilateral development partners.

The term governance has become almost synonymous with civil or political governance. In part, this is traceable to the fact that the emphasis on governance issues arose from the realisation that the presumed sound macro-economic prescriptions were by themselves not yielding the predicted improved economic performance in Africa. Inappropriate political environments, in particular the poor governance practice of states, has been identified as a major impediment to economic reforms and growth. But there is also another important reason why the emphasis on political governance is well-deserved: political governance defines the context in which economic governance and corporate governance – the other two main dimensions of governance – are practised. The relationship among political, economic and corporate governance is analogous to a series of concentric circles in which political governance forms the outside circle, followed by the economic governance circle, with corporate governance at the centre (Figure 10.1).

An explanation of the relationship is important. Political governance sets the orientation of the economy – for example, whether a country will be a market economy, mixed economy or centrally planned economy.[1] Regardless of the type of economic system, an effective corporate governance framework is vitally important,[2] which explains the location of the corporate governance circle at the centre of our concentric circles. In the centrally planned economy and the state-dominated mixed economy, the dominant corporate form is the state-owned enterprise (SOE), while in the market economy the dominant corporate form is the incorporated private sector company. Political governance also supplies the institutional infrastructure for economic governance. By institutional infrastructure is meant both the rules of the game (what economists refer to as institutions) and the organisational structures (what are popularly called institutions). In turn, economic governance provides the context in which corporate governance is practised, by providing the laws under which corporations are established; the regulatory framework for the conduct of corporate affairs; and the macro-economic framework. Thus corporate governance stands at the intersection of law, public policy and business practice.

There are at least three reasons why special attention should be given to corporate governance in Africa. First, there is a growing consensus about private-sector-led development and the need to strengthen the regulatory capacity of the state in such an economic context. Second, the privatisation process in Africa – however slow and uneven it might be across the region – is bringing nearer a time when private firms rather than SOEs will have a great influence on the lives of people in Africa. Moreover, privatisation is taking many African governments from the familiar terrain of governance of SOEs to the unfamiliar territory of creating the legal and regulatory framework for the governance of private sector firms. Individual country experiences in this area vary considerably, however. Third, the financial crises that hit East Asian countries in 1997 have been attributed partly to a wide range of poor corporate governance practices, especially in the areas of securities market regulation, accounting and auditing standards in financial institutions, and bankruptcy laws. This should serve as a wake-up call to Africa on the importance of corporate governance issues, particularly as the countries in the region begin the transition from state-led to private-sector-led development.

Typically, the corporate governance framework is subject to two types of influences: those of the internal stakeholders and those of the external stakeholders. The internal stakeholders include the shareholders, the company board and management. The external stakeholders include the suppliers, employees, customer, bankers, the community where the corporation operates, the larger

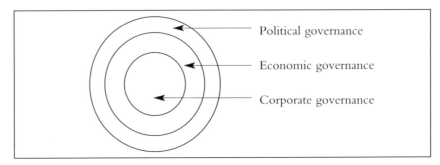

Figure 10.1 Concentric Circles of Governance

public and the state. There are complex linkages and interactions between the internal and external stakeholders. For example, in many cases, the internal stakeholders turn to the public through the law courts to adjudicate their internal disputes, or to public opinion to validate their viewpoints. Moreover, most of the so-called internal rules of the corporation are buttressed by the legislation of the state.

The main argument of this chapter is that a number of current trends and developments serve to highlight the influence of the external stakeholders on corporate governance. In this chapter the term contemporary external influences is used to describe these trends and developments. Many of these contemporary external influences not only opportunities but also constraints for corporate governance. Most notably, these external influences reinforce the layer of external regulations on corporate governance. By external regulations is meant the body of codes, norms or laws imposed on the corporation, either by the state or through international agreements. These laws, codes or norms cover such areas as anti-trust, securities and environmental laws, etcetera. By contrast, internal regulations refer to the rules and bye-laws established by the owners of the corporation (shareholders) and the controllers (the board and management) to ensure effective management of the corporation. Some of these rules deal mainly with problems that arise from the separation of ownership form control. Of course, it may be noted that historically the evolution of corporate governance has been influenced by external developments. The analytical challenge, then, is both to identify such current trends and their implications for corporate governance, and to indicate the policy challenges they pose for Africa.

Conceptual Issues in Corporate Governance

Corporate governance is defined in several ways and it may be helpful to distinguish them. It is defined either in terms of relationship, or of supervision and control, or of leadership. Thus, it has been defined as a 'relationship among various participants in determining the direction and performance of corporation. The primary participants are the shareholders, the management (led by the chief executive officer) and the board of directors' (Monks and Minow, 1996). It is also defined as involving 'a set of relationships between a company's management, its board, its shareholders and other stakeholders. Corporate governance also provides the structure through which the objectives of the company are set and the means of attaining those objectives and working performance are determined' (OECD, 1999).

Corporate governance has also been defined as 'the process of supervision and control (of governing) intended to ensure that the company's management acts in accordance with the interests of the shareholders. Governance is thus distinguishable from executive decision making, the former being the process by which managers are held accountable for their performance of the latter function' (Parkinson, 1994). The Commonwealth Association on Corporate Governance views it 'as essentially about leadership – leadership for efficiency, leadership for probity, leadership with responsibility, leadership which is transparent and which is accountable' (CACG, 1999).

There are two main models of corporate governance: the shareholders' and the stakeholders' models. In the stakeholders' model, corporate policies and strategies take into account not only the interest of those who invest in (shareholders), work for (managers) and direct the affairs of the corporation (the board of directors) but also the employees, suppliers and workers' union. By contrast, in the shareholders' model, the prime focus is on earning returns to the shareholders, the board and management (Otobo, 1999: 9–14).

Corporate governance is not synonymous with the private sector. The private sector is the universe in which firms – the basic unit of business organisation – whether incorporated or unincorporated, operate. Throughout this chapter, the words firm, company and corporation will be used interchangeably; and will be used to refer to the private sector corporation. The private sector can be likened to a pyramid with the informal sector firms at the base and the very large firms at the apex (Figure 10.2). As can be gleaned from its various definitions above, corporate governance pertains to the way in which the incorporated firms are controlled and managed. Though the informal sector enterprises may have their

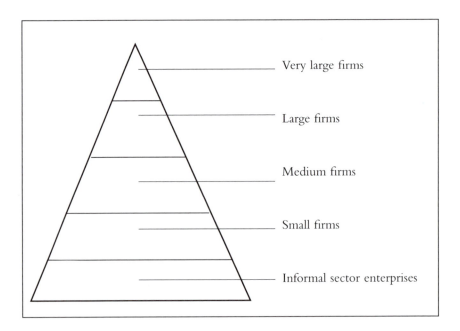

Figure 10.2 The Structure of the Private Sector

governance structures, strictly speaking the term 'corporate governance' does not include them. This is because informal sector enterprises are not recognised by law. By contrast, the corporation is a creature of state law, though not owned by the state. Instead, the incorporated firm is established, on application by its owners to the state, to serve the aims that the owners (shareholders) intend. It may be noted that all public firms are incorporated, but not all incorporated firms are public. The use of the term public refers to listing on the stock exchange, rather than to public enterprises or SOEs. But listing on the stock exchange is only one dimension of the public life of the corporation or company.

A separate dimension of the public nature of the corporation relates to its being viewed as serving or being responsible to the interest not only of the shareholders, but also of the larger society. This turns critically on the question of the accountability of the corporation. The traditional view holds that the corporation should be accountable only to its owners (shareholders) through the management. In this view, the role of company law is to provide the rules that protect the interests of the shareholders and enable a company to make maximum profits for them. Accordingly, public purpose is best served through the profit-maximising behaviour of the corporation, because this leads to more wealth creation for the society. If the corporation is required to incorporate social considerations, or to accommodate any other public interest in its operation, this should be set out explicitly by law.

Set against this view is the notion that corporations, especially large corporations, must be seen as social enterprises because their activities affect not just the shareholders but also the larger local or sometimes global society. In particular, the decisions of the big corporations can affect unemployment, trade and the physical environment. The corporation, therefore, should act as a socially responsible citizen; it should incorporate social as well as profit considerations into its operations. This is the idea of corporate social responsibility, which entails incurring costs for socially desirable but not legally mandated action, in return for which no compensation can be claimed (Brudney, quoted in Parkinson, 1994). It involves a corporation giving up some profits, by either taking on additional costs in its operations, or making financial transfers or payments to communities and others in the hope that the company will do better. The term 'profit-sacrificing corporate social responsibility' has been used to describe this behaviour (Parkinson, 1994).

Corporate social responsibility[3] has two categories: 'relational' and 'non-relational'. Relational responsibility refers to attempts to promote the welfare of groups such as employees, customers or neighbours who are affected by the conduct of the company's mainstream business activities. It involves limiting the damaging impact of the company's processes or products (self-regulation) or treating more 'fairly' the groups with which the company comes into contact as a necessary part of carrying on its business. Relational responsibility, in turn, can be subdivided into two types of self-imposed constraints: 'prudential constraints' and 'other-regarding constraints'. Prudential constraints are reflected in rules and practices that require a sacrifice of profits in the short term, but have long-term profit pay-off for the company. The purpose of prudential constraints is to prevent long-term profitability from being put at risk by attempts to make short-term gains.

On the other hand, 'other-regarding constraints' are adopted not with the ultimate goal of protecting profitability but for the sake of the relevant interests themselves. They are thus a response to supposed moral imperatives that conflict with profit maximisation, not merely a self-interested response to moral preferences. These may include a commitment to higher health and safety standards than the local laws demand, or such ethical concerns as not doing business with a country where there is racial or religious oppression. 'Social activism', on the other hand, refers to conduct which is particularly beneficial to society or particular interests, but falls outside the scope of the company's ordinary commercial operations. Examples include charitable donations, arts sponsorship or scholarships to students. These examples fall into the category often referred to as philanthropic acts of business.

Corporate social responsibility mainly represents an act of corporate discretion – in other words, a 'voluntary' constraint on corporate conduct or discretion. This can be contrasted with non-voluntary constraints imposed on corporate conduct. There are two categories of non-voluntary constraints on corporations. Organic constraints are those relating to the creation, structure and management of business corporations. Economic constraints are those imposed on corporate decision making by the free market system and by the regulatory framework of anti-trust and securities laws (Milstein and Katsh, 1982). Though many of the constraints on corporate conduct are national in their origin and scope, they may also take the form of laws or codes negotiated by governments at the regional and global levels, or adopted voluntarily in response to various 'international concerns'. Figure 10.3 illustrates the various types of constraints, voluntary and non-voluntary, on corporate discretion.

As the preceding analysis has made clear, corporate governance seeks to reconcile the objective of profit maximisation with a web of constraints to corporate power and discretion. It bears emphasis that in the long run no corporation can be adjudged successful or even survive without being profitable. Separating the various constraints on corporate governance helps to shed light on the factors that affect the operating environment of the corporation and, therefore, its profitability. This provides the backdrop to a better understanding of how the various trends and developments to be described in the next section affect the environment in which corporations function, and of the implications they therefore carry for corporate governance.

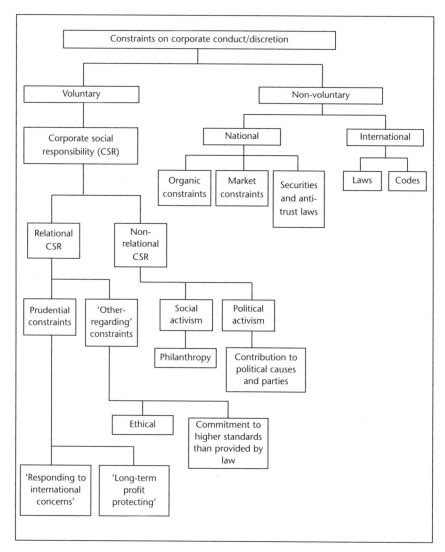

Figure 10.3 Types of Constraints on Corporate Discretion

Contemporary External Influences on Corporate Governance

The main issues that dominate the internal operating environment of corporate governance are fairly clear and straightforward. An illustrative list includes disclosure rules; directors' duty of care and diligence; rights and obligations of shareholders; role and responsibilities of the board; equal treatment of shareholders; and managerial discretions. Other issues include methods of appointment to the board; communication from the board to the shareholders; accountability to shareholders; board performance assessment; review of financial performance; and business ethics for the board and management. Many of the codes or guidelines on corporate governance, or reforms of corporate governance developed at the national or international levels, focus on these issues (OECD, 1999; CACG, 1999).

By contrast, the factors that determine the external operating environment of the corporation are mostly unpredictable and also variable over time. Yet chief executive officers (CEOs) and the board are increasingly supposed to be sensitive to the implications of these external influences on corporate governance. Indeed, there have been important instances of boardroom 'revolt' against CEOs, or shareholder 'revolt' against the board, because of incompetent handling of external influences, especially when such influences lead to the loss of business opportunities, reduction of profits or damage to the reputation of the corporation. It should be stressed, however, that there are complex linkages between internal and external factors that affect the operating environment of the corporation.

Based on the analytical framework developed in the previous section, the focus of our analysis is to examine the nature of constraints or opportunities that some contemporary external influences present for corporate governance. A selective review of such trends or factors follows.

Globalisation

Globalisation refers to the process of increasing integration of countries into the world economy and the increasing web of contacts among enterprises, institutions and peoples across national borders. It is, however, a multidimensional phenomenon encompassing economic, social, political and cultural aspects. The effects of economic globalisation on corporate governance are complex and varied. These show up mainly through trade, investment, services and technology. The new World Trade Organisation (WTO) agreements strongly demonstrate these themes. To understand how economic globalisation affects corporate governance, it is essential to make a distinction between corporate structure and corporate practices. Corporate structure refers to the unique organisational arrangements for corporate governance: for example, whether the corporation has a united or divided board; whether the positions of the CEO and chairman are combined or not; and the role of shareholders' meeting in corporate governance, including the delegation of authority from shareholders to the board. Corporate practices, on the other hand, refer to the rules and procedures that govern the operations of the corporation. These include disclosure rules, the rights of shareholders, investor protection, the board's duty of care and diligence, and auditing procedures. The corporate governance framework, consisting of the corporate structure and corporate practices, reflects the peculiar legal, historical, cultural and political context of the country of origin of the corporation.

While globalisation may not alter the corporate structure, it influences corporate governance practices in several ways, especially through the strategies it makes available on corporate finance, production and management. For example, the liberalisation of capital markets has made foreign capital more accessible and, in some cases, more attractive to the corporation. Because corporate finance now draws on international sources, corporate governance practices have become a matter of interest not only to national shareholders but also to the international investing community – including international bondholders and foreign portfolio investors from whom the corporation obtains capital. The internationalisation of production exerts similar pressure, for example on labour policy.

As a result, foreign capital not only exerts a disciplining force on managers or executives of the corporation because of the increasing international scrutiny to which the performance of the corporation is subjected, but also stimulates changes in corporate practices in at least two ways. First, the globalisation of capital has been heralded as a major force certain to cause a confluence of corporate practices. This is based on the premise that as a corporation obtains capital from other countries, it increasingly has to adopt practices that the foreign funders or investors bring. There is evidence, for example, that US investors insist on the adoption of US-style shareholder activism, including demands for a say in the operation of the company, for improved disclosure of financial results, and for reforms to improve the independence of the board of directors.[4] Moreover, the need to strengthen the confidence of the financial markets in corporate financial assessment is providing a new impetus towards common standards of auditing and accounting for transnational and global corporations.[5]

Closely related to this is the way the globalisation of finance has intensified the search for an appropriate regulatory regime for international banking. This effort, built around the Basle Committee, consisting of financial supervisory authorities of ten industrialised countries, has resulted in an agreement on the international convergence of supervisory regulations governing the capital adequacy of international banks.[6] These standards have become benchmarks, especially in assessing the financial health of banking corporations operating on a global scale. It should be stressed that special attention has been given to regulating financial flows because the volume and volatility of these flows have increased considerably with the globalisation of capital markets. The recent monetary crises in Mexico, Asia and Russia underscore the significance of these developments and concerns.

Moreover, globalisation has increased the sources of inputs and the scope of product markets for the corporation. This opens various possibilities for managers of the corporation in developing institutional arrangements for production, purchase, and distribution for its goods and services. Such arrangements could include networks, alliances, franchising, foreign direct investment and subcontracting arrangements. While these institutional devices are not new, globalisation has intensified their adoption by the corporation as strategic responses to survival in the global marketplace.

In parallel, the effort to make globalisation more humane and equitable has impelled corporations into voluntarily submitting themselves to certain international standards. An illustrious recent example is the global compact of nine principles launched by the UN Secretary-General in 1999 to engage corporations in the promotion of labour standards, respect for human rights, and protection of the environment. Corporations are requested to translate commitments to the principles in these areas into concrete management practices. The global compact is based on the conviction that weaving universal values into the fabric of global markets and corporate practices will help advance broad societal goals while securing open markets (Annan, 2000: 37).

These principles are more in the tradition of promoting corporate social responsibility and are very different from the unsuccessful efforts by the United Nations to develop codes of conduct for multinational enterprises in the 1970s, essentially as a way of regulating the economic behaviour of global corporations. Globalisation is also producing international constraints on corporate governance in other areas as well. Corporations are increasingly required not only to adapt to internationally negotiated environmental standards but also to pressures from civil society organisations dedicated to promoting various causes. As explained previously, these new standards represent a new set of constraints on the corporation.

Overall, whether in the financial markets or in other spheres, globalisation has increasingly resulted in the internationalisation of corporate regulation. Reflecting, in particular, on the situation in the financial markets, one analyst has remarked that the disruption of national systems of regulation resulting from globalisation, especially of financial markets, has deprived national states of legitimacy (Dezalay, 1994), as the several rules are set at the international level. This trend could constrain the role of the state to specific aspects of regulation.

Liberalisation

Liberalisation is the summary term for the reduction or elimination of state controls in the economy, resulting in greater reliance on price signals in free markets. Economic liberalisation usually centres on relaxing state controls in the finance, trade and production sectors. The main institutional arrangement for state intervention in these sectors was or remains the public enterprise or state-owned enterprise (SOE), quite apart from an array of rules and restrictions that were designed to regulate various economic activities.

Usually the elimination or dilution of restrictions in the financial sector has taken the form of abolition of economic regulations such as directed credit to preferred sectors, fixing of the interest rate, removal of foreign exchange control and the deregulation of exchange rates. The lifting of layers of economic regulation invariably leads to the removal of the several distortions with which managerial agents[7] of the corporation daily have to contend. With the deregulation of the foreign exchange regime and elimination of the practice of directed credit to preferred sectors, corporate finance – an important task of corporate governance – becomes less difficult. Even so, liberalisation has often resulted in higher interest rates, bank distress and financial disorders.

Liberalisation has provided an impulse for effective prudential regulation and supervision of the financial system. This is because liberalisation increases risks to the financial system – risks that arise from the volatility of financial markets; from lack of adequate information about borrowers; from the inability or unwillingness of borrowers to repay loans; and, sometimes, from speculative attacks that are not warranted by economic fundamentals.[8] It follows that while financial liberalisation potentially eases the financing of the corporation, it nevertheless contains a lot of risks. The challenge for public policy is to establish an effective regulatory framework that minimises the various categories of risk.

Deregulation, involving the opening of some hitherto 'closed' sectors, or lifting price controls, is an important component of economic liberalisation. Opening of such sectors as aviation, telecommunications and radio broadcasting has brought about increased competition in these sectors. Deregulation thus challenges managerial agents operating in the new firms to seek even greater market share, usually through improving quality of services and lowering of prices to attract customers. In sum, economic liberalisation provides a competitive policy environment for corporate governance.

Privatisation

The term privatisation is used here in a rather restricted sense. It is defined as the sale of SOEs to the private sector through private placement, public offer or competitive bidding by strategic investors. Privatisation affects corporate governance through intricate pathways. As a starting point, it is helpful to recognise that privatisation replaces one form of corporate ownership – state ownership of SOEs – with private shareholders' ownership of the privatised enterprises. However, the transfer of ownership is not necessarily accompanied by a wholesale transfer of all control and accountability functions to the private sector (Scott, 1994). To understand why, it is important to explain the effects of privatisation on ownership and control.

Before privatisation, state control over public enterprise tends to be all-embracing: the state's roles as owner, operator and regulator are fused, even if exercised discretely by various agencies of government. As an owner, the government appoints the directors or managers who manage the enterprise, makes decisions on the location of the enterprise, and exercises the property rights. As an operator, the government, through its appointed directors, makes decisions on investment, production, procurement and personnel matters. Before privatisation, the interests of government as an investor in an SOE and the public as consumer of any SOE goods or services are presumed to be protected or reconciled. This is achieved through the influence that the public exercises on government policy, either through their representatives in the legislative process, who periodically review SOE performance during budgetary debates on financial allocation to an SOE, or through public pressure on the controlling ministry of the SOE. As a regulator, the government sets technical standards for products and the prices of the products and sometimes gives directives on cross-subsidisation – for example, when it instructs a public monopoly to serve rural areas at below prevailing price or cost.

Once the ownership of an SOE is transferred to the private sector through privatisation, concerns for investor protection and consumer protection become non-convergent and public interests about the performance or conduct of the privatised enterprise are expressed through regulatory policy. With the regulatory functions of government separated from the operating and ownership functions as a result of privatisation, designing a new regulatory framework becomes imperative. It is important to recognise that state-owned enterprises operate in all three types of market structures: competitive, oligopolistic and monopolistic. Invariably, the divestiture of SOEs into competitive markets reinforces greater competition, and here regulatory reform will take the form of strengthening competitive market structure, often through anti-trust legislation and prevention of restrictive business practices.

It is entirely a different matter when public infrastructure enterprises such as electric power, telecommunications, water or piped gas, and public transport enterprises such as railways are divested. These categories of enterprises exhibit three characteristics: the volume of investment or the nature of the activity allows for one or few enterprises; products are price-inelastic, by which is meant that an increase in the price of services produced does not lead to a sharp fall in demand; and they have huge sunken costs that represent a major barrier to entry and exit. These natural monopoly characteristics explain why the state continues to exercise control in the product markets of the newly privatised enterprise, by establishing new regulatory frameworks. The innovation of privatisation plus regulation is to establish the principle that control of monopoly abuse can be achieved through very specific actions, such as control of prices and possibly of quality (Bishop *et al.*, 1996a). Indeed, the profusion of regulatory agencies as a result of privatisation is widely acknowledged as one of the major paradoxes of privatisation (McCahery *et. al.*, 1994; Hogwood 1990). But there is no contradiction between extensive privatisation and equally elaborate regulatory institutions in support of privatisation. For, as Rodrik has written, 'the freer are the markets, the greater is the burden on regulatory institutions. It is not a coincidence that the United States has the world's freest markets as well as its toughest anti-trust enforcement' (Rodrik, 2000).

The establishment of public regulatory agencies for newly privatised corporations represents a form of state limitation on corporate governance. Yet a major objective of public regulation is to make these newly privatised enterprises behave in a manner comparable to firms in a competitive market. Indeed, one of the major effects of privatisation is to foster competition in the product, factor and capital markets. In such an environment, a major task of corporate governance is to adapt to and benefit from the opportunities of competition.

Regional cooperation and integration

The relationship between regional cooperation and integration and corporate governance is mutually reinforcing. Regional cooperation can provide a platform for shaping corporate governance policies and practices. Conversely, the private sector – as an agent of corporate governance – can be a catalyst for regional integration. Increasingly, it is recognised that successful regional integration effort is not a matter for governments alone, but also for the private sector. The approach adopted here, however, is to examine how regional cooperation serves as a framework to shape corporate governance. The regional level stands at an intermediate point in the continuum stretching from the national to the global level in the regulation of corporate governance.

Regional integration is built on a foundation of harmonisation of economic and financial as well as social and environmental policies. The agreements achieved or standards set in these areas not only affect national public sector programmes, but are sometimes explicitly aimed at corporate governance. For example, governments use a regional or subregional framework to pursue harmonisation in such areas as mergers and acquisitions, competition policy, company laws and commercial practices. The European Union provides a good example of using a regional approach for harmonisation, if not standardisation, in these areas.[9]

OHADA provides a contemporary illustration of how regional cooperation is being used to shape corporate business practices in Africa. Fifteen francophone African countries in West and Central Africa signed a treaty establishing the Organisation pour l'Harmonisation en Afrique du Droit des Affaires (OHADA) in 1993.[10] The treaty aims to facilitate regional economic integration and international trade by providing unified, modern business legislation for member states, strengthening legal and judicial security for enterprises, promoting arbitration to settle contractual disputes, and providing continuing education to magistrates and judicial personnel. To date, uniform laws have been enacted for general commercial law, corporations and economic interest groups, secured transactions, bankruptcy proceedings and discharge of liabilities, debt collection proceedings and arbitration. Enforcement of the commitments made in OHADA are achieved through a variety of subregional institutions. Thus the frameworks of subregional and regional cooperation are increasingly used to reach agreements, enact laws or establish norms that define corporate practices.

Civil society activism

Civil society organisations are frequently as active in corporate governance as in political processes. Corporate governance practices are shaped not only by public regulation or international agreements but also by a range of NGO activities such as consumer campaigns, mass demonstrations, publicity campaigns, petitions and public hearings. In so doing, civil society organisations (CSOs) raise public awareness about corporate governance practices, monitor the performance of corporations and disseminate information about corporate conduct.

Vigorous, well-informed and articulate NGOs have provided an impetus for change in corporate practices. CSOs work in a diversity of areas, such as environmental preservation, protection of human rights, elimination of child and prison labour and enhancing safety and protection. The activities of CSOs in these areas have led to a change in corporate practices in various countries.

CSOs influence corporate governance in other ways. Through their agitations on specific causes, they can build public consensus around an issue where none existed. With public consensus achieved, they sometimes push for enactment of law(s) to promote or protect such a new consensus. It is worth noting, in this regard that NGOs have been instrumental in transmuting into law some public concerns on such issues as product safety, pollution or other health hazards. Once such laws are enacted, they become mandatory standards to which corporations must adhere or risk severe penalty.

Thus, the agitations and advocacy of civil society organisations can induce major constraints on corporate conduct. As a consequence, managerial agents of corporations evince considerable sensitivity to the views of CSOs, especially on issues relating to the operations of their corporation.

Coping with the Policy Challenges in Africa

Several policy challenges arise for Africa in corporate governance sections. These policy challenges are cross-cutting in that they apply to some or many of the issues examined in the previous section. The main challenges are in regulatory enforcement, incentives regime, state capacity and responsible corporate citizenship. This list is essentially illustrative rather than exhaustive. The choice of these challenges is informed by the consideration that they occur at the junctures of law, public policy and business practice – a key feature of corporate governance itself, as remarked earlier. Coping with the challenges will entail the adoption of carefully designed policy responses, including effective partnership between business and government. Set against this general principle is the recognition that African countries are diverse in several ways. Therefore, country responses will have to be tailored to their specific circumstances within a general approach.

Regulatory challenge

A common strand that runs through the analysis of issues in the preceding section is the need for an effective and sound regulatory framework for various aspects of corporate governance. Typically, a regulatory framework consists of a legislative enactment or decree that establishes a regulatory agency and indicates its functions, including its enforcement powers. The regulatory process consists of three interrelated components: setting the rules or standards, monitoring for compliance, and enforcement (Otobo, 1996). Separating these components of the regulatory process makes it easier to understand why different components of the regulatory process can be purchased at different levels. For example, as is evident in the discussion in the previous section, many norms or standards are set at levels other than the national.

Nonetheless, enforcement would invariably remain at the national level. This explains why the next subsection is devoted separately to the enforcement challenge. Here the focus of analysis is on the other components of the regulatory framework. Against the background of this essential clarification, it is possible to state that African countries confront a threefold regulatory challenge as a result of new external influences on corporate governance.

The first regulatory challenge relates to laws or norms set at the global level to guide corporate governance – whether such rules relate to capital adequacy standards for international banks, accounting or auditing standards for regulations governing the business practices of corporations in a regional or subregional context, or voluntary principles of the global compact for business conduct. The key issue here is that these standards or principles will inevitably have to be complied with, and the challenge for public policy is to ensure that such compliance will indeed occur. There are two essential components of this task. First, the relevant departments of government should be aware of the existing bodies of laws or conventions on corporate governance. Maintaining an up-to-date information base is therefore vital. Second, African countries must devote as much effort to creating and updating information on global and regional conventions as to national laws. International conventions are but one source of regulations for corporate governance. National governments will continue to have a major role in enacting regulations for corporate governance. However, the very approach used in formulating some of these international rules or norms poses a challenge to Africa and other developing countries.

The second challenge that African countries face, therefore, has two aspects. These relate to what have been described as imperial harmonisation and standardisation without representation. Imperial harmonisation refers to the practice of bringing the rules, norms or laws of developing countries into conformity with the standards of the industrialised countries; while standardisation without representation refers to the reality that, quite often, the African countries are either not represented at all, or not adequately represented, in the international policy-making bodies where these standards are agreed. Thus a number of rules that are being developed or agreed for corporate governance evince the characteristics of imperial harmonisation and standardisation without representation – two practices, it may be stressed, that are among the causes of discontent with globalisation. Tackling these two related problems requires a combination of more active involvement by African countries in the development of international regulations and a determined attempt to secure better and broader representation in the relevant international fora. Concerted African effort will be a key to success.

The third challenge is to adapt international laws and norms to national contexts. Indeed, as Rodrik (2000) has observed, 'all successful societies are open to learning, especially from useful precedents in other societies … what is important is that imported 'blueprints' be filtered through local practices and needs'. An essential step in this regard is to undertake periodic reviews of the existing array of corporate governance practices and see how international rules can be adapted to national situations. Often this can be achieved by setting up a commission of eminent persons to advise on the reform of the corporate governance framework.

Enforcement challenge

A sound legal framework without enforcement leads to lack of credibility on the part of government. Effective enforcement is central to credible regulation and up-to-date and accurate information is essential to that effort. On the other hand, failure to comply with rules and regulations damages the reputation of the corporation. Hence, both the government and the corporation have a mutual interest in transparent and consistently applied enforcement procedures.

The need to avoid concentration of power in a regulatory agency has led, in some countries, to separating the roles of adjudication and enforcement. In such instances, the regulatory agency monitors the performance of the regulated industry, ensures compliance with rules and investigates complaints; but it refers disputes to the courts or arbitration panels, which are entrusted with adjudication. The agency is then entrusted with the task of implementing the rulings of the court. Under this model, conflict resolution between the regulator and the firm or industry is assigned to the courts, while investigation and enforcement is undertaken by the agency. A key consideration for such arrangements is the need to further insulate the agency from politics. Regardless of which institutional arrangement is chosen for the investigation of enforcement and adjudication, success is largely dependent on the clarity of rules and the consistency with which they are applied.

In many instances, enforcement is through imposing sanctions, or negotiated compliance. The range of sanctions might begin with imposing a fine or exacting a public apology. The diversity of country experience and the complexities of enforcement argue for a prudent, common-sense approach, and African countries should choose the model of enforcement that best suits their circumstances.

Incentive regime

An effective corporate governance framework cannot be built on the foundation of 'sticks' without 'carrots'. Good corporate governance should provide proper incentives for the board and management to pursue objectives that are in the interests of company and shareholders, and should facilitate effective monitoring, thereby encouraging firms to use resources more efficiently (OECD, 1999). This requires effective partnership between the public and private sectors. Government has responsibility for providing an enabling macro-economic environment for corporate governance, for devising incentives for attracting investment, and for joining in dialogue with the private sector agents.

The private sector – especially the organised component of the private sector – should be able to engage the public sector in periodic dialogues. Institutional arrangements such as business–government round tables or public–private consultative forums can play an essential role in this regard. Many African countries are overcoming their suspicious attitude towards the private sector. However, the private sector would have to seize the initiative in pressing the public sector to create a propitious environment for it. There is a strengthened consensus on the major elements of a propitious sector. These include building robust financial systems, improving the business environment and investment in physical infrastructure, information technology and human resource development.[11]

State capacity challenge

The need for effective regulation, strong enforcement and appropriate incentive regimes implies that effective state capacity is vital to supporting corporate governance. It has been defined as a measure of the government's ability to implement its policies and goals. State capacity has four dimensions: regulatory, administrative, technical and extractive (Brautigam, 1996). In Africa, a particular difficulty in designing and implementing appropriate regulatory enforcement and incentive regimes is the lack of skills and institutional capacity. This raises the question of how the state should proceed in Africa, where demand for its numerous services is occurring in the context of weak or ineffective capacity. There is the view that the state should match its role to its capability (World Bank, 1997). Applying this proposition can easily turn into advocacy of a minimal role for the state.

Set against this view is the idea that there should be strategic government participation in key areas of the economy, consistent with the country's initial conditions and long-term development goals (Mkandawire and Soludo, 1999: 106). However, filling the gap in state capacity in Africa must include measures to build the capacity of the state gradually and allow the market to undertake certain functions. At the same time, there is recognition that markets must be supplemented or strengthened by an appropriate set of institutions (United Nations, 2000: 211). But, even more important, there are essential tasks that the state cannot relinquish to the markets. That is why strengthening the capacity and effectiveness of the state is so vital.

Responsible corporate citizenship

A major challenge of corporate governance is to make the corporation act like a responsible citizen. The notion of responsible corporate citizenship is very broad and almost imprecise. But it is generally thought to embrace three central ideas: that the corporation must act within the law, seeking neither to avoid nor to evade the law; that the corporation's conduct is ethical; and that the corporation is socially conscious – the notion of corporate social responsibility discussed earlier.

The chief argument for responsible corporate citizenship is that it enables the corporation to maintain its legitimacy in and retain the confidence of the society. But the corporation's key consideration in its operations – the yardstick of its success – is profit maximisation. However, there is also a role for the goodwill of the corporation. As Bratton (1992) has noted, the law makes us talk the good, but does not force us to impose it. He argues that corporations should permit external values such as the ethic of goodwill to be included, in order to enhance the legitimacy of corporate actions, as well as business purpose which is based on wealth maximisation. In reality, public policy cannot rely on the goodwill of the corporation – desirable though that might be.

The siren song of responsible corporate citizenship is often heard when the market mechanism to control corporate conduct is weak or ineffective; when there is a large regulatory void or outright evasion of the law; or when the state is unwilling or unable to enforce the laws. Thus, to achieve responsible corporate citizenship, African public policy makers should aim to make governance respond to a mix of policy instruments including compliance with the provisions of national and international laws and conventions; appeal to socially responsible conduct; and public and political exhortation aimed at the corporate conscience.

Conclusion

All dimensions of governance, whether political, economic or corporate, seek to foster the same set of attributes; namely, transparency and accountability. A major consideration in this regard is how to devise institutional arrangements to promote these governance attributes. The specific arrangements will differ, depending on the dimension and the political and legal traditions of a country. A robust corporate governance framework, for example, should respond to the demands of internal stakeholders and be sensitive to the concerns of external stakeholders. The latter is not always assured because the logic of profit is the dominant consideration of the corporation.

However, a number of contemporary external influences are forcing corporate executives to be responsive to a host of non-profit considerations. This trend is likely to continue even though the nature and complexity of such external influences will vary. This requires business–government partnership in a variety of policy areas. For African governments, the task of dealing with the challenges arising from various contemporary external influences on corporate governance underlines the need for effective state capacity, including improved coordination among the various agencies of government.

For example, effective regulation and enforcement are not possible if public institutions are riven by self-interest. Moreover, coordination, especially among the various branches of government, is essential to a well-functioning corporate governance framework. This is because the tasks of rule making or standard setting, compliance, enforcement and devising incentive structures for corporate governance are undertaken by various departments of government. Thus the same issues that dominate economic policy making generally in Africa are also pertinent to developing a robust framework for corporate governance.

Notes

1 The latter is virtually eclipsed. For a very interesting and recent analysis of the reasons for the triumph of markets over central planning or pernicious government interventions, see Yergin and Stanislaw, 1999.
2 The idea that the principles of sound corporate governance should apply as much to SOEs as to private sector corporations is emphasised in OECD, 1999 and CACG, 1999.
3 The discussion in this section on the various categories of corporate social responsibility relies on Parkinson, 1994.
4 This point of view and relevant examples are drawn from Monks and Minow, 1996.
5 Work on some of these issues is being pursued within the Global Corporate Governance Forum, sponsored by the OECD and the World Bank.
6 For a detailed discussion of the evolution of the Basle Committee standards, see Kapstein, 1996.
7 The term managerial agents of corporation and executives of the corporation are used synonymously.
8 For a discussion of the various categories of risk associated with financial liberalisation and the weakness of the financial system in Africa, see Brinkman, 1999.
9 For a discussion of the European Union approach, see Monks and Minow, 1996: 322–5.
10 The information on OHADA draws on World Bank, 2000: 80.

11 For a discussion of measures for private sector development in low-income countries, the category to which many African countries belong, see World Bank, 1995.

Bibliography

Annan, Kofi (2000): 'We the Peoples: the Role of the United Nations in the 21st Century', Report of the Secretary-General to the 55th Session of the UN General Assembly, New York: United Nations.

Bishop, Matthew, John Kay and Colin Mayer (1996) 'Introduction', in Matthew Bishop, John Kay and Colin Mayer (eds.), *The Regulatory Challenge*, Oxford: Oxford University Press.

Bratton, William W. (1994) 'Public Values, Private Business and US Corporate Fiduciary Law', in Joseph McCahery, Sol Piccioto and Colin Scott (eds.), *Corporate Control and Accountability: Changing Structures and the Dynamics of Regulation*, Oxford: Clarendon Press, pp. 23–39.

Brautigam, Deborah (1996), 'State Capacity and Effective Governance', in Benno Ndulu, Nicolas van de Walle, *et al.*, *Agenda for African Economic Renewal*, New Brunswick, USA: Transaction Publishers, pp. 81–108.

Brinkman, Henk-Jan (1999) 'Financial Reforms in Africa and the Lessons from Asia', in Barry Herman (ed.), *Global Financial Turmoil and Reform. A United Nations Perspective*, Tokyo: United Nations University Press, pp. 213–46.

CACG (1999) *Guidelines: Principles of Corporate Governance in the Commonwealth – Towards Global Competitiveness and Economic Accountability*, Malborough, New Zealand: Commonwealth Association on Corporate Governance.

Dezalay, Yves (1994) 'Professional Competition and the Social Construction of Transformational Regulatory Expertise', in Joseph McCahery *et al.*, *Corporate Control and Accountability*, pp. 203–16.

Hogwood, Brian W. (1990) 'Developments in Regulatory Agencies in Britain', *International Review of Administration Sciences*, 56, 4 (December).

Kapstein, Ethan (1996) *Governing the Global Economy: International Finance and the State*, Cambridge, Mass: Harvard University Press.

McCahery, Joseph, Sol Piccotto and Colin Scott (1994) 'Introduction: Corporate Control – Changing Concepts and Practices of the Firm', in Joseph McCahery *et al.* (eds.), *Corporate Control and Accountability*, pp 1–20.

Milstein, Ira M. and Salem M. Katsh (1982) *The Limits of Corporate Power: Existing Constraints on the Exercise of Corporate Discretion*, New York: Macmillan Publishing Co. Inc.

Mkandawire, Thandika and Charles C. Soludo (1999) *Our Continent, Our Future: African Perspectives on Structural Adjustment*, Trenton, New Jersey: African World Press Inc.

Monks, Robert A. G. and Newll Minow (1996) *Watching the Watchers: Corporate Governance for the 21st Century*, Cambridge, Mass: Blackwell Publishers Inc.

OECD (1999) *OECD Principles of Corporate Governance*, Paris: Organisation for Economic Cooperation and Development.

Otobo, Ejeviome E. (1996) 'Regulatory Reform: an Imperative for Successful Privatisation', paper presented at the Annual Conference of the African Privatisation Network, Accra, Ghana, 4–6 November 1996.

—— (1997) 'Regulatory Reform in Support of Privatisation. Patterns and Progress in Africa', *African Journal of Public Administration and Management*, 8–9, 2: 25–50.

—— (1999) 'Institutions and Economic Governance for a Market Economy: Pathways for Africa', *Development Policy Management Network (DPMN) Bulletin*, 6, 1 (November).

Parkinson, J. E. (1994) *Corporate Power and Responsibility: Issues in the Theory of Company Law*, Oxford: Clarendon Press.

Rodrik, Dani (2000) 'Development Strategies for the Next Century', paper presented at the conference on 'Developing Economies in the 21st Century', Institute for Developing Economies, Japan External Trade Organisation, Chiba, Japan, 26–27 January.

Scott, Colin (1994) 'Privatisation, Control and Accountability', in Joseph McCahery *et al.*, *Corporate Control and Accountability*, pp. 231–46.

United Nations (2000) *World Economic and Social Survey*, New York: United Nations.

World Bank (1995) *Private Sector Development in Low-Income Countries*, Development in Research Series, Washington, DC: World Bank.

—— (1997) *The World Development Report: the State in a Changing World*, New York: Oxford University Press.

—— (2000) *Can Africa Claim the 21st Century?*, Washington, DC: World Bank.

Yergin, Daniel and Joseph Stanislaw (1999) *The Commanding Heights: the Battle Between Government and the Market Place That Is Remaking the Modern World*, New York: Touchstone Book, published by Simon and Schuster.

PART III
Obstacles to Good Governance and Development

11

The Refugee Problem
Julia A. Duany

During the last quarter of the twentieth century, the increase in the incidence of ethnic strife in Africa has resulted in massive short-term and long-term displacements of people. Until recently, African leaders viewed the refugee population as a problem for the United Nations; the UN, for its part, perceived the problem as being temporary in nature. As time went on, the world became increasingly aware that the quality of life among refugee populations around the world, and especially among the African refugees, has been declining and that the refugee problem has not only come to stay but is on the increase.

Many subregions of Africa are afflicted by recurring bouts of drought, famine and war. Although generally ignored by the international community, African catastrophes have become front-page news on some occasions. The events deemed newsworthy include famine in the former Biafra (1967), Ethiopia (1973–4, 1983–4) and the Sudan (1984–5, 1988–9, and 1998); military interventions in Ethiopia (1977–83) and Somalia (1992–5); and genocide in Rwanda (1992–5). Ethnic conflict ravages the African continent. People in many countries live in fear of holocausts, but the average citizen in the West knows nothing about this. The genocide in Sudan has been going on for so long that now the international press barely recognises it for what it is. Perhaps the most hideous variation of genocide has occurred in Sierra Leone and Liberia. There, not every human victim is exterminated; some are allowed to live, but only after their hands or feet have been crudely amputated.

The negative impact of Africa's conflicts is made manifest at every level of society. The economic, social and political instability perpetuates a vicious circle of self-destruction, and the most vulnerable groups are women and children. The most common war crime committed against women is sexual violence. Rape continues to haunt the victims long after the fact with its devastating physical, emotional and social consequences. An important underlying fact of the refugee crisis in Africa is the enormity of the refugee population. According to the statistics of the United Nations and what is now the African Union, there are 21 million refugees in Africa. Sudan alone is said to account for 3 million refugees. In addition, Sudan has five million internally displaced people, most of whom are women and children.

It was in this context that I went back to the Sudan, hoping to elicit the active participation of refugees in analysing their conditions. My goal was to enter into dialogue with refugees, especially those whose experience had been different to my own, to compare their conditions with those of Sudanese refugees living abroad; in so doing I hoped to avoid the biases of foreign relief workers as well as their jargon, in order to see the faces and hear the voices of real human beings. In time, I became frustrated and angered by what I saw as the expansion of the Western 'welfare state' to include the refugees of the so-called 'Third World'. I felt that I needed to challenge the perception of the helpless, impotent African refugee. Disaster services are important, but by themselves they eventually leave people divested and demoralised – a helpless nation. In Southern Sudan, people do not want to become dependent upon outside services, but until very recently self-reliance has not been given the least attention by the international relief community.

Learning from the Survivors

In November 2000, Bade Onimode of the African Centre for Development and Strategic Studies (ACDESS) asked me to contribute this chapter on the African refugee problem from an African refugee's perspective. I wondered what I could say about a subject that suggests no hope. Or about a continent that has witnessed unending violence, suffering and death for decades. However, as I reflected back on my life, I realised that, if nothing else, I had survived. I came to feel that my own experience, as well as those of other refugees, might help point the way to solutions.

Who is a refugee? A refugee is a person who lives outside of his or her country because of a well-founded fear of persecution based on race, religion, nationality, political opinion or membership of a particular social group. He/she either cannot or does not want to return home. Internally displaced persons (IDPs) are people who have been forced to leave their places of residence but are relocated within the internationally recognised border.

I will never forget the day, several years ago, when my niece and I visited the Jabal Aullia camp for internally displaced persons near Khartoum. It was home to over 25,000 people, all Dinka from Southern Sudan. While we were walking through the camp, people carrying buckets of water ran past us. My niece and I followed. We found a crowd of people gathering around a woman giving birth, lying on a dirty mat. It was unthinkable: a Sudanese child, born out in the open with men, women and children watching! I wanted to provide help to the woman, but there was nothing that I could do. I could only ask the other women to gather around and hold up their *tobes* to give the new mother some privacy. I wondered, 'How did it come to this? Could the UN High Commissioner for Refugees (UNHCR) not have provided a birthing tent? Or could the government not have taken the woman to a maternity clinic in the city? Is this camp the best that we can offer to these people?'

Since that day, I have visited other refugee camps and have learned many things about refugee conditions. My awareness of the refugee experience continued to grow during my years in the United States, where I have lived as a refugee since 1984. As greater numbers of Sudanese refugees arrived in the United States, I became involved in their resettlement. There were many misunderstandings and arguments, as well as some major incidents of personal pain and hurt, which happened because both refugee and host communities were poorly prepared for the challenge of resettlement. Many refugee immigrants from the Horn of Africa arrive in the United States with a mixture of fantastic expectations and fear. Most of these people have had no previous experience either of travelling or living abroad. Their expectations of America have been formed by what they have seen on television. To the African, America is at once a dream world of freedom and affluence and a nightmare of violence and poverty.

Immigration to the United States under peaceful and normal conditions is a stressful process, but for the refugee it is also a process of profound loss. When I arrived in the United States I had hoped to regain those non-material things that I had lost: peace, happiness, and a sense of belonging to a community. Instead, I found myself torn apart. One part of me mourned over the loss of my culture and another part of me desperately struggled to find a place in the strange, new one. For any refugee working through the pain of loss, culture shock takes a long time. My own struggle lasted for a period of years. For that reason, I fully understand why so many of us who are refugees feel that we are forever outside trying to look inside. This awareness gives me courage to expose, as an African refugee, the pain of the refugee experience.

But it is not enough simply to analyse the experience. I am convinced that if Africa is to get to the root of its refugee crisis, it must proactively involve the community in the process of finding solutions.

Root Causes of the Refugee Problem in Africa

Africa is as vast and diverse as the refugee problem confronting it. Many factors contribute to the increase of refugee populations in Africa. Rising poverty, population expansion, increasing urbanisation and natural disasters such as droughts or floods all unfold against varied geographical and historical backgrounds.

Mankind frequently escalates natural events into catastrophic proportions. Man-made disasters include economic uprooting, the breakdown of political structure, violence (ranging from banditry and internal conflict to international war) and the displacement of entire peoples. The nature of political power in modern African states together with the real and perceived rewards of capturing and maintaining power are key sources of crisis across the continent.

Colonial legacy

The modern African state is the child of its colonial father. The Europeans divided Africa into colonial territories at the Congress of Berlin in (1884–5). This division resulted, nearly 70 years later, in the newly independent Africa governments inheriting a multitude that in some countries defied any attempt at national unity. The difficult issues of governance that ethnic animosities have created have been compounded by the tendency to overcentralise power and the means of production.

The use of technologically superior weapons has enabled comparatively few Europeans to control vast territories. The colonial ruler needed clerks and other subordinates to support the colonial administration. This gave rise to a new class of Africans educated in Western ways and language. This in turn created disparities among various ethnic groups which have had lasting economic, occupational, social and political consequences.

The Africans of the new élite or class were taught to regard traditional African values as inferior to Western ones. Yet because they were Africans, the élite were opposed to colonial rule. They evolved into a class of professional politicians leading the countries of Africa into independence, and into a future in which they planned to play the key role, little realising that much of what they had learned about government from their colonial rulers would prove to be their undoing.

Post-colonial years: a centralised system controlled by the few

The post-colonial African state, in spite of its hopeful beginnings, could not escape its colonial legacy. This legacy is built upon a process of subordination and is inherently violent; it is even more problematic because of Africa's historical background of ethnic conflict. Thus post-colonial state building in Africa has become a history of violent conflict. In the Sudan, for example, state building has come to mean acquiring the monopoly of the instruments of force and the imposition of Islamic dominion.

Throughout Africa, the struggle to transform the constitutional state collapsed during the 1960s into totalitarianism. Even then, a strong presumption existed that the independent nation states would emerge as modern societies, fashioned by the new African élite and drawing on Western intellectual traditions in political science and technology. Indigenous culture was identified as an obstacle to progress – and to political power – and condemned to eradication. But a culture can be intentionally eradicated by the state only through repression and ultimately by genocide (as in the case of Rwanda and Sudan). Those who become partners in eliminating tribalism sooner or later find themselves partners in genocide.

The adoption by the African élite of Western theories of an egalitarian, centrally controlled, socialist society has proved to be a costly failure. To the loss of human life must be added the widespread dislocation of domestic trade; the breakdown of communication networks; the sharp decline in agricultural production; urban decay and the terrible economic conditions of rural areas. Insecurity resulting in massive displacement of the rural population makes Africa the best-represented continent in the refugee population of the world. Within the African states, communities united by a similar culture are still struggling to obtain a measure of self-determination or independence as nation states. Thus the state as it exists today has yet to become an organic part of the African political and social process. Consequently, there exist enormous discontinuities between the rhetoric of the post-colonial state and the realities of African societies.

Early refugee populations

The earliest post-colonial struggles for decolonisation and nation building produced early refugee populations. The refugees who appeared during the mid-1950s and early 1960s were usually freedom fighters struggling and fleeing from colonial oppression. Very much the product of their time, they were greeted genuinely and generously by their neighbours as brothers and sisters; people who could stay as guests and then almost certainly return home within a discernible time horizon to be leaders, business people or farmers in their own newly independent states.

The refugees lived with local populations with whom they were often ethnically linked, or in settlements, and were welcomed into the host country's labour force. They retained their dignity as members of the human family. As President Julius Nyerere once recalled, it was an age of innocence, both for the refugees and the rulers. The future looked so bright that the next generations of refugees did not anticipate the obstacles they were about to meet on the road toward the shining future.

Ethnic conflict: Africa divided

Ethnic identification is a sensitive, emotional issue, and one that is manipulated. Until either international war or civil war breaks out, violent ethnic conflicts in Africa are usually confined to one subregion. They tend to be played down or even denied by the government concerned and the outside world takes little notice of them. Nevertheless, ethnic conflicts are frequently the forerunners of civil wars, as was the case in Burundi, Rwanda, South Sudan, and the Democratic Republic of Congo. Kenya is an example of ethnic conflict that was threatening to escalate before the Presidential and parliamentary elections of December 2002 which put in power a truly representative government. The availability of weapons in Africa guarantees that ethnic conflicts are likely to become increasingly common in the future. They are not a natural phenomenon. They are caused by people and in many cases are exploited by individuals (usually those in power) to promote their own interests.

The new players, such as warlords, occupy pivotal roles. As in the case of Sudan and Angola, the most powerful warlords enrich themselves at the expense of the starving population by controlling relief operations. Food aid has created a wealthy commander class who live, removed from the field of battle, in big houses in large cities. The problem is no longer considered temporary and is virtually out of control, and every aspect of the African refugee crisis has changed dramatically.

The evaporation of the high aspiration of independence has produced crumbling social systems in Africa. The main source of refugee populations in this environment has become politicised and militarised beyond recognition. Refugees are rarely welcomed as guests by their neighbours these days and the African states are increasingly following the lead of other regions of the world in closing their doors to refugees (UNHCR, 1995). Conflicts always have an important negative impact on the development prospects of a country.

The Refugee World: the Swelling Population of Africa's Limbo

According to the latest report of the UN's Food and Agriculture Organisation, some 34 million people in Africa (one person in 15) are suffering from war-related factors. Countries that are particularly affected are Sierra Leone, Liberia, Somalia, Eritrea, Ethiopia and Sudan. Even in countries where war has ended, such as Mozambique and Angola, people still suffer from the effects of many years of conflict.

According to the latest UN estimate, 15 million people from sub-Sahara Africa have been expelled from their homelands. They still live in their countries of origin, but under the same conditions as refugees. Their own governments offer little in the way of aid programmes. An additional seven million people have fled beyond the frontiers of their own countries and are living mostly in refugee camps.

Hostile hosts

A major concern of refugees is rejection by their host communities in Africa, where resources are scarce. As the refugee crisis has evolved into a permanent feature of African society, the refugee population itself has changed, becoming more sophisticated and even devious in claiming places of refuge or obtaining emergency food rations and shelter. At the same time, the most vulnerable among them, such as women and children, have become specific targets of predators.

The movement of mass refugee populations brings problem both for the country from which they have fled and the country of refuge. In the former, the loss of large sections of the population can disintegrate local economic and political structures. The migration of the refugees upsets the balance of supply and demand in regional markets. Many of the refugees leave behind cultivated fields, whose crops, an integral part of the regional supply, are neglected. In the host countries, the sudden and drastic increase in population also puts strain on the economic system and usually has a devastating effect on the environment. The high population density of the refugee camps unavoidably leads to excessive strain on natural resources. In Africa's fragile ecological system, for example, mass felling of trees for fuel and shelter can inflict lasting damage on local productive capacities.

The increase in the population of refugees leads to higher local prices or pillaging. Competition for resources often escalates into violence between refugees and locals, and contributes towards creating general insecurity in the region. This destructive cycle has an adverse effect on the local quality of life and on the willingness of local people to accept the refugees.

Short-term outlook

Many refugees, especially those in Africa, suffer from adverse living conditions. These conditions range from the threat of violence to lack of appropriate health care facilities, poor nutrition and limited educational and employment opportunities. African refugees are especially vulnerable to long-term deprivation, because the international community is growing increasingly weary of responding to what essentially can be termed a man-made disaster.

Assistance to refugees is generally part of the United Nations' overall humanitarian aid programme. In some countries, the UNHCR, NGOs and other agencies have stepped in and become the only sources of care for refugees and other conflict victims. In countries most devastated by conflict, basic medical and social services, which are generally weak under the best of circumstances, are weakened even more or collapse completely. In such circumstances, the local citizens suffer along with the refugees.

In the context of Africa's present political environment, the needs of refugees should be seen as long-term. African countries need to be supported in 'taking ownership of the problem' through developing their own health and social services sectors to be able to handle the population. Taking ownership of the refugee problem may also provide an incentive for stopping violence in many African countries.

Ideally, refugees should be dealt with by several government ministries: education, labour and employment, social welfare and healthcare. Such an integrated approach is necessary if the whole range of issues related to refugee assistance is to ensure that refugees have a voice in the decision-making processes that affect their lives and the lives of their families. Where international agencies have had to step in and offer services, they should work to integrate the refugees with the local community, thus changing the focus of humanitarian assistance agencies from providers to facilitators.

A short-term outlook is inadequate, because the refugee crisis is not temporary. But the African governments and the international community both need to redefine their effort to accommodate and integrate the refugee population as an immigrant population for the long term.

Refugees with special needs

Another aspect of this problem is the failure to identify refugees or IDPs who have special needs. Individuals who have been physically disabled, such as victims of landmines, must be a focus of special assistance. Not only have they suffered violently and most directly, but their ability to recover has been impaired. At the same time, a broader definition of refugees with special needs is not only possible, but also often desirable. This definition can include families or communities as a whole. Nevertheless, using a broader definition for programme planning should benefit families and communities without displacing attention and resources from the complex needs of the refugees themselves. For example, a broad-based community development programme in an area of heavy conflict should not be considered as short-term assistance, but should address the community's basic needs related to that particular refugee culture. Broad-based community development programmes have traditionally ignored the social and mental problem of the refugees. These must be explicitly built into the planning of the refugee programmes.

Humanitarian targets

One of the consequences of the permanent nature of the refugee crisis is that NGOs have become a target of harassment and, sometimes, killing. Resentment on the part of refugees is generated by the belief that the NGOs are benefiting from their tragedy. UNHCR field staff and members of other agencies, who until recently had worked on the periphery of conflict and were respected by all as Good Samaritans, now find themselves working in impossible physical conditions. They are sometimes abused, and/or accused of spying, or are forced to make life-or-death decisions. According to a 1999 UN report, a total of 36 UNHCR staff members were killed or reported missing during one crisis. I have seen, for example, the growing insecurity of the UNHCR personnel in Uganda. Their offices have become fortresses surrounded by barbed wire and are heavily guarded. The workers fear to venture far from the compound.

Time for a holistic approach

Helping refugees to address their concerns is a task that is best accomplished through the proactive initiative of all African leaders, undertaken jointly with local communities, especially local organisations, the international community and the NGOs, both non-religious and religious. Agencies assisting refugees, especially during the early stage of their entrance into new settlements, must adopt a holistic approach to their concerns. This means transforming the process of delivering services from a service-based model to a client- or market-based model. This model (Table 11.1) will assist the refugees, both individually and as a community, in understanding the roots of the crisis, in using their skills and experience to find solutions to problems, in developing their capacities for self-reliant living and in making positive contributions to the host community.

Aiding refugee populations should be based on a holistic approach. African communities should adopt policies of non-segregation in camps and provide a non-dehumanising enabling environment. In Kakuma refugee camp, for example, the Kenya government forbids the refugees from owning any assets.

Support from the international aid community must focus on local capacity building, health, education, complete rehabilitation and true socio-economic integration of the refugees into the host community. While there are no guarantees that the host community will not stigmatise the refugees, a long-term integrated approach can begin to address the problem. The international aid community must consciously work to ensure that its own programme and support do not encourage or add to the stigmatisation of refugees.

Table 11.1 Shift from Service-Based Model for Human Services to Market-Based Model

At issue	The service-based model	The market-based model
Who's in charge	Professionally driven	Citizen/client is partner
Contribution of professionals	Professional provides answers	Professional is a resource
Process	Usually diagnosing a single cause and cure	Understanding multiple causes and seeking ongoing change
Procedure	Bureaucratic	Informal
What's valued	Credentials	Experience
Communication	Largely one-way	Collaborative
Focus of problem solving	Individual deficiency	Capacities developed through interaction
Exchange	None – only Western nations contribute	Mutual benefits to refuges, host, and international communities

Source: Lappé and du Bois, 1994

Because the increase in humanitarian aid has become a major challenge world-wide, a number of initiatives over the last few years have drawn up recommendations and standards for action. Some examples include the United States and Canadian resettlement programmes. These are not problem-free, but they do encourage complete rehabilitation and socio-economic integration of the refugees into the host community. Even though these are affluent countries, it is still our challenge to do what we can as Africans to integrate refugees into our own communities. To create a better world, one in which human rights are respected, African leaders must assume the ownership of the refugee crisis and must be willing to change the way their camps are administered.

Vision for the Future

Aid processes

Africa has a big role to play in alleviating the refugee crisis. Improving present conditions requires the participation of refugees in the decision-making and implementation processes that affect their daily affairs. Human activities provide insight into daily living, since what people do is often different from what they say they do and what they think they do. Life in the refugee camp, through adaptive social habits and ordinary activities, produces tolls of survival. Changing structures to involve refugees in decision making will generate solutions from within the refugee community. These solutions should rely first and foremost on the internal strengths of the refugee community and translate into initiatives taken in cooperation with agencies sympathetic to its problems and aspirations.

It requires much effort to move the issues of the refugee beyond the initial stage of dependency to the stage of self-help. At the stage of dependency, the refugees are helpless, fearful and easily intimidated. But it is at the stage of self-help that the refugee really begins to develop self-confidence and integrate into his or her new community. To move refugees forward to the stage of self-help, culturally sensitive, trust-based relationships must be built in two areas. First, the refugees must learn to trust each other, and, second, they must learn to trust other people in their new community. This process demands open communication between the agency and refugee community.

Involving refugees in designing solutions to their problem is a major step in the process of integrating them into the community at large. Within the context of a self-help support group, both the new and the more experienced refugees should analyse their problems and work in coordination with the provider agency to design solutions.

Since many refugees are women, it is helpful to establish support groups among them. It is important to encourage the women to organise themselves. It must be their initiative and they must take ownership. Women are the ones who are at the centre of service to the family, who spend the most time with the children and who play the most important role in the provision of family health care and nutrition. And it is the African woman refugee who is most likely to become isolated in the host community. By encouraging the women to organise themselves and to take some initiative we show our confidence in them, which in turn gives new refugee women the confidence they need to make a healthy adjustment to life in their new 'home'.

The African host communities should enter into partnership with the NGOs in integrating refugees into local community life. As we encourage refugees to learn to trust other people in their new community, we should make an effort to sensitise the local people about the refugee culture. Again, the refugees can and should be part of the solution, since when it comes their own culture, they are the experts. The host and the refugee communities can help to educate each other.

Developing a long-term transitional outlook will help the refugees to adjust to their new lives. Refugees need acceptance, respect and a lot of help. It is not enough to maintain refugees and their families at survival levels. Care for mothers and children, health, education, disease prevention, family planning, language and literacy classes, consumer education, and training in the skills of daily living are all necessary to improving their quality of life. But from the beginning we must be culturally sensitive as we plug refugees into the new system and help them make necessary changes. We must step out of our comfort zone to help them. We must build a relationship of trust in a cross-cultural framework.

Funding

Inadequate funding will always be a problem, but there are ways to make this limitation easier to deal with. First, agencies such as NGOs and the UN must communicate openly with the refugee communities that they serve. This is the only way in which misunderstandings about the use of funds can be avoided. Second, agencies must not fear losing control by involving refugees in the decision-making process. Knowledge is power. Our goal should be to empower the refugees economically.

On the regional or local level, relief efforts, both public and private, rely on Western nations for resources. These resources are not as forthcoming as they once were. Therefore, African nations should take the initiative to contribute their own resources. On the international level, however, reasons for the limitation of resources are more difficult to understand. The international community is severely underfunded. Early in 2000, for example, we saw the European nations responding very quickly to stop bloodshed in Kosovo. It is disheartening to see that in countries considered more 'civilised' than Africa, race relations still play a role in decision making.

This is why Africans must take the lead in solving their problems. We cannot expect outsiders to do our work for us. We have the knowledge, ability and cultural insight that can be key factors in making effective use of resources and services to deal with refugee issues. Refugees adjust best when they are allowed to organise themselves into self-help support groups that focus on solving problems. The women's organisation effort in Nigeria is a very good example of working through trust-based relationships.

Minimise duplication of services

Cooperation between NGOs and the UNHCR is needed to minimise the duplication of services. A voluntary, self-controlling regionally focused association could devise measures for programme evaluation and incentives to develop local capacity and enhance participation in what should be joint efforts. The goal is to bring people together in partnership to achieve reforms and results, and not to undermine each other.

NGO and UNHCR staff quality

As their aid operations have become high-tech, multibillion-dollar industries, NGOs and the UNHCR have attracted some people who may not be as concerned with humanitarian mission as they are attracted by well-paying jobs. Agencies working with the refugees must take care to supplement, rather than overwhelm, existing local resources.

There is a concern that many of the foreign-assisted operations in Africa are run by inexperienced aid staff who have little or no knowledge of the culture and way of life of people they have been sent to serve. Ignorance puts personnel in a defensive posture when they are challenged or intimidated by their African counterparts, who have the advantage of knowing the culture and the people. Such an atmosphere may create conflict within the agency and will certainly serve to exclude refugees from participating in any decision making. External agencies would be wise to bring in indigenous experience when training and preparing their staff for service in the field. The easiest way to do this is to involve refugees in the training and in filling staff positions from the pool of refugees.

Peace and Stability

The real answer to the refugee crisis is peace. Peace is a dynamic, constructive expression of human energy. Contrary to what most people believe, governments cannot make peace. They can only exercise a temporary control over individual human energy. True peace is the product of liberty, and liberty is the product of self-government. Peace is something that happens when men and women have the freedom to apply their creativity and energy to solving problems like hunger, disease, illiteracy and violence. Peace is a total way of life.

That wars cause hunger, deprivation and suffering is self-evident. Attacking villages, looting, rape and confiscating land contribute to destroying harvests and productive inputs. Destruction of a country's infrastructure – its roads, bridges, public transport links and marketplaces – hinders trade between subregions. Thus, some subregions have a food deficit and areas are left uncultivated. Landmines are a particular threat; they severely hamper recovery of the economy and food supply, long after the war is over. Sudan has an estimated 10 million landmines. These are all buried in the southern part of the country where ten million people live. Experts reckon that it will take no less than 30 years to clear the land of these mines.

Arms control

Africa consistently has been overlooked in international arms control agreements. As a result, Africa has become a hot market for arms. Africa has become a continent where the AK 47 rules. The flow of weapons into Africa is a moral issue that the international community cannot continue to ignore. The availability of weapons destabilises effort to reform government, law and education by sustaining a way of life that encourages Africans to kill Africans.

The international community must consider and include the nations of Africa in future arms control agreements. People who are interested in Africa must begin to view arms control as a public relations problem. To get support from the international community, Africans must learn to market the message in a positive, proactive way.

Decentralisation and democratisation

Reform in government is needed to shift the base of the African state from central control to local control. A more accountable democratisation will accompany the development of community-based governance.

Systems of law and order need to incorporate African norms of governance. If the rule of law is to mean anything, Africa needs to go back to its roots and re-discover its indigenous conflict resolution mechanisms. These use local actors and traditional, community-based judicial and legal decision-making mechanisms to manage and resolve conflicts within or between communities. This is being done with some success as a people-to-people peace and reconciliation process in the Upper Nile region of Southern Sudan.

Education

Refugee education has been neglected. Reliable data are not available as to the magnitude of this neglect but it is colossal. Sudan is an example of a country where two generations have had no formal education because of war. The present system of education in Africa is based on models that produce white-collar workers. The models ignore the African context and push forward a prescribed programme regardless of what the people actually need or want. Educational objectives need to be looked at afresh. On leaving the primary level, children should have acquired enough knowledge to enable them to cope with the practical situations of everyday life. UNCHR could establish a collaborative research effort with NGOs on finding ways to provide adequate and affordable educational services. This could be undertaken in collaboration with the host countries. Adult education and training in the field could step up scientific research on the food crops grown by local farmers, or strengthen local communities through self-help programmes. Technical skills could make a life-or-death difference to people in thousands of villages.

Conclusion

What African communities need most is peace. This is where the challenge lies for African leaders in the 21st century if Africa is to claim the century. It must rely increasingly on its traditional mode of governance; that is, look back in order to be able to move forward. African leaders should concentrate on improving conditions for all people within their countries. Humanitarian assistance, whether to refugees or to citizens, should shift from paternalism and aim at improving people's ability to make the decisions that affect their lives. This shift can only succeed in a politically stable atmosphere in which human rights are respected and people have sufficient security. In this light, resolving Africa's refugee problem will require a strong commitment from African leaders and the international community to developing a political environment that fosters economic and individual freedom, democracy and decentralisation.

Bibliography

Ali, Taiser M. and Robert O. Mathews (eds.) (1999) *Civil Wars in Africa: Roots and Resolution*, Montreal and Kingston: McGill–Queen's University Press.

Beacon, Jonathan (1998). *Losing Place: Refugee Population and Rural Transformation in East Africa*. Refugee and Forced Migration Studies, Vol. 3, New York: Berghahn Books.

Belz, Mindy (2000) 'We Have Nothing but We Have Everything', http:/www.worldmag.com/world/issues/06-7-00international_asp

—— (2000) 'Blue Nile Blackout'. http:/www.worldmag.com/world/issue/06-10-00

Bercovitch, Jacob and Richard Jackson (1997) *International Conflict: a Chronological Encyclopedia of Conflicts and Their Management 1945–1995*, Washington, DC: Congressional Quarterly.

Burr, J. Millard and Robert O. Collins (1995) *Requiem for the Sudan: War, Drought, and Disaster Relief on the Nile*. Boulder, CO: Westview.

Food Aid for Development (FAD) (1994) *Food Supply Situation and Crop Prospects in Sub-Saharan Africa*, July Special Report, Rome, Italy: FAD.

Harrell-Bond, B. E. (1986) *Imposing Aid: Emergency Assisitance to Refugeees*, Geneva: Oxford University Press.

Lappé, Frances Moore and Paul M. du Bois (1994) *The Quickening of America: Rebuilding Our Nation, Remaking Our Lives*, San Francisco: Jossey Bass Publishers, Inc.

Mawson, Andrew N. M. (1991) 'Murahalen Raids on the Dinka, 1985–89', *Disasters*, 15: 137–49.

UNDP (1994) *Bericht zur Menschlichen Entwicklug*, Bonn: United Nations Development Programme.

UNHCR (1993) *The State of the World's Refugees: the Challenge of Protection*, Harmondsworth: Penguin Books.

—— (1995) *The State of the World's Refugees: in Search of Solutions*, Oxford and New York: Oxford University Press and UNHCR.

—— (1997) *The State of the World's Refugees: a Humanitarian Agenda*, Oxford and New York: Oxford University Press.

—— (1999) 'Africa: Innocence Lost. The 30th Anniversary of the OAU Refugee Convention', *Refugees*, 2, 115.

12

The External Debt Crisis: Strategies and Policies
Mike I. Obadan

Currently, many African countries, like some other Third World countries, have continued to stagnate and be frustrated under the burden of heavy external debt obligations. African countries, especially those in sub-Sahara Africa (SSA), are among the most indebted of developing countries, considering standard debt indicators and income levels. In the year 2000, out of 34 countries classified by the World Bank as severely indebted low-income countries (SILICs), 28 were in Africa. These countries included Angola, Ethiopia and Nigeria. Out of 18 moderately indebted low-income countries, eight were in Africa – Zimbabwe, Togo, Senegal, Kenya, Ghana, the Gambia, Chad and Benin. With respect to less-indebted low-income countries only Lesotho is African, while out of 41 less-indebted middle-income countries, only five are African – Swaziland, South Africa, Egypt, Cape Verde and Botswana. Countries have been classified as low-income if their 1998 GNP *per capita* was $760 or less, and as middle-income if it was more than $760.

Low levels of savings and income, and the attendant shortage of investment capital, led many African countries to rely heavily on official development assistance (ODA) and foreign borrowing to close widening resource investment gaps. Then the increasingly hostile international economic environment from the early 1980s and the collapse of commodity exports forced Africa and the rest of the South into a horrendous external debt crisis (Onimode, 2000: 5). This, of course, does not overlook the role of poor domestic policies and improper deployment of loans contracted, with the result that the returns on investment have not been adequate to meet maturing obligations and leave a balance to support domestic economic growth. This issue of inefficient use of borrowed funds, along with other factors, has translated into higher debt *per capita* for heavily indebted poor countries in relation to others. And SSA's debt has tended to be a bigger burden than that of other highly indebted regions because of greater poverty and the more structural weaknesses of African economies (Hussain and Underwood, 1991: 22).

The SILICs of Africa are characterised not only by low *per capita* incomes but also by low social indicators (high illiteracy and infant mortality, etcetera), poor infrastructure and low economic diversification. All these suggest the need for genuine debt relief for African countries as a basis for their exit from the debt trap. But so far, the initiatives, strategies and measures have not gone deep down enough to address this debt problem realistically.

The External Debt Burden

Eighteen years after the international debt crisis erupted in the early 1980s, the external debt stock of African countries has maintained an upward trend. Tables 12.1, 12.2, 12.3 and 12.4 show various indicators of the African debt problem from 1980. From an estimated US$8 billion in 1970, the total external debt stock of African countries rose to US$111.9 billion by 1980. This figure rose by 177.6 per cent to US$310.7 billion in 1997.

Table 12.1 Africa's Total External Debt

	Sub-Sahara Africa (US$ million)	North Africa (US$ million)	All Africa (US$ million)	Ratio of SSA to all Africa's debt (%)
1980	60,641	51,281	111,922	54.2
1988	150,535	99,695	250,229	60.2
1989	157,351	101,530	258,881	60.8
1990	177,400	92,973	270,373	65.6
1991	183,595	90,862	274,457	66.9
1992	182,555	88,746	271,301	67.3
1993	188,707	86,680	275,387	68.5
1994	219,670	94,054	313,724	70.0
1995	233,687	99,659	333,346	70.1
1996	229,467	97,859	327,321	70.1
1997	219,322	91,413	310,735	70.6

Source: World Bank, 2000c.

Sub-Sahara Africa has had a larger and rising share of debt stock, moving from 54.2 per cent in 1980 to 70.6 per cent in 1997. Indeed, the trends of SSA point to an even more dramatic increase in external debt burdens. The total external debt stock of SSA rose from US$84 billion in 1980 to US$219.4 billion in 1997 (Table 12.2). The figure in 1999 was a little changed from a year earlier at US$231 billion. Of the total, long-term debt represented 78 per cent; public and publicly guaranteed debt was 7.4 per cent; while private non-guaranteed debt constituted just 4 per cent of the total. Although new disbursements increased in 1999

Table 12.2 External Debt of Sub-Sahara Africa, 1980–98 (US$ Million)

	1980	1988	1989	1991	1992	1993	1994	1995	1996	1997	1998
Total debt stocks											
(EDT)	84,049	164,981	171,236	183,218	183,218	195,399	219,696	233,750	229,537	219,445	225,751
Long-term debt	58,448	135,476	140,735	155,315	151,349	158,897	175,576	184,174	178,255	171,070	175,956
(LDOD)	(69.5)[1]	(82.1)	(82.2)	(84.8)	(82.6)	(81.3)	(79.9)	(78.9)	(77.7)	(78.0)	(77.9)
Public and publicly guaranteed	53,881	130,663	135,764	145,963	146,250	158,811	165,383	174,183	169,842	163,273	168,502
Private non-guaranteed	4,567	4,813	4,813	5,402	5,099	5,086	10,193	9,991	2,41478	1,798	7,454
Use of IMF credit	3,033	7,000	6,380	6,603	6,345	7,019	7,920	8,673	8,445	7,393	2,400
	(3.6)	(4.2)	(3.7)	(3.6)	(3.5)	(3.6)	(3.6)	(3.7)	(3.7)	(3.4)	(3.3)
Short-term debt	22,568	22,505	24,121	22,003	25,525	29,484	36,200	40,903	42,856	40,981	42,395
	(26.9)	(13.6)	(14.1)	(12.0)	(13.9)	(15.1)	(16.5)	(17.5)	(18.7)	(18.7)	(18.8)
Of which interest arrears on LDOD	250	6,294	7,608	10,829	13,135	16,897	18,568	20,663	20,2211	18,336	18,301
Official creditors	152	4,418	5,707	7,760	9,898	12,892	14,302	16,141	16,450	15,592	-
Private creditors	98	1,876	1,901	3,069	3,242	4,005	4,266	4,522	3,771	2,744	-
Memo: principal arrears on LDOD	1,201	13,921	14,016	21,388	25,691	31,790	35,483	41,293	40,184	38,041	37,946
Official creditors	513	7,415	8,718	12,895	16,400	20,520	23,241	28,765	30,238	30,929	-
Private creditors	688	6,505	5,235	8,492	9,292	11,211	11,642	12,528	9,945	7,112	-
Memo: export credits	-	42,639	49,912	55,348	52,685	50,776	47,197	45,729	45,705	47,306	-

Note: 1. Figures in parentheses are percentage shares.

Sources: World Bank, 1996; World Bank, 1999.

Table 12.3 Sub-Sahara Africa's External Debt Indicators: Summary Debt Data (US$ Billion)

	1980	1990	1998	1999
Total debt stocks (EDT)	60.8	176.9	230.1	231.1
Long-term debt (LDOD)	46.6	149.4	180.2	179.1
Short-term debt	11.2	20.9	42.5	44.7
Total debt service (TDS)	6.7	10.9	14.1	15.2
Debt indicators				
EDT/XGS (%)	65.5	209.6	238.9	225.1
EDT/GNP (%)	23.5	63.0	72.3	75.8
TDS/XGS (%)	7.2	12.9	14.7	14.8
INT/GNP (%)	3.8	6.3	5.4	5.1
RES/MGS (Months)	1.4	1.9	1.7	1.7

Notes: See Notes to Table 12.4. In addition:
RES = External reserves
MGS = Imports of goods and services
Source: World Bank, 2000a

compared to the level in 1998, net transfers on debt were negative at US$2.7 billion.

The issue of negative net transfers brings into sharp focus the burden of debt service payments. With the sharp increase in the magnitude of the debt stock, total debt service payments have increased *in tandem*, rising from US$6.7 billion in 1980 to US$15.2 billion in 1999 (Table 12.3). The severity of the debt problem can be better appreciated by examining some debt indicators, especially the external debt/ export goods and services (XGS) ratio, the external debt/GNP ratio and the total debt service (TDS)/XGS ratio. These debt ratios have risen very sharply over the 1980–99 period. The ratio of external debt to exports of goods and services rose from 65.5 in 1980 to 225.1 in 1999, implying that as at that year all indebted African countries would require more than two years of export earnings to pay off debt. Relative to GNP, total debt rose from 23.5 per cent in 1980 to 75.8 per cent in 1999. These ratios suggest heavy debt burdens in relation to conventional critical values. The TDS/XGS ratio, ranging from 7.2 to 14.8 per cent between 1980 and 1999, appears low in relation to the critical value of 20–25 per cent. However, the relatively low debt ratios hide more than they reveal. Arrears and debt relief reduced payments to a proportion of all scheduled obligations. But many African countries have been facing liquidity problems. Given their inability to meet debt obligations, as and when due, a fair proportion of the obligation had been accumulated as payments arrears. These arrears on payments of interest and principal accounted for two-thirds of the growth in African debt since 1988 and reached US$64 billion in 1996 (Onimode, 2000: 5). Thus, as a result of the wide divergence between scheduled and actual debt service payments, against the background of poverty and deficient export earnings, there has generally been a significant difference between SSA's ratio of actual debt service to export earnings and the ratio of scheduled debt services to export earnings. The scheduled debt service to export earnings ratio, which is the more accurate measure of the pressure of debt service on export earnings and on the economy, has been on the high and burdensome side in many African countries.

Besides the insights provided by the above debt ratios, the results of debt sustainability analysis by the IMF/World Bank of 41 highly indebted poor countries (HIPCs) for the period beginning 1995/6 and projected into the future for periods of up to ten years and beyond showed that the debt positions of some African countries were unsustainable (IMF/World Bank, 1996). This implies that the countries would not be able to meet their external obligations in full without (1) future recourse to debt rescheduling or relief; or (2) the accumulation of arrears over the medium or long term; or (3) compromising economic growth. Countries with unsustainable external positions included Mozambique, Sudan, Zambia and Zaire. Four countries were classified as possibly stressed: Cameroon, Tanzania, Uganda and Côte d'Ivoire. In spite of Nigeria's highly adverse debt indicators, it was left unclassified because of the considerable uncertainty regarding the outlook for policy adjustment, and the difficulties in making acceptable assumptions about possible debt rescheduling terms. However, Ajayi (1991) had concluded that Nigeria's external debt was unsustainable. Thus, in the light of the deteriorating debt indicators, it is appropriate to state that SSA is a debt-distressed region, with only about five countries having been described as less-indebted in 2000 – Lesotho, Swaziland, South Africa, Cape Verde and Botswana (Table 12.4).

Causal Factors of the Debt Crisis

Against the background of the debt crisis which began as a creditors' crisis in August 1982, when Mexico declared its inability to service its foreign debt following the sharp rise in short-term interest rates, combined with a recession in the industrialised countries that caused export volumes to drop and commodity prices to plummet, Africa's debt difficulties acquired significant dimensions in the 1980s and 1990s. The debt difficulties derive variously from the nature of the economies, long-standing internal and external imbalances, poor economic policies implemented by governments and exogenous factors. African economies are characterised by heavy dependence on a few primary export commodities (usually between one and three) and the export trade is highly concentrated. The industrial sector, which is still in an incipient stage, depends heavily on imported inputs. The economies, therefore, have been very vulnerable to external shocks.

Table 12.4 Key Indebtedness Ratios of African Countries, 1996–8

Country	EDT/XGS	PV/XGS	EDT/GNP	PV/GNP	TDS/XGS	INT/XGS
Algeria	212	206	68	66	32	14
Angola	250	236	292	276	28	9
Benin	250	159	75	48	9	4
Botswana	17	14	12	9	2	1
Burkina Faso	465	274	56	33	18	6
Burundi	1,441	806	124	69	39	11
Cameroon	427	356	117	97	23	10
Cape Verde	120	75	50	32	9	2
Central African Rep.	576	358	90	56	19	5
Chad	365	211	69	40	12	4
Comoros	405	268	101	67	12	1
Congo, Dem. Rep. of	822	774	720	678	1	1
Congo, Rep. of	312	286	92	84	3	1
Cote d'Ivoire	288	246	151	129	27	14
Egypt Arab Rep. of	168	129	2	32	10	5
Equatorial Guinea	88	72	90	73	2	1
Eritrea	45	27	19	11	1	1
Ethiopia	1,065	898	166	140	12	5
Gabon	142	143	93	94	10	6
Gambia, The	197	111	120	68	11	3
Ghana	252	172	83	57	25	8
Guinea	420	306	93	68	19	7
Guinea–Bissau	2,406	1,733	415	299	20	12
Kenya	235	174	69	51	18	6
Lesotho	103	73	57	41	8	3
Liberia	-	-	-	-	-	-
Madagascar	532	396	120	90	15	6
Malawi	403	226	111	62	14	4
Mali	472	322	124	85	12	4
Mauritania	578	318	256	141	25	9
Mauritus	91	92	59	60	11	6
Morocco	174	157	61	55	23	9
Mozambique	1,619	539	256	85	21	8
Niger	506	340	86	58	19	4
Nigeria	190	184	83	81	8	3
Rwanda	997	554	70	39	17	8
Senegal	266	187	86	60	22	7
Sierra Leone	1,123	745	159	105	18	8
Somalia	-	-	-	-	-	-
South Africa	67	66	18	17	12	4
Sudan	2,599	2,448	207	195	9	0
Swaziland	22	17	18	14	2	1

Table 12.4 cont.

Country	EDT/XGS	PV/XGS	EDT/GNP	PV/GNP	TDS/XGS	INT/XGS
Tanzania	648	484	109	81	21	10
Togo	207	143	99	68	6	2
Tunisia	122	118	60	57	15	6
Uganda	516	311	62	37	21	4
Zambia	546	438	207	166	16	6
Zimbabwe	161	140	63	55	34	7

Notes:

EDT Total Debt Stock	XGS Exports of Goods and Services
PV Present Value of Total Debt Stock	GNP Gross National Product
TDS Total Debt Service	INT Interest Payments

Source: World Bank, 2000a

Against this background, the governments of many African countries accumulated external debt in their bids to finance savings–investments gaps and development. In the late 1970s and early 1980s, a period of excess loanable funds in the Western world, international commercial banks and their surrogates cast off all restraints in marketing loans to often unsuspecting developing countries in the guise of assisting economic development efforts. Most African countries fell for their sales talk and, consequently, borrowed heavily and accumulated trade bills. But most of their development projects had been designed to improve domestic industry and infrastructure rather than to boost export production and earnings directly. While increases in economic growth and export production hardly materialised, debt servicing problems surfaced and multiplied. In short, external borrowing, rather than bringing in the expected results, brought a number of negative results and led many SSA countries into what is now popularly called the debt trap (Ani, 1997a).

No doubt, poor economic management reflected in wasteful and unproductive expenditures, as well as management of borrowed funds by inefficient public enterprises, contributed to the debt problems of African countries. Poor economic management led to the use of borrowed funds by many debtors to finance consumption, delay adjustment, or invest in projects with low rates of return. Much of the funds borrowed in the 1970s were used to sustain declines in national savings and to finance capital flights or projects that were not viable at prevailing market prices. Indeed, some of the debtors were considered underborrowed by the creditors, who were too wiling to lend to them without ensuring the viability of the projects. Even in some cases where funds were invested wisely *ex ante*, unforeseen adverse movements in interest rates and the terms of trade made the *ex post* rates of return inadequate. Finally, poor economic management was also reflected in the highly inflationary fiscal policies of the SSA countries, which contributed to debt accumulation. Besides expansionary fiscal policy and outright borrowing for consumption, many SSA countries pursued policies that weakened their external positions. Growing fiscal deficits and surging private credit demand led to rapid monetary expansion in many countries. Most of the policies increased borrowing needs and lowered export earnings, thus reducing the ability of SSA countries to meet rising debt service obligations. In some countries, like Nigeria and Congo (Democratic Republic), a large scoop of the foreign loan windfall was swindled into secret foreign bank accounts.

However, the role of exogenous factors, largely beyond the control of the countries, was also pervasive in Africa's foreign debt crisis. The two oil price shocks of 1973–4 and 1979–80 led to record balance of payments deficits for many countries, while a few oil producers accumulated surpluses. Even then, external debt also accumulated in several oil-producing countries during the mid-1970s as a result of declining real prices (Gabon) and production difficulties (Congo). Furthermore, after 1977, Nigeria, the leading SSA oil producer, began to borrow heavily in commercial markets. Another very potent factor was the drastic deterioration in the external economic environment in the form of higher interest rates, lower commodity prices and severe recession in the industrialised economies. The 1981–2 recession in the North, which was induced by tight money, triggered systemic difficulties and posed threats to both debtors and creditors. The terms of trade of the borrowing countries deteriorated throughout most of the 1980s. For example, over the period, 1980–98, the terms of trade of SSA countries declined by 85 per cent from 176.9 to 95.6. This deterioration in the terms of trade caused or aggravated acute foreign exchange problems. Also of note were the financial and economic policies of the industrialised countries, as reflected in measures which slowed their economic growth (and thus reduced export opportunities for African countries) and sharply raised interest rates, thus further jeopardising the debtors' ability to service debts. The phenomenon of natural disasters – drought, desertification and decimation of crops by insects – also compounded the debt problem. They reduced commodity exports and led to increases in food import bills. Thus, both domestic and exogenous factors significantly aided the external debt build-up and debt servicing difficulties of African countries and the Third World countries in general.

Consequences of the Debt Burden

The debt crisis had a severe impact on African economies, exacerbating the problems arising from the sharp deterioration in primary commodity prices (Greene and Khan, 1990: 12). Real growth, investment rates and exports have fallen sharply since 1980. The constraining influence of the external debt burden became more pronounced as the African economies failed to grow sufficiently to reduce the burden to a sustainable level. In order to service increasing interest and amortisation liabilities, debtor countries had to commit a large proportion of their export earnings to debt service payments. One implication of the dramatic increase in the stock of debt and debt payments, coupled with reduction in foreign exchange earnings, is curtailment of import capacity. Import compression, reflected in declines in capital goods and intermediate goods imports, has had serious repercussions on the ability of African countries to finance and undertake development projects and achieve respectable growth rates. Another implication of the constraint imposed by the debt burden on resource availability for domestic use is that the resultant development resource gap has often been financed by money creation or borrowing from African central banks. The African economy, as a result, has been characterised by inflationary monetary and fiscal policies which impose high costs (on the economy) in terms of crowding out private credit, discouragement of badly needed foreign capital, and capital flight triggered by inflationary pressures and the poor investment climate.

Related to the foregoing is the fiscal dimension of Africa's external debt burden. As the composition of the debt is heavily tilted towards the public domain, the responsibility for debt service also falls heavily on the public sector. The heavy debt service payments have inevitably put great pressure on budgets, leading to rising fiscal deficits in the highly indebted countries (Iyoha, 1999: 17). The implications of this are many; one is that increased tax to service the debt and reduce the deficit has the effect of depressing investment – this is the debt overhang effect. Second, forced reductions in public investment, especially on social services – education and health – also result from the stiff demand of high debt service payments on the budget. This diversion of resources from public investment to foreign debt service payments is related to the 'crowding out' hypothesis mentioned in the previous paragraph.

The overhang effect of heavy debt burden has been most debilitating in many African countries. The debt overhang, which can be related to the difference between the present value of a country's contractual debt obligations and the expected resource transfers that will be made to service the debt, has an *illiquidity effect* and a *disincentive effect*. The illiquidity effect results from credit rationing. In this context, debt overhang implies that many countries are shut out of international credit markets and cannot borrow. Many high-yielding investments – human capital accumulation, investment in technology and physical infrastructure, etcetera – therefore remain unexploited in such debtor countries. Any credit rationing arising from a debt overhang crowds out many such desirable investments (Bowe and Dean, 1997: 22). The *disincentive effect* of the debt overhang arises from the possibility that an increase in the output of a country with a debt overhang also leads to an increase in its debt-service transfers to foreigners. The debt overhang reduces investment on two fronts. It discourages debtor governments from undertaking adjustments and reform because the accruing benefits may be appropriated by foreign creditors in the form of augmented debt service transfers. It may also inhibit private investment, because the requirement to service debt in the future raises taxes, thereby reducing the after-tax return on investment. The size of the disincentive effect depends on the ability of creditors to tax output increases by channelling them to debt service obligations.

Iyoha (1999: 24), in his econometric analysis of the effects of external debt on economic growth in SSA countries, found empirical support for the negative effects of debt overhang. The analysis showed that SSA's external debt stock and debt service payments act to depress investment and lower the rate of economic growth through both the debt overhang and the 'crowding out' effects. Indeed, gross domestic investment collapsed in Africa in the 1980s and 1990s. Available World Bank data show that investment as a proportion of GDP declined from 28.3 per cent in 1975–9 to 23.4 per cent in 1980–4 and 19.1 per cent in 1990–3. Real GDP growth similarly performed poorly, declining from 3.1 per cent in 1975–9 to 1.9 per cent in 1980–4, and 1.4 per cent in 1990–3. In another econometric study of the external debt burdens of African countries, Odedokun (1993) found that the existing level of external debt overhang makes it difficult for the countries to meet their debt obligations, resulting in a vicious circle of debt overhang. Therefore, in the light of the empirical findings, significant debt relief, in terms of debt stock and debt service reduction, will have positive effects on economic recovery and growth.

The external debt overhang has not only depressed incomes, investment and living standards, but has also seriously constrained the scope of macro-economic policy making, and has had damaging effects on economic and financial institutions (Greene and Khan, 1990: 24). Economic policy making in many African countries has been reduced to crisis management, with longer-term strategies being shelved in order to meet the day-to-day needs: foreign exchange, debt service payments and necessary imports for production and consumption.

Finally, the debt burden has forced many indebted African countries to seek rescheduling agreements with their creditors. One major condition for this is the adoption of IMF and World Bank SAPs. Increasing amounts of time have been devoted to successive debt rescheduling and short-term adjustment programmes. The SAPs have generally failed in African countries, while debt rescheduling has proved to be an inadequate debt resolution strategy. Countries have had to reschedule over and over again while the debt stock continues to build up.

Existing Debt Management Strategies and Policies

The early international debt strategy

The creditors' response to the debt crisis which erupted in August 1982 was an international debt strategy which emphasised case-by-case, market-based approaches – rescheduling (to preserve the contractual present value of the debt), adjustment and new money (to increase the present value of the debt). The underlying assumption was that sovereign debtors were temporarily illiquid but not permanently insolvent. Accordingly, creditors continued to treat most debtors as effectively illiquid, rather than being in any sense insolvent. That is, no matter how severe the debtors' cash-flow strains might have been, their longer-term ability to service debt was assumed to be fundamentally unimpaired (Cohen, 1989: 4). Creditors thus believed that the debtor countries would ultimately service their debt in full. But this has turned out to be erroneous, as most debtors are actually insolvent, and not just illiquid.

The case-by-case strategy expected that if rescheduling/refinancing worked well, then obligations would be postponed, while the debtor gains, thus affording it an opportunity to implement corrective policies. On the other hand, the requirement of strong adjustment programmes, supported by determined structural reforms, was aimed at increasing domestic resource mobilisation, attracting non-debt creating flows, reducing impediments to growth and preparing the ground for debt service. On a case-by-case basis, creditors and donors were to ensure the provision of adequate external financing in support of such adjustment programmes.

Against the background of the goal of the debt management strategy being to facilitate the return of budgetary solvency, debtor countries that pursued strong adjustment policies were faced with the need to restrain imports and raise exports, thus generating surpluses to enable them to meet their debt-servicing obligations. However, the adjustments entailed high costs in terms of reduced investment and output, and compressed domestic consumption and wages. According to Cohen (1989), the real tragedy of the prevailing strategy is

> the extent to which it discourages investments in debtor countries, thereby depriving them of the very means they need – an expansion of productive capacity to help them earn their way out of their difficulties. In macro-economic terms, the obligation to pay full external debt service requires a corresponding reduction of domestic expenditures in order to release resources for transfer abroad. In budgetary terms, the obligation requires extra public revenues in order to pay foreign interest costs. In practice, therefore, debtors must undertake some combination of spending cuts and tax increases, both of which fall especially hard on capital formation. The result is a cut in investment rates in debtor countries. Therefore, the prevailing strategy virtually condemns debtor countries – even those committed to serious policy reforms – to frustration and failure.

By 1985, the failure of the strategy was clearly manifest. Debt service ratios were rising. The banks' initial flow of new lending had dried up, and net financial transfers (new lending minus principal repayment minus interest payments) from debtors to creditors had turned seriously negative. And despite rescheduling and new money, the banks were receiving more interest and principal from developing countries than they were dispensing in new loans.

From the Baker Plan to HIPC Initiative

Against the background of the failure of the original 1982 debt strategy, since the mid-1980s a number of initiatives, beginning with the celebrated Baker Plan, have been pioneered by creditors and the Bretton Woods institutions to address the debt problems of developing countries, particularly the SILICs and the severely indebted middle-income countries (SIMICs). The initiatives aimed at resolving the debt problems of the SILICs under the Paris Club protocol are the following: Venice Terms (1987); Toronto Terms (1988); Trinidad Terms (1990); Enhanced Toronto Terms (1991); Naples Terms (1994) and the HIPC Initiative (1996). On the other hand, the initiatives directed at the debt problems of the SIMICs are the Baker Plan (1985); the Brady Plan (1989); and the Houston Terms (1990). These various initiatives are highlighted below, beginning with the initiatives for the SIMICs.

1   *The Baker Plan.* Aimed at the debt crisis of middle-income countries, this plan was enunciated by the US government and presented by James Baker, US Treasury Secretary, during the World Bank–IMF meeting held in Seoul in October 1985. The plan called for increased bank and official lending to 15 heavily indebted middle-income countries in return for commitments from them to adjust their economies in growth-oriented directions. Specifically, the banks were to provide the countries with new money to the tune of US$20 billion. The plan rejected a bankruptcy approach entailing debt cancellation, and aimed rather at increasing economic growth in the debtor countries and the restoration of creditworthiness that would pave the way for voluntary commercial lending. It stressed a menu of market-based options which included discounted buy-backs, interest and currency switching, securitisation and debt conversion. Much of the official lending, however, was implicitly used to finance interest and principal repayments to the banks, as evidenced by the enormous negative transfers from debtors to creditors. (In this respect the scheme resembled carousel-style financial scams.)

2   *The Brady Plan.* The need to find a more satisfactory solution to the debt problem led to the enunciation of the Brady Plan in 1989. It was an explicit official recognition that new lending and adjustment policies alone were insufficient to reduce the debt overhang. Introduced by another US Treasury Secretary, Nicholas Brady, the initiative was essentially a reformulation of the Baker Plan as it contained many of features of the latter, such as the discounted buy-backs, securitisation and continued support from creditor governments through official bilateral debt rescheduling and new export cover. Against the background of the adoption of adjustment programmes by debtor countries, the Plan stressed voluntary market-based debt and debt service

reduction as a complement to new money lending and the prevention of free riding. Moreover, the Bretton Woods institutions were to provide funding to eligible countries for total debt and debt service reduction. Thus, the thrust of the initiative was to shift official strategy from coordinated lending to debt reduction. The new strategy was, however, to eschew mandatory write-downs in favour of a voluntary, market-based approach. Needless to say, this plan failed.

3   *The Houston Terms.* Proposed by France and the United States at the Houston Summit of the industrialised countries in July 1990, these terms were directed at the lower middle-income countries with high levels of official debt. The features of the terms included:

- rescheduling of ODA loans with a 20-year maturity, including up to 10 years of grace;
- rescheduling of export credits and official loans, other than ODA, with a maturity of 15 years and up to 8 years of grace; and
- possible selling or swapping by creditor governments of ODA loans as well as a limited amount of non-concessional credits through debt conversion programmes.

These terms have not solved the problem.

4   *Venice Terms.* Under these terms, agreed upon at the Venice Summit of June 1987, those of the poorest countries that were undertaking adjustment programmes were to be considered as possible recipients of lower interest rates on their existing debt as well as a longer repayment period (20 years) and a longer grace period (10 years) to ease the debt burden. These terms have also failed.

5   *Toronto Terms.* Approved by the major Paris Club creditors participating in the Toronto Summit of June 1988, and adopted at the IMF–World Bank meeting in Berlin in October 1988, these terms involved a menu of options for countries (IDA-only) with very low *per capita* income, chronic balance of payments problems and SAPs under implementation. These terms have the features of a partial debt write-off, lower interest rates, and a further lengthening of maturities to 25 years, including 14 years' grace for rescheduled concessional debt. For non-concessional debt, creditors were to choose from a menu of three options: partial write-offs (cancelling one-third of the principal due during the consolidation period); longer repayment period; and concessional interest rates. These terms have not worked, either.

6   *Trinidad Terms.* The inadequacy of the Toronto Terms, in offering very little relief to the debtor countries, particularly the poor and highly indebted ones,

led to the adoption of Trinidad Terms by the meeting of Commonwealth Finance Ministers held in Trinidad in late 1990. The major features of the Trinidad Terms were the cancellation by creditors of two-thirds of the stock of debt owed by eligible countries in a single operation, and the rescheduling of the remaining debt over 25 years (including 5 years of grace) with interest payments capitalised for the first five years. The repayment schedule was to be flexible, depending on the debtor country's export capacity. The terms recognised that the initiative would not solve the problem.

7   *The Enhanced Toronto Terms* (now also called the London Terms). Adopted in December 1991 by the Paris Club to replace the Toronto Terms, the Enhanced Toronto terms provided for additional debt relief of up to 50 per cent of the eligible debt in net present value terms. Under the terms, the maturity of ODA debts increased from 25 to 30 years. For non-ODA debt, the amount of partial write-off of debt service due during the consolidation period was increased from 14 to 23 years of grace. The notable special feature of the terms was the combination of interest reduction and partial interest capitalisation. But the terms remained inadequate for resolving the problem.

8   *The Naples Terms.* These reflected the need for a high degree of concession-ality in rescheduling, and a fundamental restructuring of the entire stock of the Paris Club debt. The Naples Terms, also known as 'exit rescheduling', were adopted by the Paris Club in December 1994 following a July G7 Summit in Naples. A notable feature of the Naples Term was that for the first time the Paris Club was prepared to grant relief on a country's total stock of debt, provided its restructuring programmes were sufficiently advanced. Other features of the menu of options included:
   • a reduction by 67 per cent in the debt stock in net present value terms;
   • lengthening the maturities up to 33 years under service reduction options, and 40 years for rescheduled ODA debts; and
   • maintenance of greater flexibility on the types of debts covered for rescheduling.
In order to benefit from the terms, debtor countries were to prove their ability to respect agreements as reflected in the establishment of a solid track record under both rescheduling agreements and an IMF–sponsored SAP. The problem has outlasted these terms, too.

9   *The HIPC Initiative.* The various initiatives from the early 1990s, entailing one form of debt reduction or another, reflected an admission by the creditors of the ineffectiveness of the traditional market approach, mainly involving rescheduling of debts. But the reductions did not go far enough, more especially as they did not cover debts owed to multilateral institutions such

as the World Bank and the IMF. These institutions were intransigent in not granting reliefs on debts owed them, as they considered these debts as superior to all other debts: they must be repaid. This stance, however, changed with the introduction of the HIPC Initiative in the fall of 1996. The initiative, jointly proposed by the IMF and the World Bank, permits debt reduction by official creditors, including the multilateral institutions, 'as long as their financial and preferred creditor status is preserved'.

The HIPC Initiative covers a group of 41 developing countries. It entails coordinated action by the international financial community to reduce the debt burden of developing countries to sustainable levels – that is, to levels that will enable them to comfortably service their debt through earnings, aid and capital inflows. Sustainable debt was defined originally as a stock of debt with a net present value of 200–250 per cent of annual exports. And for extremely open economies, it was defined as a debt-to-government revenue ratio of 280 per cent. Apparently, in response to criticisms that this did not go far enough, these parameters were lowered in 1999 to a debt-to-export ratio of 150 per cent and a debt-to-revenue ratio of 250 per cent. That boosted the net present value of potential debt reduction from $12.5 billion to $27 billion.

To qualify for assistance under HIPC, a country must adopt adjustment and reform programmes supported by the IMF and the World Bank, and pursue those programmes for three years. It must also be ESAF-eligible, IDA-only, and facing an unsustainable debt after the full application of traditional debt relief mechanisms. Apart from these eligibility criteria, there are two key elements of the design or architecture of the initiative, namely:

- debt sustainability analysis (DSA) which is the key analytical linch-pin of HIPC discussion for each country;
- performance criteria, in terms of three years of track record to get to a decision point based on the DSA, and three years to the completion point.

Essentially, therefore, relief under the HIPC Initiative is tied to firm evidence of the country's implementation of SAPs. Qualifying countries reach a decision point after displaying a track record of implementing an SAP for three years. At that decision point, donors assess the prospects of the country and decide how much debt relief is needed to reduce its debt to sustainable levels. Under the set of conditions, three more years of SAP policies were then needed to reach the completion point, when the debt relief is actually granted in terms of flow re-scheduling on concessional terms, debt reduction or debt service reduction, debt buy-backs, or grants. The debt reduction can be up to 80 per cent in present value terms. Donors, however, decided in 1999 to have a floating completion point. Instead of a three-year rigid requirement, a country is deemed to have reached completion point when it fulfils a set of reform requirements.

By April 1997 Uganda had become the first country to reach the decision point and be found eligible for assistance under the HIPC Initiative; upon reaching its completion point it was to receive debt relief of approximately US$340 million in net present value terms. So far, Bolivia, Burkina Faso, Côte d'Ivoire, Guyana, Mali, Mozambique and Uganda have qualified for debt relief – of US$3.4 billion. Benin and Senegal have been considered ineligible because their debt has been judged sustainable without recourse to extraordinary measures (World Bank, 2000: 176). Preliminary reviews are said to have been completed for Ethiopia, Guinea-Bissau, Mauritania, Nicaragua and Tanzania. However, the procedures of the HIPC Initiative entailing a number of stages are rather complex and time-consuming for the desired timely impact on the debt burdens to be made. Indeed, African countries have expressed strong concerns on different aspects of the Initiative relating to eligibility and performance criteria; debt sustainability analysis; the treatment of the fiscal burden of debt service; the length of completion period before countries become eligible for the facility; the level and commitments of funding of the facility; and the difficulties of dealing with non-Paris Club creditors.

Specifically, it is felt that the required performance period before a country can obtain relief from the Initiative – namely, the first three-year period leading to the decision point and the second three-year period leading to the completion point – is too long. And according to Ani (1997a: 16–17) the work-out period can be up to nine years. This derives from the reasoning that

> the HIPC Initiative would appear to envisage that a country which had not benefited from the Enhanced Toronto Terms should start from there. It would then move to the Naples Terms, which presupposes the implementation of a three-year adjustment programme. If measures taken at those stages prove insufficient to bring the beneficiary country's debt stock to a sustainable level within another period of three years, it could then be allowed to receive support under the HIPC Initiative. Therefore, for countries which had not had a Toronto Terms treatment, the work-out period may not be less than nine years.

The feeling that the period is long is also in view of the need for governments to take quick action in the areas of social, economic and infrastructure investment. Another criticism is that the performance criteria used under the Initiative's mandatory SAPs are too stringent, while the DSA carried out to determine eligibility for the different stages of the Initiative and the basic assumptions underpinning this analysis might be unrealistic. Thus, the set range for the criteria – originally net present value of exports to debt ratio of 200–250 per cent and debt service to exports of 20–25 per cent – might not suffice. Besides, concern has also been expressed about the lack of inclusion of domestic debt in the calculation of debt service burden. The exclusion of Nigeria from the HIPC Initiative on flimsy grounds has also been strongly questioned.

In view of the above concerns, it will hardly be surprising if many years after the adoption of the Initiative it will have had little impact on the debt burden of

Table 12.5 African Countries' Multilateral Debt Relief Agreements with Official Creditors, January 1980–December 1999

Country	Number of agreements	Range of dates of agreements	Amount consolidated (US$ million)	External debt stock (US$ million) 1980	1997)
Algeria	2	1 June 1994–21 July 1995	12,285	19,365	30,890
Angola	1	20 July, 1989	365	6,290*	10,160
Benin	4	22 June 1989–24 October 1996	372	424	1,627
Burkina Faso	3	15 March 1991–20 June 1996	152	330	1,297
Cameroon	5	24 May 1989–24 October 1997	5,289	2,588	9,293
Central African Rep.	7	12 June 1981–25 September 1998	163	195	885
Chad	3	24 October 1989–16 July 1996	57	284	1,027
Congo, Rep. of	4	18 July 1986–16July 1996	4,362	1,527	5,071
Côte d'Ivoire	8	4 May 1984–24 April 1998	6,797	7,462	15,609
Egypt	2	22 May 1987–25 May 1991	26,263	19,131	29,850
Equatorial Guinea	4	22 July 1985–15 December 1994	139	76	283
Ethiopia	2	16 December 1992–24 January 1997	555	824	10,079
Gabon	6	21 January 1987–12 December 1995	4,233	1,514	4,285
Gambia, The	1	19 September 1986	19	137	430
Ghana	1	29 March 1996	93	1,398	5,982
Guinea	5	18 April 1986–26 February 1997	848	1,134	3,520
Guinea–Bissau	3	27 October 1987–23 February 1995	214	140	921
Kenya	1	19 January 1994	517	3,383	6,486
Liberia	4	19 December 1980–17 December 1984	76	686	2,012
Madagascar	8	30 April 1981–26 March 1997	2,584	1,250	4,105
Malawi	3	22 September 1982–22 April 1988	84	830	2,206
Mali	4	27 October 1988–20 May 1996	221	727	2,945
Mauritania	6	27 April 1985–28 June 1995	464	840	2,453
Morocco	6	25 October 1983–27 February 1992	7,614	9,258	20,162
Mozambique	6	25 October 1984–9 July 1999	4,352	4,163*	5,991
Niger	9	14 November 1983–19 March 1996	727	863	1,579
Nigeria	3	16 December 1986–18 January 1991	13,668	8,921	28,455
Rwanda	1	21 July 1998	54	190	1,111
Senegal	12	13 October 1981–17 June 1998	1,799	1,473	3,671
Sierra Leone	6	8 November 1980–25 April 1996	554	469	1,149
Somalia	2	6 March 1985–22 July 1987	221	660	2,561
Sudan	3	18 March 1982–2 May 1984	988	5,177	16,326
Tanzania	5	18 September 1986–21 January 1997	3,544	5,322	7,177
Togo	9	20 February 1981–23 February 1995	934	1,049	1,339
Uganda	7	18 November 1981–24 April 1998	697	689	3,708
Zaïre	6	9 July 1981–23 June 1989	4,845	4,770	12,330
Zambia	7	16 May 1983–16 April 1999	4,594	3,261	6,758

Note: *1988 Debt figures.

Sources: World Bank, 2000a; World Bank, 2000b: Analysis and Summary Tables.

many of the 41 heavily indebted poor countries, 33 of which are in Africa. And on the basis of preliminary analysis of debt sustainability, only 16 of the 33 African countries identified for the Initiative were potentially eligible to benefit (ECA, 1997: 83). Thus the resolution of the HIPCs' debt problem appears to be beyond the HIPC Initiative.

A brief appraisal of the various initiatives

What is clear from the foregoing is that within the framework of the various initiatives were different degrees of various measures, such as rescheduling or refinancing, debt reduction, buy-back, debt conversion, collateralisation, etcetera. The endorsement of these measures by the creditors and the international financial institutions was usually predicated on the implementation of credible economic recovery and SAPs by debtor countries, as a means of achieving long-term sustained economic growth. No doubt some debtor countries have benefited from some of the initiatives and measures, particularly those which entailed debt and debt service reductions. The initiatives have brought little respite, however, to the lower middle-income African countries, the bulk of whose debts consist of official Paris Club and non-Paris Club bilateral and multilateral debts. That they have not succeeded in lifting debt-distressed African countries into the path of resumed growth is owing to a number of factors such as the short consolidation period (12–18 months for Paris Club debt); unfavourable moratorium interest rates that increase the debt burden; politics of debt between the creditors in the Western world and the debtor countries in the developing world; and the inherent nature of debt rescheduling.

Debt rescheduling, the primary tool for the alleviation of the debt burden since the debt crisis of the 1980s, has aimed at cash flow relief rather than debt stock reduction in net present value terms. But while temporary cash flow relief is being provided, the debt stock builds up. As Ani (1997 b: 14) has argued, the operation of the Paris Club's rescheduling arrangements make it a debt-inducing rather than a debt-reduction mechanism. Using Nigeria's debt stock for illustration, he has observed that by the end of 1996, after paying off a total of US$6.75 billion (principal and interest) from a debt stock of US$17.66 billion, rescheduling still left the country owing as much as US$19.091 billion.

Indeed, for many indebted countries, the traditional debt relief mechanisms have not been enough, even where the countries have undertaken strong reform policies to make their external positions sustainable. Generally, these mechanisms have not been successful in resolving the problem of the long-term indebtedness of the highly indebted countries in a sustainable manner. The failure of the various initiatives to alleviate the debt burden shows the defects inherent in them. During the period January 1980–December 1995, 22 African countries renegotiated their commercial bank debt a total of 58 times. In the same period, 35 African countries renegotiated their debt with official creditors in the Paris Club 51 times. Some countries, such as Senegal, undertook 11 reschedulings with the Paris Club, yet still continued to be plagued by external debt problems. Other countries that were supposed to have 'graduated' from the Paris Club still experienced debt problems (ECA, 1997: 83). Table 12.5 shows that between 1980 and 1999 African countries entered into numerous multilateral debt relief agreements with official creditors, yet their debt stocks have continued to grow.

At the dawn of the 21st century, the HIPCs have continued to face the problem of 'external viability' – a requirement that debtor countries, while achieving sustainable growth, should be able to meet their external resource requirements, including debt servicing, without debt rescheduling or accumulation of arrears. In order for sub-Sahara Africa, for example, to achieve external viability, it has been estimated that it will require external support equivalent to an annual reduction of 35 per cent in scheduled external debt service. This certainly calls for substantial debt relief from creditors, in terms of debt and debt-service reduction (cancellation) as well as highly concessional ODA or grants.

Desirable Strategies and Policies for Resolving Africa's Debt

Debt cancellation

The original market-based strategy for resolving the debt problem has gradually given way to an emerging consensus among segments of the creditor community that debt cancellation/forgiveness is a strategy worthy of consideration. This has perhaps been due to the realisation that the market-based strategies and solutions have been incapable of bailing out most of the debt-distressed countries, more especially as it has turned out that these countries' inability or unwillingness to service their debt was not as a result of temporary bad luck: they have indeed been and remain insolvent, not just illiquid. So far, the impact of all the various initiatives of the 1990s (including the HIPC Initiative) that entailed some form of debt reduction has been very limited. And many African countries remain insolvent and burdened by debt overhang and liquidity constraints. There is, therefore, the strong need for outright and unconditional cancellation by the creditors of a large portion of the debts. The creditors have continued to resist any substantial reduction of debt obligations on a number of grounds:

- possible 'contagion effects' of a widespread write-down of developing countries' debt obligations;
- loss of creditworthiness in terms of the damage that debt relief could do to the long-term credit standing of developing nations;
- weakening of discipline in terms of possible deleterious effects on the policies pursued by debtors;
- moral hazard issue, in terms of the risk that some developing countries might

deliberately take steps to lower their economic performance in order to qualify for debt relief;

- need to surmount legal issues by any plan for debt relief; and
- injection of politics into the creditor–debtor relationship by any scheme for debt relief: it may be noted, though, that the debt issue is already highly politicised, and that the broad balance of bargaining power between debtors and creditors has always been in favour of the latter.

While some the above concerns of the creditors are legitimate, they nevertheless have self-serving elements. They underrate the concerns and commitment of debtor countries themselves to put their houses in order, and overcome the trauma of being trapped in external debt. It is therefore desirable for creditors to soften significantly their resistance to debt forgiveness, as the Jubilee 2000 coalition has been urging. This option is the most complete and effective strategy for debtor countries to recover from debt-induced depression and resume sustainable growth. Not only is the principal extinguished, but also the steady accumulation of debt that comes from repeated rescheduling and the resulting capitalisation of interest and arrears. Besides, debt forgiveness would relieve African countries of the heavy administrative and financial costs associated with repeated rescheduling under the Paris Club (Greene and Khan, 1990: 19).

Collective action

Extracting concessions on debt relief from creditors by debtor countries does not come easily. There is, therefore, a need for effective collective action on the part of the debtors. They will have to be organised in order to bring about appropriate agreements among the parties concerned. Some form of the much-talked about debtors' cartel is indispensable in view of the persistent resistance of the creditors' cartel in the Paris and London Clubs. It will enable debtors to forge a common front which would improve their capacity to proffer credible options in negotiations with the creditors. But then debtors will have to muster the political will to overcome the potential obstacles of:

- diversity of economic conditions and prospects among the debtors, which tends to overshadow their common interest in debt relief;
- the myopic tendency of national sovereignty, which encourages each government to seek the best possible deal for itself while failing to see the broader picture; and
- the fear of a possible coordination of efforts by debtors becoming counterproductive in terms of reprisals from creditors.

Should these obstacles continue to rule out collective debtors' action, then the option of collective inaction may become appealing. This entails non-payment of debt service, thereby saving valuable foreign exchange for development purposes.

And, as Cohen (1989: 17) has argued, the more the default trend persists, and is exemplified by significant debtor nations, the greater will be the ultimate erosion in the bargaining power of the creditors.

Use of Africa's looted funds in creditor countries for debt relief

This is the *debt-for-loot swap* and it is imperative, especially after the recovery by the Jewish people of gold looted in the holocaust, that the African gold and money in secret foreign accounts should also be returned.

Complementary market-based debt relief

As creditors tend to be more comfortable with market-based debt relief in comparison with outright debt cancellation, they should endeavour to increase their debt reduction initiatives through the greater access of debtors to options such as buy-backs, exit bonds and debt–equity swaps. A number of debtor countries have benefited from these schemes in the past, although with different degrees of impact and success. Debt buy-backs permit a country to repurchase or buy back its debt on the secondary market for cash at a discount, using either its own or donated resources. The transaction can also take place directly between the debtors and creditors.

Exit bonds are new bonds issued at a discount in exchange for old debt. Because exit bonds are generally either collateralised or made senior to the remaining old debt, they can be exchanged for old debt at a fraction of their face value.

Debt–equity swaps are exchanges of bonds/debt instruments for ownership rights to equity in the debtor country. Typically, a third party investor is involved: the original creditors sell debt at its secondary market price to an investor who then swaps the debt through the debtor-country's debt conversion programme for local currency that must be dedicated to the equity investment (Bowe and Dean, 1997: 32). Essentially, therefore, a debt–equity swap is a buy-back linked to equity investment at a subsidised exchange rate. In 1992, Nigeria bought back $3.395 billion of commercial debt due to the London Club at 60 per cent discount. In addition, the sum of $2.054 billion was collateralised as a 30-year bond with the London Club. With this arrangement, the yield of the bond within a 30-year period would offset or pay for the collateralised amount.

However, in view of the limitations on the scope and impact of the various market-based schemes, they can only complement the outright debt cancellation strategy. Creditors generally are unwilling to sell claims with heavy discounts, and unless donors provide the funds for debt buy-backs, they do not lead to the inflow of new money and merely serve to divert scarce domestic official resources. Very often, it is difficult to sustain debt–equity swap programmes because of their inflationary effects. This is because most central banks simply print money to pay for the swap.

Sound macro-economic management

Certainly poor management has played a role in the economic stagnation and debt crisis of African countries. The debt overhang only compounded the underlying structural and institutional problems retarding development. The need for good policies and sound economic management in debtor countries, therefore, cannot be overemphasised. The implementation of appropriate macro-economic policies along with debt reduction packages will ensure that debt reduction provides a much-needed stimulus to investment recovery and growth in African countries. The call for debt relief for these countries is not a suggestion, however, that the debtor countries should postpone putting their houses in order through necessary reforms and recovery programmes. The point is that African countries should be able to design and implement their own programmes to meet their recovery and growth needs instead of implementing failed IMF–World Bank SAPs aimed at generating funds to service external debt at the expense of the development of African economies. The ECA's document on an Alternative African Framework to Structural Adjustment Programmes (AAF–SAP), prepared in 1989, can be the framework for each country's home-grown adjustment. African countries must also learn to gauge properly the nature and extent of external shocks so as to undertake timely adjustments, and thus avoid recourse to excessive borrowing. Some desirable elements of sound economic management in Africa are discussed below.

1 *Macro-economic stability.* This entails avoidance of expansionary fiscal, monetary and exchange rate policies that produce huge budget deficits and inflationary financing. Macro-economic instability hurts savings, investment and growth, and encourages debt accumulation. There is, therefore, a strong need for fiscal discipline among African countries as they may not have the taxing capacity or the domestic savings required to service external loans used for financing fiscal deficits. Domestic or external credit cannot be a permanent substitute for fiscal discipline because, sooner or later, total expenditure will have to be reduced to the level of total resources. External financing cannot postpone this need indefinitely.

2 *Boosting of domestic savings* to reduce the reliance on foreign financing. A policy of fiscal balance or reduced fiscal deficits can increase public savings. Private savings can be increased through a variety of measures aimed at removing distortions in the financial markets, and at the same time appropriate interest rate policies have to be designed and implemented for eliminating tax disincentives and fostering a climate of confidence and stability (Obadan and Odusola, 1999: 21). Particularly helpful are regimes of low inflation, stable exchange rates and positive real interest rates. Funded compulsory pension schemes and functional capital markets are also indispensable in the savings promotion drive.

3 *Favourable investment climate* and policies to promote foreign direct investment.

4 *An appropriate economic role for government.* This means that the government should do only those things that no-one can do better, such as providing basic infrastructure and social services, while leaving to private sector/market providers what they can do best. In other words, African governments should not expand the public sector into areas that the private sector is in a good position to cover, and should carry out sensible privatisation of failed enterprises in which the public sector at present has an overbearing presence.

Sound external debt management policy

1 As external loans must be repaid in foreign exchange, external borrowing decisions must be linked to a general economic policy framework that will guarantee both the profitability of the invested borrowed funds and the generation of sufficient foreign exchange for external debt service. If external loan proceeds are devoted to satisfying immediate consumption needs, then external borrowing will have no other long-term effect than creating an advanced call on future external earnings. The developing countries that fared best in the successive shocks to the international economy in the past were those with balanced rather than asymmetric integration, and those that made a conscious allocation of external saving to productive projects. It is therefore important that external loans, over time, must create the ability to service the loans. The only sustainable way of achieving that objective is to ensure that such loans are invested in productive activities with rates of return sufficient to service the loans. In addition, the investment must enhance the borrower's capacity to earn foreign exchange, since foreign debt has to be serviced in foreign currency. In other words, a good debt management policy is one which stresses the investment of borrowed external funds in export-increasing or import-decreasing activities and projects.

2 It is important also to design a debt management framework that ensures:

   • hands-on information providing an early warning signal of debt crisis – a comprehensive overview detailing sources of loans, projects financed, return on the projects, loan maturity, debt-servicing profile and other critical elements of effective debt tracking and monitoring (this implies the full computerisation of debt management functions and the achievement of cost-effectiveness in the management of external debts);

   • an appropriate currency composition of external debt and hedging to minimise exchange rate and interest rate losses from possible shifts in the terms of trade and the balance of payments;

   • national controls over volatile and speculative international capital movements – these cause capital flight, exchange rate instability and monetary disorders as in Mexico, Asia and Russia. Some governments thus demand that foreign capital inflow must remain in their countries for at least one year before it can move out, in order to prevent destabilisation.

Bibliography

Ahmed, M. and L. Summers (1992) 'Tenth Anniversary Report on the Debt Crisis', *Finance and Development*, 29, 3 (September).

Ajayi, S. I. (1991) *Macro-economic Approach to External Debt: the Case of Nigeria*, AERC Paper, Nairobi: Initiative Publishers.

Ani, A. A. (1997a) 'Debt Burden in Developing Countries. Options for Africa', address to the All Africa International Public Relations Professional Development Conference, Cairo, 19–21 November.

—— (1997b) 'Nigeria's Debt Profile: Problems and Challenges', keynote address at the Central Bank of Nigeria Seminar on 'The Debt Problem and the Nigerian Economy – Resolution Options', Abuja, 28–29 October.

Bowe, M. and J. W. Dean (1997) 'Has the Market Solved the Foreign Debt Crisis?', *Princeton Studies in International Finance*, 83 (August).

Cohen, B. J. (1989) 'Developing-Country Debt: a Middle Way', *Princeton Essays in International Finance*, 173 (May).

ECA (1997) Financial Sector Reforms and Debt Management in Africa. Vol. 1. Proceedings of the Sixth session of the conference of African Ministers of Finance. Addis Ababa: Economic Commission for Africa.

Greene, J. E. and M. S. Khan (1990) *The African Debt Crisis*, AERC Special Paper 3, Nairobi: Initiatives Publishers.

Hussain, I. and J. Underwood (1991) 'The Problem of Sub-Saharan Africa's Debt – and the Solutions', in I. Hussain and J. Underwood (eds.), *African External Finance in the 1990s, a World Bank Symposium*, Washington, DC: World Bank.

IMF (1999) *IMF Survey*, 28, 17 (30 August).

IMF/World Bank (1996) *Debt Sustainability Analysis for the Highly Indebted Poor Countries*, Washington, DC: International Monetary Fund/World Bank.

Iyoha, M. A. (1999) *External Debt and Economic Growth in Sub-Saharan African Countries: an Econometric Study*, AERC Research Paper 90, Nairobi: AERC.

Obadan, M. I. (1990) 'The International Debt Problem', paper presented at the 1990 Concluding Seminars of the Senior Executive Course No. 12, National Institute for Policy and Strategic Studies, Kuru, Jos, 8 October.

—— (n.d.) *Foreign Capital Flows and External Debt in Nigeria* (in press).

Obadan, M. I. and A. F. Odusola (1999) 'Savings, Investment and Growth Connections in Nigeria: Empirical Evidence and Policy Implications', National Centre for Economic Management and Administration (NCEMA) *Policy Analysis Series*, 5, 2.

Odedokun, M. O. (1993) 'Econometric Analysis of External Debt Burdens of African Countries: Debt Rescheduling and Arrears of Interest', *African Development Review*, 5, 2 (December).

Ojo, M. O. (1995) 'Africa's Debt Burden in Historical Perspective', *CBN Economic and Finance Review*, 32, 2.

Onimode, Bade (2000) 'Unequal Exchange: External Debt and Capacity for Development-

Oriented Policies in African Countries', paper presented at the Millennium Conference of the Nigerian Economic Society, Abuja, September.

Payer, Cheryl (1992) *Lent and Lost*, London: Zed Books.

Uchendu, O. A. (1994) 'The Determinants of External Debt Service in Africa', *CBN Economic and Financial Review*, 32, 1 (March).

Usman, I. (1995) 'Issues of Debt Management Strategy for Africa' *CBN Debt Trends*, 1, 1.

World Bank (1996) World Debt Tables, 1, Washington, DC: World Bank.

—— (1999) *Global Development Finance*, Washington, DC: World Bank.

—— (2000a) *Global Development Finance*, Washington, DC: World Bank.

—— (2000b) *African Development Indicators*, Washington, DC: World Bank.

—— (2000c) *World Development Indicators*, Washington, DC: World Bank.

13

Human Development Deprivation: Water and Sanitation
Oluwafemi Odediran

Water is, perhaps, the most precious asset on earth; hence the saying that *Water is Life*. This colourless, odourless and tasteless liquid is essential for all forms of growth and development – human, animal and plant. Water is the most essential thing for life, after air. It is a fundamental basic need for sustaining human and economic activities. Access to water and environmental sanitation (defined below) is also a basic human right, which is guaranteed by international conventions ratified by almost all the countries in the world, including the Convention on the Rights of the Child. Providing water in the desired quantity and quality and at the right time and place has been a constant endeavour of all civilisations.

Civilisation is in some sense a dialogue between people and water. The earliest civilisations settled on river banks, lakes and sea coasts only because of proximity to water. The importance that a country accords to the need for an adequate and wholesome water supply is an index of its civilisation, growth and development. No other natural resource has had such an overwhelming influence on human history. As the human population increases, as people express their desire for a better standard of living, and as economic activities expand in scale and diversity, the demands on fresh water resources will continue to grow. Today, 60 per cent of people in developing countries live without an adequate supply of drinking water, and children and women spend eight or more hours daily carrying water from distant sources. Scarcity of potable water may also lead to people using contaminated sources of water. An adequate supply of safe water is thus a prerequisite for significant socio-economic development.

Rapid industrialisation, urbanisation and population growth have hastened the degradation of the environment and the depletion of natural resources. But it is the development processes that we have practised so far that have polluted the earth. In providing the desired quality of life for a privileged few, the process of development has caused a marked decline in the quality of life for the bulk of humanity. The deterioration of public health has taken place due to unhygienic conditions and the pollution of the environment. To maintain proper public health, environmental sanitation has become one of the important topics and needs of today.

The World Health Organisation (WHO) has defined environmental sanitation as the control of all those factors in man's physical environment which exercises or may exercise a deleterious effect on his physical development, health and survival. Environmental sanitation is a broad term and it includes water supply, waste (solid and liquid) disposal, food sanitation, insect and rodent control, atmospheric pollution control, ventilation and air conditioning, lighting, housing, institutional sanitation, occupational health work, accident protection and the eradication of health-threatening nuisances.

The list of the various aspects of environmental sanitation/protection is very long. Since in all developing countries, as in Nigeria, resources are limited, in order to achieve maximum results priorities have to be fixed. An adequate supply of safe drinking water and a non-polluting excreta disposal system are important parts of environmental sanitation. Their provision is listed by the WHO expert committee on environment in rural areas and small communities. The others are the control of insect and animal vectors of disease in places where these are of significance. It has been established that 80 per cent of communicable diseases like dysentery, cholera, typhoid and hookworm can be controlled by adopting safe water supply and excreta disposal systems. Thus, for achieving environmental sanitation and thereby public health, these systems should be accorded top priority.

The Global Scenario of Fresh Water and Sanitation

Increasing knowledge of the ecological processes that constitute the global hydrological cycle has helped society to better understand the atmospheric and terrestrial movements of water, enabling people to improve and regulate its availability. Such initiatives were originally confined to minor technical interventions such as small-scale diversions, canals and shallow wells. In the past century, however, the range and intensity of technical interventions have greatly expanded, so that people are now capable of storing large volumes of water, moving them over long distances and using these resources several times before they are released back into the natural hydrological cycle. All these features have resulted in a dramatic increase in the global consumption of fresh water.

The limit of sustainable use of these resources in a given climatic region is determined by local climate, hydrological and hydro-geological conditions. In many parts of the world the amount of water being consumed has exceeded the annual level of renewal, creating a non-sustainable situation. In many regions with scanty rainfall, particularly in the industrialised countries, levels of utilisation are already so high that most possibilities of diverting water away from the natural flow into storage facilities have been exhausted. Today, more than ever before, there are growing concerns over water and sanitation, particularly in the domains of the supply of water, the transmission of diseases and the social and economic costs of both water and sanitation.

Drinking water supply

The situation regarding the status of drinking water supplies has caused particular concern. The United Nations, for example, declared the 1980s the International Drinking Water Supply and Sanitation Decade. Other international declarations have also clearly recognised that access to water is a fundamental right of people.

Fresh water lakes and rivers, which are the main sources of water consumed by people, contain an average of 90,000 cubic kilometres of water, or just 0.26 per cent of total global fresh water reserves. This tiny fraction is distributed in a very uneven manner on earth, creating a wide range of environments, from arid regions and deserts to humid areas, which experience regular flooding. In many parts of the world, the rainfall pattern is highly skewed and is characterised by small periods of intensive precipitation followed by long, dry periods. Great disparities may even be seen on the same continent: about 20 per cent of the total global run-off flows in the Amazon River of South America, while the Sahara Desert has consistently received no rainfall.

Such variations become very important as human activities diversify geographically and in scale. Wherever water is scarce, human engineering initiatives have been geared towards balancing this spatial inequity. In south-western USA, for example, engineering interventions in the form of extensive dams have already exhausted most possibilities for enhancing fresh water availability. In many other parts of the world, future options are becoming extremely complex and uncertain as the levels of total fresh water consumption approach the limits imposed by the annual renewal of fresh water resources.

The cost of inadequate water supply in terms of human suffering is enormous. Authoritative estimates indicate that around 80 per cent of communicable diseases are water-borne or water-associated afflictions. Health benefits from the heavy investments made in water supply in developing countries since 1980 have been severely limited due to lack of progress in sanitary waste disposal. Improper disposal of human wastes, half of which remains uncollected, denies nearly 2.3 billion people an adequate standard of living and remains one of the developing world's most serious public health problems. Lack of sanitation to promote hygiene and behavioural change are responsible for the transmission of diarrhoea, schistosomiasis, cholera, typhoid and other infectious diseases affecting thousands of millions of human beings. The 1999 World Health Report estimates that 2.2 million people died in 1998 from diarrhoeal disease, including more than 1.8 million children under five years of age. Millions of people suffer from parasitic worm infections stemming from the presence of human excreta and solid wastes in the environment. Multiple infections with several different parasites, including hookworms, roundworms and amoebae, are common and often contribute to nutritional deficiencies. Both the health and social consequences of this deplorable state of affairs are especially harsh for women, girls and children.

At the same time, incentives to tackle sanitation are often lacking. For governments, there is neither prestige nor political capital to be gained in focusing on the sector, because the people most in need of sanitation have little political power. Communities are not motivated to initiate sanitary improvements because there is little understanding, either of the relationship between unhygienic waste disposal and disease and child survival, or of the fact that, appropriately transformed, waste might have some economic benefits.

The inadequate and unsanitary disposal of infected human excreta leads to contamination of ground water supplies. In most developing countries, the bacterial and viral diseases caused by contaminated water, account for 80 per cent of the morbidities. Infected waste often provides opportunities for other species of flies to lay their eggs, breed, feed on the exposed material and to carry infection. It also attracts domestic animals and rodents and other vermin, which spread the faeces, creating an intolerable and health-threatening nuisance level.

There is a relationship between environmental sanitation and the state of health of the population. The relationships are both direct and indirect in character. The direct effect is exemplified by the reduced incidence of certain diseases such as cholera, typhoid, paratyphoid fever, dysentery, infant diarrhoea, hookworm, ascariasis disease, bilharziasis, water-borne disease and other intestinal and para-intestinal infestations. The indirect relationship of environmental sanitation and the state of health of the population are that:

1 improvement in hygiene promotes a state of well-being in the public that is conducive to its social development;
2 improved environmental sanitation is accompanied by a marked decrease in morbidity from other diseases, the etiology of which is not directly related to either excreta disposal or contaminated water supplies;
3 various economic benefits, such as those resulting from an increase in life expectancy, result from the proper implementation of environmental sanitation programmes.

Transmission of diseases from excreta

The faeces-borne infections and infestations – such as cholera, typhoid and para-typhoid fevers, dysenteries, infant diarrhoea, hookworm disease and ascariasis – are the causes of untold death and morbidity. All these diseases can be controlled through proper sanitation, especially through proper excreta disposal. To transmit disease, the following factors are necessary:

• a causative or etiological agent;
• a reservoir or source of infection;
• a mode of escape from this reservoir;

- a mode of transmission from the reservoir to the potential new host;
- a mode of entry into new host;
- a susceptible host.

If any one of these six conditions is absent, then the communicable diseases cannot spread. The duty of health/sanitary workers is to guard against all modes of transmission of these diseases; thus the objective of sanitary excreta disposal is to isolate faeces so that the infectious agents in the faeces cannot reach the new host.

Social and economic costs of water and sanitation

Those living on the margins of society are agricultural, construction and service workers. Their losses in terms of nutrition and health hurt family units, stunt community growth, and cripple national economies.

In Africa, labour used in gathering water is estimated at 40 billion hours valued at US$2 billion a year. And in just ten weeks, a cholera epidemic in Peru cost US$ 1 billion in agricultural export and tourism revenues. Three million children die every year from water-related diseases. And for future generations, the horrendous costs of a polluted environment caused by not managing water and wastes are incalculable.

During the 1980s, the world coordinated its efforts to put an end to this social and economic attrition. Attempts were made to involve communities and there were laudable advances in all development programmes. Water is now considered the only commodity whose costs are coming down.

Despite the significant successes of the Water Decade, global achievements fell short of expectations. Population and pollution increases played their parts, but it has also become clear that the community approach and appropriate technology were not used to their full potential.

These inefficiencies must be overcome before the environment deteriorates so far that it becomes unmanageable. Water and sanitation provision for the excluded has to pick up speed. Programmes need to progress about three times faster for water and about four times faster for environmental sanitation. To do this, costs must be halved and resources doubled.

The Way Forward

Community-based approach

A reconceptualisation is moving development from a mental map that casts people as ignorant and dependent on experts to diagnose their way forward, to one which sees people as the most dependable experts on what is good for them. This paradigm shift sees humanity as the most important factor in development, and development in community clusters as a good strategy for national development.

The centrality of the community in providing potable water at community level is based on the understanding that the most important health workers are mothers, not the doctors, and the most important health centres are homes, not hospitals. Clearly, sustainable development and the empowerment of communities are mutually dependent. Communities should determine their own needs, control the course of their own lives, manage their resources and gain access to the services to which they are entitled.

Experiences gathered around the world lead to the conclusion that a water and environmental sanitation programme cannot be successful without the active participation of the total community. The success of such a programme is also measured on the basis of its power to sustain itself and grow. To succeed, the programme should gain popular support and overcome popular objection. In both water and environmental sanitation, hygiene education of the public plays a very important role. Technical improvement of the environment without proper education of the public in water management, sanitation and hygiene, based on local traditions, customs and beliefs, has always proved futile.

Attention must be given to the structure and organisation of the programme, which must fit into the local social and economic system. More important still is bringing the people into the programme as partners. One of the ultimate objectives of the water and sanitation programmes in a community is to get the family to solve its own water and sanitation problems. It is important that each family should participate in some way in the execution of a sustainable solution. Only when the families are willing to participate in the scheme and to learn a new habit should water and sanitation schemes be launched. When water management, sanitation and personal hygiene become habits, then water and sanitation programmes will have tremendous success and be sustainable.

The need for advocacy

Hard work is not enough to keep water resources and environmental sanitation from deteriorating. Strong advocacy is also indispensable. By fostering political commitment to restructure debt, reallocate resources, help communities, and organise and raise new funds, programmes can begin to reach the vast majority of those in greatest need.

Because the appropriate technology exists and well-informed planners know how resources can be more equitably distributed, our humanity impels us to take action. If only key people know about the critical nature of this situation, they will be mobilised to take action. To make this happen, better communication and dialogue are required, ranging from political advocacy to community management.

Advocacy is a popular term for the process of making an issue stand out, getting people's attention and changing minds. But advocacy is more than selling an idea. It searches for the higher ground and the common good. Therefore, in looking for support for water and environmental sanitation programmes, beware of thinking of them as an isolated sector, with isolated interests. This is not the time to stand alone. It's time to work with other groups. Advocacy means building partnerships and alliances with the overall goal of human development.

Activists in the field of water and environmental sanitation are in a good position to attract allies. Because water is essential to life and because communities are willing to organise and help pay for it, water offers an important entry point for primary health care, child survival, women's role in development, environmental issues and economic initiatives.

All these converging interests present a historic moment for water and environmental sanitation because supporters of those interests are coming to the conclusion that their efforts need strong community involvement in order to be sustainable. They also recognise that most development programmes do not have enough community involvement to make them sustainable. They can be convinced, therefore, that there is benefit in joining with water and sanitation efforts because water is one issue that can galvanise a community and prepare it to improve itself in other ways, including the hygienic use of water and the disposal of wastes.

By building on water's importance and the strengths of water programmes at the community level, advocacy for water and environmental sanitation can take advantage of the readiness of natural allies, and create the momentum to spur political commitments and financial support. Since advocacy is based on building partnerships and alliances, this is an especially propitious time for water and environmental sanitation workers to make a leap forward – and those other development interests can be tapped along the way.

Women's participation

The peace, welfare and harmony of a society are normally ensured if women are given due respect and participation in the society. As the society around us has undergone changes, respect for women has deteriorated in male-dominated societies where women are considered as objects of exploitation in various ways. Despite the achievement records of women in history, they are not given their rightful place in the development of our society. Therefore, for the healthy growth of society, the active participation of women is a must in all fields. The participation of women in water and environmental sanitation programmes can have several benefits. It can contribute to the achievement of programme objectives and also to the attainment of wider development goals. Women's participation can also be of both direct and indirect benefit to themselves. In order to achieve water and sanitation programme objectives, women certainly have a greater role to play than their male counterparts. Women can be of greater help than men because in their everyday lives they are more concerned with environmental sanitation, hygiene and the regular functioning of water facilities. They have more control as far as environmental sanitation is concerned, and their involvement has proved to have tremendous benefits, some of which are discussed below.

1 Water- and sanitation-related diseases are responsible for most of the morbidity and mortality in developing countries. When there is improved water supply and sanitation, there will be significant reduction in these diseases. Women play a key role in this process because traditionally they manage domestic water use and household hygiene, educate and care for young children, and provide health care in the household and often in the community. Women make decisions on the use and, to some extent, the maintenance of water supply and sanitation facilities.

2 When women become involved in water and sanitation programmes, the traditional skill and knowledge of managing households can benefit the projects. Drawing on this skill – by selecting women as community workers, local committee members and candidates for training and the development of experts in health education and maintenance – improves the status of women in the community.

3 Involving women in water and sanitation programmes also leads to economic benefits, direct as well as indirect. When women are involved, the income they earn can be spent on basic family needs such as food, clothing, utensils and other commodities, and also for maintaining proper sanitary conditions. This makes women valued partners in the family.

4 The introduction of water supply and sanitation programmes has welfare benefits, since the time and energy spent on collection and disposal of waste is reduced. The benefits women derive differ considerably according to their household and socio-economic situations. Liberated time and energy may be utilised in domestic, economic and community development work. In rural areas, women are actively involved in agriculture and animal care. In poor families, women work for others for some income. Other women are able to devote more time to community and educational activities.

Since the beginning of the International Drinking Water Supply and Sanitation Decade (1981–90), the basic role of women as users and managers of water has been emphasised. The need for women's participation, not only as passive beneficiaries but also as active agents in planning, maintenance and management, has been recognised. But, in practice, water management systems fail to involve women in a meaningful way. A study done by the United Nations Development Programme reveals that the involvement of women in a skilled and organised way contributes significantly to the effectiveness and efficiency of such projects.

Cost-effective appropriate technology

If power is to be shared, such empowerment also demands an ability to transfer technology effectively, and indeed to define and recognise appropriate technology in terms that are truly appropriate. The past decade has demonstrated that there is no single level of technological 'appropriateness'. Remote sensing through satellites, investments in up-to-date deep-well drilling equipment and improved hand-pumps, and traditional techniques of water harvesting and conservation known centuries ago all come together today in tailoring strategies to the needs of particular communities. Many developing countries, held back by vested interests or heavy dependence on external agencies, are yet to innovate their own technological capabilities or acquire access to technologies that are more appropriate to their needs.

The technologies that are appropriate for low-income areas are those in which the technical and organisational characteristics of the infrastructure are adapted to the socio-economic and environmental conditions in the community. The reverse is common as municipal service providers are focused on conventional systems. The prevailing technical standards and regulations often hinder the application of appropriate technologies, and the systems are not adapted to actual need and demand in low-income areas. Municipal engineers, moreover, are not trained in low-cost technologies, which they regard as substandard.

Many so-called appropriate technologies have been developed for the rural areas, but their adaptability for use and operation in low-income urban areas is not always clear. In the first place, the type of land and the density of the area requires a specific technology; second, the community must be able to meet the operation and maintenance requirements of the chosen system. A third point that needs careful consideration is the environmental impact of technologies in the high-density conditions prevailing in most urban areas. Finally, appropriate technology options at community level will have to link up with the network of the whole city – usually articulated on hierarchical lines – and cannot therefore be developed in isolation.

In order to ensure that the right benefits are derived from the use of cost-effective technology, therefore, the following actions are necessary:

- development of an approach that ensures that the community has a choice in the level of technology and service delivery, while being aware of the cost implications;

- ensuring that the technology selected can be managed by the community and does not have a negative impact on the environment;

- training local engineers and technicians in low-cost technologies;

- supporting the development of technologies that are appropriate for conditions in low-income areas;

- ensuring that the technology and services and provisions links up with the municipal-level network.

Conclusion

Acknowledging certain fundamental elements with regard to water will facilitate vital long-term objectives of sustainable development. Among the multiple functions that water fulfils, the basic human ecosystem needs are of paramount importance. Water is also indispensable for food production, for industrial development and for a wide range of activities and processes in the landscape as well as in society. It is argued that the allocation of finite water resources must be given to the various functions that water fulfils in society and in the landscape. Intersectoral coordination and priorities in allocation are particularly demanding and current sectoral allocation may have to be reviewed. In particular, the issue of national food sufficiency versus national food self-reliance needs to be addressed in national policies and in international agreements on global food security.

The involvement of users and the sharing of responsibilities and management tasks is a prerequisite for the proper choice of technological and organisational approaches. The most effective water policies and institutions involve the users of water as explicit participants in water management, planning and decision making. Experience has repeatedly shown that major decisions made without involving local communities and those affected by decisions are considerably more likely to fail. International water conferences and meetings have consistently recommended that water managers and planners should be obliged to seek public participation in and community discussions about allocations and priorities in order to facilitate the user-pay approach, and generally to encourage democratic decision making. Acknowledging the role of women at community and other levels appears to be particularly effective and valuable. However, greater efforts are needed through education and training programmes to ensure that women take an active role in water management and institutions.

Bibliography

Ling, Jack C. S. and Cynthia Reader-Wilstein, 'Water – a Vital Wellspring for Human Development: a Case for Advocacy', paper prepared for the International Water and Sanitation Centre, www.irc.nl/themes/communication/vital.html

Lundquist, Jan and Peter Gleik (1997), 'Sustaining Our Waters into the 21st Century', paper prepared for the International Water and Sanitation Centre, www.irc.nl/products/publications/ajw/v8no5.html

Nigam, Ashok, Biksham Gujja, Jayanta Bandyopadhyay and Rupert Talbot (1997) *Fresh Water for India's Children and Nature, Learning from Local-level Approaches*, New Delhi: UNICEF.

Singh, S. K. (1997) 'Role of Women In Environmental Sanitation', *Journal of Institution of Public Health Engineers* (India), 3 (July–September).

Wegelin-Schuringa, Madeleen (2000) 'Strategic Elements in Water Supply and Sanitation Services in Urban Low-Income Areas', *Waterfront*, 14 (April), UNICEF.

WHO (1995) *Expert Committee Report on Environmental Sanitation*, WHO Technical Report Series, 30, 9, Geneva: World Health Organisation.

14

Poverty and HIV/AIDS:
Instruments for Regulating African Insecurity?
Yves Ekoue Amaïzo

Although it started as an informal meeting, they ended up organising the strategic defence of the interests of Western countries. The G8 countries – the US, Japan, France, Germany, Canada, the United Kingdom, Italy and Russia – succeeded in clouding the issues. Those advocating the cause of Africa's debt, AIDS and development funding returned empty-handed. In this way the G8 governments, unbeknown to the majority of the world's citizens, seem to have launched a new concept based essentially on security, in the case of neighbours such as Russia, and on insecurity in the case of countries with inconsequential influence like the African states.

Viewed from this angle, it is no wonder that the G8 failed to meet the aspirations of those who were hoping for outright debt cancellation and energetic action on the treatment of AIDS in Africa. However, we must not think that nothing was achieved. As regards Africa, the thrust was to treat the debt issue and AIDS as new tools for world governance: namely, the regulation of African insecurity. Is it phobia or an attempt to ease the Western conscience? In any event, the stark reality of statistics on debt and AIDS provides a clear perspective on the issue. African leaders are becoming aware of the situation. But do the conferences designed to arouse awareness on AIDS, like the one held in South Africa in July 2000 and the one which followed in Nigeria at the end of the year, suffice to relaunch the initiative in favour of the population, despite by the exorbitant cost of the solutions proposed and the ill-will of certain people?

Because of the emphasis on debt relief in the media (BBC, 2000) and NGO expectations, many Africans believed that something important would emerge from the G8 meeting held on the island of Okinawa, Japan, in July 2000. The disappointment was all the more upsetting not only because the rich countries failed to honour their commitment to cancel the debt, but also because they demonstrated how little importance they attach to problems affecting Africa. Even Secretary-General Kofi Annan criticised the rich countries for failing to live up to their promise to cancel the debt of the countries qualifying as poor countries, amounting to US$100 billion, at the end of the year 2000:

> Mr Annan said that so far less than half of the world's 40 most heavily indebted countries have qualified for the relief which has mounted to only US$15 billion. The debt relief has been slow in coming because the leading industrialised countries require the poor nations to introduce wide-ranging economic reforms and to promise not to use their relief to fund wars. (*Ibid.*)

Following the crises hitting emergent states, mainly in South-East Asia, the principle of non-contagion of financial markets was given pride of place – which principle was then applied to AIDS, considered as a real threat to sub-Sahara Africa.

Debt and AIDS: Rapid Escalation in Sub-Sahara Africa

What can be the possible relationship between a disease like AIDS and the debt burden of Africa south of the Sahara? Obviously, it is the exponential growth of those two indicators in Africa that catches the eye. The total stock of the African debt rose from US$61 billion in 1980 to US$226 billion in 1999, of which US$7.5 billion (3.3 per cent) is private debt not guaranteed by the state (World Bank, 2000a). The loans contracted from the IMF amount to US$7.4 billion; that is, equivalent to a virtual cover for the risk undertaken by the private sector and corresponding to the share of public debt not guaranteed by the state. In the absence of reliable statistics on AIDS for the 1980s, it suffices to articulate the Joint United Nations Programme on HIV/AIDS (UNAIDS) statistics to realise that the AIDS growth curve looks strangely like the debt curve.

It is acknowledged that approximately 34.3 million adults and children in the world are infected and live with the HIV/AIDS virus. In Africa, out of a population estimated at 627 million, over 24.8 million are infected, including 24.5 million in sub-Sahara Africa as against 0.9 million in North America and 0.5 million in Western Europe. Of the adult African population (ages 15–49), 8.57 per cent are affected, including 12.9 million African women: the disease does not spare the children, for all that. Over one million children aged 0–14 years are infected in sub-Sahara Africa. Although at first they clung to their age-old habit of resorting to opacity, it then dawned on African government authorities that it was in their interest to gather transparent information on AIDS, even if the reality is still far from the declaration of good intentions.

The countries that agreed to play the game of transparency and information are also the first to achieve promising results. With improvements in statistical surveys (Table 14.1), they are in a position to work out the percentage of the population infected. From this it is possible to get an idea of the impending disaster due to the progression of the disease and the attendant loss of income of all sorts in Africa.

Table 14.1 Population Living with the AIDS Virus: Selection of a Few African Countries South of the Sahara (Estimated, 31 December 1999)

Country or region	Adults and children (0–49 yrs)	Adults as % of the total pop.	Rank
Sub-Sahara Africa	24,500,000	8.57	
South Africa	4,200,000	19.94	03
Benin	70,000	2.45	18
Burkina Faso	350,000	6.44	15
Burundi	360,000	11.32	08
Cameroon	540,000	7.73	14
Democratic Republic of Congo	1,100,000	5.07	16
Côte d'Ivoire	760,000	10.76	10
Djibouti	37,000	11.75	07

Source: UNAIDS, 2000

AIDS or Debt: What Do We Choose?

It must be recalled that the growth in *per capita* income in sub–Sahara Africa has been negative (– 0.2 per cent) between 1965 and 1997, and between 1997 and 1999 (– 0.4 per cent), the latter percentage representing about US$510 per inhabitant, which contrasts sharply with a *per capita* income approaching US$22,350 for the European Union. More than 75 per cent of the African countries had a lower *per capita* income in 1998 than they did in 1965. The average annual growth rate of the population in SSA was 2.8 per cent between 1965 and 1997 (higher than the GDP growth rate), thus confirming the worsening of poverty. To this must be added the amount earmarked annually by each African country for health care, which amounted to 33 dollars per head between 1990 and 1998, with about one doctor per 10,000 inhabitants. For the European Union, the number of doctors per 10, 000 inhabitants was 37 during the same period, and each European spends an average 1,974 dollars per annum for medical care and is covered by social security and a social insurance scheme (Table 14.2).

If the cost of health is such that we need an entire life's wage to restore our health, then the African, afflicted by AIDS and debt, has no prospect on the horizon of achieving any significant development of 'Africa without the Africans', that is perhaps implicit between AIDS and debt (Fukuyama, 1992). Some people may even talk of AIDS or debt interchangeably. The choice does not appear to be basically different.

A young man above the age of 15 in the year 2000, living in Africa in the areas most exposed to the disease, must come to terms with the reality that over 15 per cent of his age mates will die within 10–15 years. Around the world, over 13.2 million children below the age of 15 years have become orphans since the AIDS

Table 14.2 Selection of a Few Countries in Africa South of the Sahara: Comparison between *per capita* Income, Received Aid and Health Expenditure *per capita*

Country or region	GDP *per capita* US$ (1998)	Aid received *per capita* US$ (1998)	Health expenses *per capita* US$ (1990–8)
Sub-Sahara Africa	510	21.4	33
South Africa	3310	12.4	246
Benin	380	35.3	818
Burkina Faso	240	37.0	95
Burundi	140	11.6	508
Cameroon	610	29.6	311
Democratic Republic of Congo	110	2.6	16

Source: UNAIDS Report, 1999

epidemic broke out. In sub-Sahara Africa, 12.1 million children are without parents. Over 2.2 million died of AIDS in 1999 in Africa as against the 18,000 cases recorded in East Asia, where the population density is much higher than in Africa (UNAIDS, 1999).

Certainly, the mode of management of HIV/AIDS should be called into question and revised. To remain on firm ground, let us review the local African realities that are still difficult to accept. With fewer children attending schools in certain regions of Africa, it is difficult to find enough funding to ensure the functioning of schools. Since the parents of the children are dead and the close family members often are not in a position to shoulder the additional burden, the surviving family unit can hardly provide for their daily subsistence. But the difficulties do not end there! The teachers posted to the rural areas are often infected with the disease. In Côte d'Ivoire, for instance, statistics indicate that in certain rural areas seven out of ten teachers die of AIDS. On the farms where the majority of African children live, fewer adults are available for farming. The destruction of the subsistence/survival structure may end in the destabilisation of Africa as a consequence of AIDS.

Contrary to what happens in the rich countries, an important segment of the African population, especially those under 15 or over 64 years, are often cared for by the active population. In 1998, it was this part of the population that bore most of the burden. This is expressed in terms of the dependency ratio. The ratio is 50.3 per cent in the OECD countries, 58.9 per cent in Asia and the South Pacific, and 60.6 per cent in Latin America and the Caribbean. In sub-Sahara Africa it is 91 per cent (UNDP, 2000) (Table 14.3). This important characteristic applying to Africa is often overlooked and not taken into account during major discussions on the issue of development assistance. When you look into the regional distribution

Table 14.3 Comparison between Debt Servicing, Aids Dependency Ratio and the *per capita* Balance of Accounts: Selected Regions and African Countries

Country or Region	Total debt servicing as % GDP in 1998[1]	Dependency ratio: proportion of aid received as % GDP in 1998[1]	Dependency ratio of non-active pop. to active pop.[2] (in %)	Total external debt *per capita* ($)[3]
Selected regions				
Sub-Sahara Africa	4.5	4.1	91.0	367.0
Latin America & Caribbean	6.5	0.2	60.5	156.8
E. Asia & Middle East	5.2	0.5	58.9	367.4
Selected African countries				
South Africa	3.4	0.4	63.9	602.7
Benin	2.7	9.2	98.3	274.5
Burkina Faso	2.1	15.5	100.4	127.2
Burundi	3.5	8.8	97.2	159.8
Cameroon	6.5	5.1	90.0	702.1
Congo (Democratic Republic)	0.3	2.0	103.1	269.3
Côte d'Ivoire	13.5	7.8	88.5	1060.8
Ethiopia	1.8	10.0	95.8	169.7
Ghana	7.7	9.3	88.7	382.4
Kenya	4.8	4.2	89.7	241.7
Madagascar	3.4	13.4	71.2	292.9
Malawi	4.7	24.4	99.6	222.2
Mozambique	2.8	28.2	92.8	482.8
Nigeria	3.4	0.5	87.7	250.5
Uganda	2.4	7.0	108.3	187.3
Rwanda	1.0	17.3	93.6	153.2
Senegal	6.9	10.8	90.4	429.0
Tanzania	3.0	12.4	93.6	237.6
Togo	2.7	8.6	96.7	362.0
Zambia	6.4	11.0	99.7	686.5
Zimbabwe	16.6	4.7	82.1	393.2

Sources:
[1] World Bank, 2000:10–14, 248–56, 342–6; Djibouti and Liberia have been omitted from the list of African countries by the World Bank Report.
[2] UNDP, 2000: 223 *et seq.* The non-active population equals the population under 15 and above 64 years.

of OECD development assistance in 1998, it emerges that there is no particular priority given to Africa. On the contrary, development assistance to SSA has fallen from 28 per cent of the total ODA in 1993 to 24.5 per cent in 1998 (World Bank, 2000a: 345). It is within this context that it must be recalled that in 1998 over 4.5 per cent of the GDP of SSA went for debt servicing, which was higher than the aid received; aid represented 4.1 per cent of GDP. The other regions of the developing world are in a situation where they reimburse practically up to 30 times what they receive as development aid. It is therefore surprising that developing countries, and most particularly those in Africa, have not sought to organise themselves with a view to defending better their collective interests and getting payments rescheduled over longer periods while demanding the review of the methods of debt calculation. Emphasis is systematically put on debt cancellation, which will only be possible under increasingly drastic conditionalities. When emphasis is placed on the debt ratio per inhabitant, then the depth of the iniquity and the absurdity of the reimbursement system emerge so clearly that it becomes a mere euphemism to say that the repayment regime is systematically and deliberately despoiling Africa (Table 14.3).

The paradox lies in the fact that the more sub-Sahara Africa reimburses, the higher its debt rises through the effect of interest payments. This region ought normally to able to pay its entire external debt by making a one-time payment of US$367 per inhabitant, whereas it has only a global US$510 annual *per capita* income; and health care per inhabitant amounts to only US$33 per annum. We happen to sign debt reduction accords, which impose stringent political and economic conditionalities, in order to qualify for debt cancellation of our total debt (of US$367 per inhabitant) over an indeterminate period, instead of focusing attention on facilitating the creation of non-debt generating resources (Amaïzo, 1998: 200) by introducing more transparency within the institutional environment. After more than doubling between 1980 (US$6.7 billion) and 1997 (US$14 billion), debt servicing by sub-Sahara Africa rose in 1998 to US$14.5 billion – US$23.1 per inhabitant – while the aid per inhabitant received over the same period was US$21.4.

Poverty Reduction and Eyewash Economic Development

It is impossible to contemplate poverty reduction, as trumpeted from the rooftops by the major rich industrialised countries, without taking into account the factors needed to generate revenue perennially through industrial production. According to their agents in the bilateral and multinational institutions for development support, it seems increasingly difficult to push through Africa's requirements, perceived from the point of view of the African civil society. It has therefore become urgent and indispensable to organise ourselves collectively to present the AIDS and debt issues as a global problem in the same way as we would table a global problem in the interest of the common weal. Without planned geo-economic arrangements and without evident effect on the population, we cannot continue to decimate health care budgets in order to organise the payment of the public external debt owed by African countries – when this debt most often results from the actions and omissions of certain bureaucratic managers wielding power in the central administration. By indirectly accepting this line of reasoning during the meeting held in Okinawa, Japan, in July 2000, the G8 showed that the authorities of the powerful nations are not interested in debt repayment so much as in the insecurity that the African continent may inflict from afar on their own domestic well-being.

The official theme of the G8 in relation to the developing countries was poverty reduction and economic development (Ministers of Finance, G7, 2000). The five main issues that dominated discussions are outlined below.

1 *An integrated approach to development* wherein the international community is expected to take action to make sure that developing countries respond to forces of globalisation in order to play their role in the world economic system. This selective process marginalises developing countries and forces them to adapt their structures and role to the needs and interests of the highly influential countries (Amaïzo, 1998).

2 *Debt relief in favour of the most indebted poor countries* where, in addition to nine countries already on the list (Benin, Bolivia, Burkina Faso, Honduras, Mauritania, Mozambique, Uganda, Senegal and Tanzania), 11 others will be granted the right to figure among the lucky few (Cameroon, Côte d'Ivoire, Guinea, Guinea-Bissau, Guyana, Malawi, Mali, Nicaragua, Rwanda, Chad and Zambia). They will then be compelled to embark on a new Programme for Strategic Poverty Reduction (PSPR), in line to replace the notorious SAP, which is fast becoming obsolete for the most indebted nations of the world. The PSPR provides for the association of international financial institutions, civil society and donors, and requires them to be taken into account. This involves only US$35 billion in nominal value, which represents approximately US$20 billion in real value. These amounts will be recorded not only as public debt relief, but also as a transformation of the private commercial debt considered as a counter-donation. It must be recalled that about 20 countries could not qualify for this scheme for diverse reasons. Four countries – Angola, Kenya, Vietnam and Yemen – cannot be considered as most indebted countries. Two countries, Ghana and Laos, have refused to participate in the programme. Two other countries, Madagascar and São Tome, have not provided sufficient statistics to benefit from the programme, although they seem to enjoy other forms of relief under the traditional IMF programmes. At the time the G8 countries were meeting, 12 countries had not submitted their case for inclusion

in the scheme, known as the Poverty Reduction and Growth Acceleration Programme. Without this prerequisite and the attendant conditionalities, the following countries cannot benefit from debt relief: Burundi, Central African Republic, Democratic Republic of Congo, Congo, Ethiopia, Liberia, Myanmar, Niger, Sierra Leone, Somalia, Sudan and Togo. It is true that the G8 harbours some doubts about the effective use of debt relief to promote poverty reduction schemes.

3 The issue of *organising the post-relief operations* was also on the agenda. The idea here is to favour the countries deemed 'serious' while refraining from encouraging the countries that persist in incurring exorbitant, unproductive expenditure. The control measures will be put in place by the OECD to officially ensure the seriousness of the applications that are accepted.

4 *Enhancement of the environment for trade and investment* remains a priority, notably within the framework of the agreements signed in the WTO. Proposals were made for poor countries to gain by building the capacity in their trade-related structures in order to foster a propitious environment in those countries and facilitate the integration of the world economy. We may therefore wonder, as do certain American economists such as Dani Rodrik of Harvard University, whether the very principle of forcing rapid integration of the world economy is not the way to supplant, progressively but surely, the very concept of development strategy (Rodrik, 2000).

5 *Acceleration of the integration of the world economy*, of course, is the ultimate goal. But it has been noticed that the numerical gap between the rich and the poor in terms of access to and production of information may turn out to be just an additional impediment to the integration of the poor countries in the world economy. Funding of our economic needs has been left in the hands of development merchant institutions, without indicating any specific conditions. It is to be hoped that the information highways will not be built as roads and railways were in colonial times, when they were used mainly to facilitate the evacuation of the essential part of Africa's resources – while the benevolent will of the colonialists ensured that there was no interconnection between the networks of rival colonial powers. Today and tomorrow, effort will bear more on controlling the content of the information disseminated. Thus, the position of the G8 is somewhat out of tune with the aspirations of the African population. Even the first recommendations by the experts of the United Nations Conference on Trade and Development (UNCTAD) appear to differ from the stand adopted by the G8. Regarding Africa's dependence on aid, UNCTAD experts are proposing a solution requiring gradual but persistent reduction of public aid in order to give a decisive impetus to African economies by reducing their aid dependency within one decade – a wide-ranging

integrated and growth support programme which mobilises domestic resources and encourages the generation of domestic savings and a massive inflow of foreign capital (UNCTAD, 2000a). It would have been interesting to see the UNCTAD experts examine the means for the generation of non-debt-incurring resources to bolster their proposal, which, in case of failure or non-cooperation on the part of foreign private investors, stands the risk of having a negative impact on Africa and aggravating the current crisis. During the next millennium, if there is a massive influx of capital on the basis of non-productive indebtedness, Africa stands the risk of becoming not only a colony but also an outright trading post – that is to say, the antechamber of world trade. Paradoxically, the reality in unbalanced world trade seems to open only a dim prospect for industrial production and local ownership of the production tools. In the specific case of AIDS, if we must follow the logic of production outside Africa and distribution in Africa, one would be led to believe that aid – the contribution by the Western taxpayers – will serve mainly for preventive measures, given the prohibitive cost of the other therapies.

The main argument advanced by UNCTAD experts is that 'History teaches us that the influx of private capital follows growth rather than promoting it' (UNCTAD, 2000b). Where this technical assistance programme is rejected, the proliferation of AIDS risks will lead to the disintegration of African societies. To be sure, this will neither contribute to attracting private capital, nor to boosting growth. This vicious circle of debt–AIDS–lack of growth is liable to benefit those advocating a population control policy in Africa under the pretext of insecurity. Without collective organisation, Africa will be faced with countless deaths. Africa may have to see the disarticulation of its society, rather than the exogenous disorganisation inherited from colonial and neocolonial times. We must convince the Western taxpaying electorate that the cost of insecurity in Africa might become very exorbitant if Africa were excluded from producing industrially, especially basic needs and generic health products, particularly for AIDS management.

From Economic Conditionality to Political Conditionality: Exerting Pressure to Prevent Alleged African Insecurity?

One of the main issues addressed by the Okinawa meeting of the leading industrialised countries was bringing under control the insecurity and risk of contagion that Africa may represent in terms of AIDS and debt for the international monetary system. It is worth revisiting this issue from the African perspective. When we talked of the debt, it was not so much to get relief as to request that some countries be allowed to enter a list where multiple conditionalities would be minimalised, if not completely eliminated, as the mode of development management practised by creditor countries. Failing this, the creditor nations will merely be shifting from economic conditionalities to political conditionalities in offering the African nations possible debt relief. Why do Africa and Western civil societies lay so much importance on talking about debt relief for the millennium, when the issue is actually being dealt with behind the scenes, especially bilaterally, in terms of the conditionalities for access to donor funding in return for the tacit right of interference in decision making in order to protect vital Western interests, and in utter defiance of Africa's rights? In a world dominated by a system based on competition, it is difficult to glimpse any genuine will to grant Africa any debt relief that will have real impact. The measures for boosting and generating added value, notably in the raw material processing sector, according to international quality control standards, and marketing thereof within the intra-African and world markets, seem to have failed to elicit any favourable response from African decision makers.

How then are we going to convince people that local production of anti-AIDS generic products for Africans cannot wait until 2006 according to WTO terms? How are we going to convince people that such local production should, of necessity, be effected within the framework of African interdependence, with the support of pioneering countries in the field such as South Africa? This requires the demystification of the 'there are no alternatives' syndrome. Expecting everything from the Western society, especially debt cancellation, cannot be the only condition. Therefore it is high time we redefined the concept of debt. At individual or collective level, a debt is an obligation of a person (individual or body corporate) to another. With regard to the African public debt, this obligation (basically financial) gradually changed into a political obligation. If political obligation becomes political allegiance, preferably towards the external world, it stands to reason that the way will open for possible divergence, or rather figuring on a permanent list of those qualified to enjoy a hypothetical partial debt relief with the attendant conditionalties. But the mode of computing interest is such that we would in the future find ourselves in a situation hardly different from today's. Viewed from the angle of creditor countries and considering the alleged risk of systemic insecurity peddled by those seeking a scapegoat following the crumbling of the Berlin Wall, it has become preferable to focus discourse on the African debt and AIDS for the consumption of Western taxpayers, while taking no concrete action in favour of Africa, except perhaps perfecting research on the continent and using it as a guinea-pig and testing ground. Elements of the private sector in the Western world have understood very well that Africa is a new market that will entitle them to public subsidies by way of soft loans or tax relief, to cover the risk it constitutes. All techniques are applied to ensure the serenity of trade and assuage the Western conscience.

It is true that the number of countries qualified to benefit from relief under the debt reduction programme initiated by the current President of the World Bank rose from 9 to 22; but this has required the acceptance of draconian conditionalities that are detrimental to the long-term interest of Africa. A country like Nicaragua officially questioned whether it was worth the candle to continue to subscribe to conditionalities without ever really benefiting concretely from the promised debt relief. The Uganda Minister of Finance showed his exasperation by saying aloud what other Africans have been saying secretly. Uganda, erstwhile good student of the IMF and friend of the Americans, was first on the list of potential beneficiaries of debt reduction. But it would enjoy no such reduction before the end of 2000 and has yet to enjoy any sustainable debt reduction and debt cancellation. As the Uganda Minister ruefully admitted mid-way through 2000, 'Not a single dollar of debt relief has come in. By the end of this year, we will have no access to this relief, unless God intervenes. This is scandalous' (Beattie, 2000: 1). He added that the increasing number of conditionalities imposed by the Bretton Woods institutions are nothing but new instruments for regulating the alleged feeling of insecurity that Africa may provoke in Western society. President Obasanjo of Nigeria broke the taboo by affirming publicly in August 2000 that part of the Nigerian debt is illegal. Up to 1985–6, Nigeria had borrowed US$5 billion and reimbursed US$16 billion. Today, the international community is still claiming payment of US$28 billion to settle the same debt (Ajayi, 2000).

Clearly the G8 is now the main source within the international community of development strategy and major world policy options. It would appear that the G8 has established a framework for putting an end not so much to development as to the applicability of international law to Africa. The G8 is on the way to institutionalising a new world order based on the unilateral right to safeguard, without prior notice, the individual or collective national interests of the Western countries. After all, was democracy not originally segregationist? Barely half a century ago, had Western democracy not excluded colonial peoples from exercising their right to vote? It is no wonder, therefore, that international law is now deemed applicable only to those found to have acceptably sound international relations. But it so happens that international relations change, depending on the overriding interests of the powerful nations (Amaïzo, 1998). Unfortunately, most African countries are isolated and incapable of acting collectively. The diversity of their positions in responding to the shift in the interests and stance of the Western powers makes them pass for nations without clout: they are promptly blacklisted collectively whenever any African country does not toe the line. Although Africa has states that are a source of concern for the West, they pose no threat to Western military security. The main source of concern is the possibility of AIDS contagion. Perhaps South Africa failed to win enough votes to host the 2006 World Cup because in certain quarters the high incidence of AIDS in South Africa is considered a high security risk, one to be marked out with beacons. Refusal to lend tangible assistance for AIDS management by organising a substantial decrease in the cost of the products for AIDS care, and instead imposing increasingly exorbitant conditionalities without any debt reduction, are just harbingers of a new policy for global management of world problems according to a unilateralist blueprint. Only ignorance can explain, if not excuse, failure to grasp this point.

Borrowing to Buy Anti-AIDS Drugs: Who Do We Want to Help?

Not only have the G8 countries failed to provide generous debt relief and debt cancellation: they have also devised new plans for increasing Africa's debt burden via AIDS control. The American Export/Import Bank has proposed making available the sum of US$1 billion as credit at 7 per cent rate of interest, purportedly for AIDS control in Africa. This consists of providing a credit line for 24 African countries south of the Sahara to enable these countries to buy anti-AIDS drugs exclusively from the United States. The worst feature of this deal is that if African professionals in the field find cheaper generic products elsewhere, they are not authorised to purchase such products using that credit, even if they had previously entered into manufacturing licence agreements obliging them to buy AIDS management products from other sources at lower prices.

The primary objectives of the offer of credit as a gift to celebrate the millennium can thus be spelled out as follows:

- to prevent the development of endogenous solutions by refusing to fund such initiatives;
- to prevent normal competition between generic products and other products costing exorbitant amounts;
- to get American taxpayers to finance the trade expansion strategies of certain American pharmaceutical companies in Africa;
- to get Africa even further into debt with the magical argument of viable AIDS control.

Given the lack of transparency in aid management in Africa, it is almost certain that few rural inhabitants will ever have access to the appropriate drug. On the contrary, collectively they will defray the cost of decisions on AIDS taken by the central administration. It must be noted that, even with a drastic reduction in prices, American pharmaceuticals marketed under this programme will still be more expensive than generic drugs (Mutume, 2001). Despite the numerous appeals by civil society organisations, the restrictive HIV/AIDS credit programme was not withdrawn. This must get us wondering about the real resolve to save human lives in Africa and the magnanimous spirit of the US Congress which is financing the American Import/Export Bank. The average cost of AIDS treatment per inhabitant is estimated by that bank at US$2,000 per annum. Certain NGOs, notably Médecins Sans Frontières, feel that with generic products we can achieve the same results within a price range of US$200–300.

What is Africa waiting for? Why can the African Union not serve as a forum for organising a collective health defence mechanism for all Africans? The strategies resorted to by Brazil and South Africa may serve as examples on more than one score. It is well and truly a combat of cultures that must be waged at diverse levels within an interdependence network between Africans and non-Africans. The action of Western and African NGOs, with the limited resources available, must be commended, promoted and supported. When will the linkage between debt and AIDS be taken into account by African leaders and by the G8 in their collective decision making concerning Africa?

Organising African Experts in a Network

Refusing to organise collectively, refusing to organise African experts in a network to germinate collective solutions, refusing to inform the population about this new Western strategy which may soon hit the African population hard does not augur well if African expertise is to claim that its turn will come in the 21st century.

Our response must be in no way a matter of chance, but rather of choice, of regular organisation and collective defence of the most vital interests of the African continent. Continuing to think, as in the colonial days, that what befell our neighbour will never affect us is a policy that risks sweeping away the entire African continent collectively, just as AIDS and debt are doing. There is the risk of seeing the African population becoming SDF – *sans domicile fixe*, of no fixed address – because of the anticipated wave of migrations. The cumulative effect of this is another SDF – *sans développement futur*. The net long-term effect is that the land will belong to whoever has the means to seize it, with or without coercion, and not to the person who was born on it or who tills it, despite those in Africa who continue to believe in the virtues of collective land tenure.

In spite of the disastrous situation in Africa, the West is not prepared to take pity but continues to defend Western interests by all means. Only countries that pay political allegiance will make significant progress. This will involve permanent compliance with the new economic and political conditionalities to qualify for debt reduction and gain for a part of their insolvent populations access to medicines and medical treatment otherwise reserved for the rich. Africa generates no greater insecurity than Europe or North America, who for their part can take their laboratory experiments, with all the attendant risks, directly into the African forests. The West must refrain from mounting a media blitz where ethics, solidarity and interdependence ought to have been given pride of place, benefiting all the parties involved in the quest for wholesome development in Africa. Africa cannot confine itself to holding conferences on AIDS awareness (South Africa in July 2000; Nigeria in 2001). Going further, African leaders should lay the foundations for a network of African expertise and capacities that would develop anti-viral drugs and organise the manufacture of generic products. They should also ensure that Africa collectively requests withdrawal of the unfavourable conditions imposed by the World Trade Organisation. Only in this way can Africa, a continent with negligible influence, build the instruments to regulate, not African insecurity, but rather the defence of her vital interests.

Bibliography

Ajayi, Rotimi (2000) 'Nigeria's Foreign Debt Illegal?', *http://www.vanguardngr.com/14082000/Cll50800.htm*

Amaïzo, Yves Ekpue (1998) *De la dépendance a l'interdépendance. Mondialisation et marginalisation: une chance pour l'Afrique?* Paris: Editions l'Harmattan.

BBC (2000) 'Annan Joins G8 Critics', British Broadcasting Corporation, Saturday, 22 July, at 19 H 58 GMT.

Beattie, Alan (2000) 'Debt Relief Lobby Accuses Rich Nations of Breaking Pledges', *Financial Times*, 3 July.

Chomsky, Noam (2000) 'Washington, audessus du droit international: L'Amerique, "Etat voyou"', *Le Monde Diplomatique*, August, pp. 4–5.

Fukuyuma, Francis (1992) *The End of History and the Last Man*, New York: Avon Books.

Minister of Finance, G7 (2000) *Poverty Reduction and Economic Development,* Report of the Minister of Finance of the G7 to Heads of State and Government, Okinwa, Japan, 21 July. *www.g8kyushu-okinawa.go.jp/e/documents/poverty.html*

Mutume, Gumisai (2001) 'Pressure Mounts for Cheaper Anti-AIDS Drugs', Third World Network, *www.twnside.org.sg/title/mounts.htm*

Rodrik, Dani (2000) *Can Integration into the World Economy Substitute for a Development Strategy?* Havard University, May.

UNAIDS (2000), *New UN Report Estimates Over One-Third of Today's 15-Year-Olds Will Die of AIDS in War-Affected Countries*.

UNCTAD (2000a) 'Capital Flow and Growth in Africa', UNCTAD/GDS/mdpb, September.

—— (2000b) 'How to Reduce Africa's Dependence on Aid? UNCTAD Proposes a Solution', press release, 14 July 2000, TAD/INF/2859. *http://www.unctad.org*

UNDP (2000) *Human Development Report*, New York: Oxford University Press and UN Development Programme.

World Bank (2000a) *World Development Indicators,* Washington, DC: World Bank.

—— (2000b) *Global Development Finance*, Washington, DC: World Bank.

PART 4
Regionalism and Development

15

Regional Economic Integration: a Development Paradigm for Africa

Lawrence O. C. Agubuzu

In April 1980 the member states of what was then the OAU and is now the African Union, with the support of the organisation's General Secretariat, the ECA and other relevant institutions, organised the first African Economic Summit. That Summit adopted the Lagos Plan of Action (LPA) and the Final Act of Lagos (FAL). The FAL called for the establishment of the African Economic Community (AEC). Thus, African countries adopted the strategy of regional integration as a development paradigm. Both the LPA and the FAL emphasised self-reliance as the approach to Africa's socio-economic development.

Soon after the OAU Heads of State and Government had adopted the LPA and FAL, the World Bank published a study generally referred to as the Berg Report which propagated the view that Africa's future economic development should rely on the continued production and export of raw materials. According to the Report, African countries were best suited to that sector, in which they held comparative advantage.

By 1985 several African countries had found themselves in the throes of socio-economic crisis and embarked, with the prompting of the Bretton Woods institutions, on economic reform programmes of one form or another. Of particular significance in this regard were the SAPs of the World Bank and the stabilisation programmes of the IMF.

In response to the trend, the ECA, under the able and distinguished leadership of Professor Adebayo Adedeji, then Under-Secretary-General of the United Nations and Executive Secretary of the ECA, spearheaded a very comprehensive programme of research on the African development paradigm. In the process, the ECA launched a debate on the relevance and implications of SAPs for Africa's socio-economic development. That effort resulted in the adoption by the African Ministers of Economic Development and Planning of the African Alternative Framework to Structural Adjustment Programmes for Socio-Economic Recovery and Transformation (AAF–SAP).

This Symposium, organised by ACDESS under the initiative of Bade Onimode, is focusing on the implementation of alternative development paradigms for Africa. It seeks to rediscover our continent's own development paradigms and mobilise support, political will and popular energies for their implementation. The hope is that the conclusions of the symposium will constitute the basis for charting a bright future for Africa.

The Concept of Economic Integration

It is against this backdrop that this chapter puts forward the proposition that developmental regionalism constitutes a major element in an alternative development paradigm. Economic integration involves the application of a set of policies and measures by a group of countries with the aim of creating a regional economic space. The creation of an integrated regional economic space should enable the participating countries to achieve a more efficient utilisation of natural and human resources. This in turn should ensure high productivity, growth and competitiveness in the globalised economy – all resulting in improvement in the standard of living for the nationals of the integrating economies.

Economic integration, it is well known, can take various forms, depending on the degree of integration of the member countries. These range from a free trade area, at the lowest stage, to a supranational union at the highest level of integration. Each stage of integration has its distinguishing features. For example, in the free trade area, countries undertake to allow trade preferences regarding goods and services that circulate among their countries, but maintain different levels of tariffs and charges of equivalent effect on similar goods entering their borders from non-participating countries. Upon subsequent decision to implement a protocol agreement among themselves to unify the levels of the customs duties they impose on goods and services entering their countries from non-member countries, they reach the stage of a customs union. Beyond the stage of the customs union, when the participating countries reach the level at which they permit the free movement of factors of production among themselves, they succeed in establishing a common market.

The key policy elements that constitute the economic community/union are the successful coordination and harmonisation of economic policies with a view to creating a unified economic space. A good example is the European Union (EU), with its Common Agricultural Policy and a harmonised monetary policy that has resulted in the use of the Euro as a single European currency and the establishment by the participating countries of a European Central Bank.

The most advanced level of economic integration is reached when a supranational authority is established. This requires some surrender of national sovereignty by member countries to the supranational authority. The closest example is, again, the European Union. Africa will attain that stage if and when the envisaged African Union becomes a reality, through the achievement of the stages of economic integration listed above.

Under the Abuja Treaty, the initial stages of Africa's integration involve the establishment by the regional economic communities (RECs) of free trade areas, customs unions, common markets, and economic communities. These efforts by the RECs are expected to lead to the establishment of the African Economic Community and the African Union. In the Constitutive Act of the African Union some measures and institutions such as the Pan-African Parliament and the Court of Justice are provided for in order to underpin the supranational character of the Union.

The Historical Foundation of Regional Cooperation and Integration in Africa

Even before the signing of the OAU Charter, the struggle of African leaders against colonial domination dating back to the Pan-African Conference of 1945, had generated a vision of a Pan-African regional economic space to be administered by a Pan-African political arrangement. Thus the prime movers of early struggles against colonialism like Kwame Nkrumah and Nnamdi Azikiwe, popularly known as the Zik of Africa, spoke generally in terms of the economic and political emancipation of Africa. Later, as some African states gained independence, declarations in the 1960s by the likes of Gamal Abdel Nasser, Nkrumah and Jomo Kenyatta were replete with calls on African leaders to create a continental government with a common market and monetary zone. Nkrumah even wanted the creation of an African Military High Command. But the environment at that time did not make it possible for the concretisation of such advanced forms of economic integration and political unification.

Nonetheless, prior to the signing of the OAU Charter in May 1963, some countries had developed various forms of regional economic cooperation and integration in Africa. There already existed, for example, the East African Community, the Community of French West Africa, and other similar arrangements on the African continent that had their origins in the colonial past of the countries involved.

In this context, one might wish to cite the Ghana–Guinea–Mali Cooperation Agreement as one of the early forms of regional grouping that emerged in the post-colonial era and served as a precursor to the forms of economic cooperation fashioned in the OAU Charter. Subsequent ministerial and summit declarations of the OAU – from the Kinshasa Declaration to the Monrovia Declaration of Commitment to Guidelines and Measures for National and Collective Self-reliance in Economic and Social Development for the Establishment of a New International Economic Order (NIEO), and the adoption of the LPA and the FAL, which called for the formulation of a treaty establishing the African

Economic Community – constituted landmark instruments aimed at creating the basis for economic cooperation and integration in Africa.

The rationale for economic integration and cooperation in Africa is both political and economic. Through integration and unity, Africa can acquire greater voice and bargaining power in the community of nations. Integration is also expected to assist Africa in overcoming the problems associated with the smallness, fragility and structural weakness of inherited colonial economics.

Background to the Treaty of the African Economic Community

Articles II (1)(b) and (2)(b) of its Charter mandate the OAU to promote regional cooperation among its member states. This mandate was subsequently reaffirmed in Resolutions CM/Res. 123 (IX) and CM/Res. 125 (IX), adopted in Kinshasa in September 1967, in which the leaders of Africa state their conviction that an expanded African market covering the entire continent should be established.

The significance of the LPA and the FAL, adopted in April 1980, lay not only in the reaffirmation of the plan to establish the African Economic Community (AEC) but also in the identification of stages for bringing this about, as well as in the decision to set up a ministerial drafting committee to formulate an appropriate treaty. This process culminated in the signing of the treaty establishing the AEC in Abuja on 3 June 1991. The Abuja Treaty came into force on 12 May 1994.

Approaches to regional economic cooperation and integration in Africa

In accordance with the Abuja Treaty, two basic approaches to African integration have been adopted. The first is the regional geographical approach. This approach seeks to use existing and future regional economic communities (RECs) as building blocks of a continental community. The AEC is to evolve into a continental system built on such entities as ECOWAS, COMESA, the SADC, ECCAS and AMU.

The second (and parallel) approach in fostering integration is the sectoral approach. A number of sectoral projects have been sponsored by the OAU/AEC or co-sponsored with other RECs. A protocol providing for legal, institutional, functional and organic links between the AEC and the RECs has been operational since February 2000. On the basis of this instrument, the OAU/AEC is to formulate and jointly implement sectoral projects with the regional institutions. This approach is in line with the provisions of the first stage of the Abuja Treaty, which calls for the strengthening of the RECs.

Trade liberalisation and free movement of capital in Africa

During the fourth stage in the evolution of the AEC, under Article 6 (2)(d) of the Treaty, member states are expected to coordinate and harmonise their tariff systems in order to establish an African Customs Union.

This would have been preceded at the third stage of the process by the establishment of free trade areas by the respective RECs, through the observance of a timetable for the gradual removal of tariff and non-tariff barriers to intra-community trade and the setting up of their respective regional customs unions.

Eventually, during the fifth stage, an African Common Market should emerge and set the scene for the free movement of all factors of production, followed by the establishment of the African Monetary Union at the sixth stage. This in turn would facilitate the free movement of capital within and among the countries.

Towards the realisation of the above objectives, the RECs, like ECOWAS, COMESA and the SADC, have developed their trade liberalisation programmes to various levels of implementation. Similar efforts have been made in monetary and financial cooperation.

Subregional Cooperation

West African region

In this subregion, there are well over 40 intergovernmental organisations (IGOs), which seek to promote regional cooperation and integration. These include the CEAO which was transformed into UEMOA. This IGO was created around the CFA Franc Zone in the subregion, which already had its own Central Bank, the BCEAO. However, the umbrella institution is ECOWAS, which since its creation in 1975 has developed several sectoral projects.

Since 1 January 1990, ECOWAS has run a trade liberalisation scheme whereby 400 products have been placed on a Common List of Preferences. There is also a compensation system for loss of revenue resulting from intra-ECOWAS tariff elimination. The process of harmonisation of various instruments to facilitate intra-ECOWAS trade has been in operation for some time, and has resulted in the use of a certificate of origin and common customs declaration forms.

Intra-ECOWAS trade is still only about 8 per cent of the region's external trade. This relatively low level is due mainly to a number of factors such as lack of a trade information network covering tradable products in member countries. Poor and non-existent trading channels as well as the absence of trade finance facilities also contribute to low intra-ECOWAS trade. There are also problems of non-tariff barriers like the numerous roadblocks that customs and immigration officials have installed between the various borders of the ECOWAS countries. Another obstacle to the expansion of trade in goods of intra-community origin is the massive influx of relatively cheap products from non-African sources.

In the area of liberalisation of payments in the ECOWAS subregion, we note that in accordance with the objective of achieving convertibility of national currencies as a means of promoting intra-ECOWAS trade, the Heads of State and

Government of the ECOWAS countries established in August 1997 an *ad hoc* committee to work towards the establishment of a single monetary zone by the year 2000. To this end, the majority of the countries are taking steps to comply with the ECOWAS macro-economic convergence criteria. Also in preparation is a Guarantee Fund to support the proposed multilateral payments system of ECOWAS by the first quarter of year 2000. In the same spirit of monetary cooperation, ECOWAS had planned to launch its travellers' cheque system by July 2000. Furthermore, 13 countries have adopted a programme that enables ECOWAS citizens to pay their airport taxes, hotel bills and air tickets in local currencies. This is a policy that underpins the advanced stage that ECOWAS has reached in implementing its protocol on free movement of persons.

Within the framework of the programme of trade promotion and private sector investment, the ECOWAS organised its first regional trade fair in Dakar, Senegal in June 1995 and the second in Accra, Ghana in March 1999. In order to enhance the processing of customs and statistical data to facilitate intra-regional trade, ECOWAS is using the Automated System of Customs Data Analysis (ASYCUDA) and EUROTRACE programmes.

Although one cannot say that the transport and communication situation in the subregion is satisfactory, one should note that ECOWAS intra-regional trade is being enhanced by the completion of the axes of the Trans-West African Highway network; namely, the Trans-Coastal and Trans-Saharan highways, which have reached implementation levels of 83 per cent and 87 per cent respectively. The road transit systems and the ECOWAS Brown Card Insurance Scheme for vehicles are part of various legal measures aimed at the free movement of persons and goods.

ECOWAS has also implemented the Second Telecommunication programme and other measures for the promotion and development of energy infrastructure, particularly the promotion and implementation of the Africa Gas Pipelines Project which links Nigeria to Ghana through Benin and Togo. The above are some of the concrete projects that have been put in place by ECOWAS. It must be stated that one of the remarkable achievements of ECOWAS is its rapid progress with the implementation of its protocol on free movement of persons, right of residence and establishment. In this connection, it may be noted that all 15 ECOWAS member states have abolished visas and entry permits for the citizens of other ECOWAS countries. In addition, five of those member states have already adopted the ECOWAS travel certificate to facilitate and enhance the free movement of citizens in the region.

It has often been stated that 'Without peace there can be no development, and that without development, peace cannot be durable.' In the case of ECOWAS, one can hardly deny that ensuring subregional peace and security has been one of the sectors in which it has made a remarkable impact. As if foreseeing what would happen in Liberia and Sierra Leone, the ECOWAS member states had signed a non-aggression pact and eventually established a mediation committee and an observer group commonly known as ECOMOG. Among other achievements, ECOWAS has facilitated the return to democratic constitutional rule in Liberia and also ensured the re-establishment of a legitimate regime in Sierra Leone. In addition, the meeting of ECOWAS Ministers of Foreign Affairs and Security held in Yamoussoukro in March 1998 took the decision to create a regional mechanism for conflict prevention, management and resolution.

In 1999, the Heads of State and Government decided to launch a 'fast track' approach to the implementation of the ECOWAS Treaty. Ghana, Nigeria and Mali have decided to lead the vanguard, with the aim of securing an ECOWAS single monetary zone soon and speeding up the trade liberalisation process.

CEN–SAD

CEN–SAD is an acronym for the Sahelo-Saharan States, which was formed by eight member states of the OAU: Burkina Faso, Chad, Libya, Mali, Niger, the Sudan, Eritrea and the Central African Republic. It was established on 4 February 1998 in Tripoli, the Great Socialist Peoples Libyan Arab Jamahiriya. Nigeria joined CEN-SAD in 2000. It has the following characteristics: one state is from north and seven from south of the Sahara; two are Arab states; five are French-speaking and one English-speaking; one is a member of AMU, two of COMESA, four of ECOWAS and two of ECCAS.

It is also interesting to note that apart from Eritrea, which has not yet signed the Abuja Treaty establishing the AEC, all the others have signed and ratified it and have deposited their instruments of ratification. In this regard, the lack of territorial contiguity of the participating member states of CEN–SAD should be noted. The treaty establishing CEN–SAD, in its preamble, draws inspiration from the Charter of the OAU and Abuja Treaty and aims at the following objectives:

- peace, stability and security of the Sahelo-Saharan space; and
- economic, political, cultural and social integration.

Indeed, the Secretary-General of CEN–SAD has signed a protocol establishing an organic and functional relationship with the OAU General Secretariat and the RECs, and has established a technical working relationship with the OAU. According to Article I of the CEN–SAD Treaty, the establishment of an economic union is envisaged. Hence CEN–SAD will foster monetary cooperation and remove all restrictions which impede integration in order to ensure the free movement of persons and goods and the right of residence.

The institutional arrangements cover the Conference of Heads of States, the Executive Council, and a General Secretariat. There are two other important organs: the Development Bank and the Economic, Cultural and Social Council, its functions to be determined by the Executive Council. The General Secretariat is temporarily located in Tripoli, in conformity with Article 11, and during the transitional period of one year, the Current Chairman of the Conference appoints the Secretary-General and his Assistant.

Eastern and Southern African Region

There are a number of regional organisations in Eastern and Southern Africa. These include the SADC, IGAD, COMESA and the East African Cooperation Commission (EACC), which seeks to revive the defunct East African Community.

COMESA

Trade liberalisation is the area in which COMESA is recognised as having made impressive progress. The major programme of COMESA was to establish a free trade area by the year 2000. Accordingly, on 31 October 2000 COMESA Heads of State and Government launched the COMESA Free Trade Area with nine member states reducing their tariffs on intra-community trade to 0 per cent. The nine countries are Djibouti, Egypt, Kenya, Madagascar, Malawi, Mauritius, Sudan, Zambia and Zimbabwe. Comoros, Eritrea and Uganda have reduced by 80 per cent, while Burundi and Rwanda have reduced by 60 per cent. Seychelles was expected to join the COMESA Free Trade Area in June 2001. The other members that have not yet reduced any tariffs are Angola, Congo Democratic Republic, Ethiopia, Namibia and Swaziland.

In the area of trade promotion and trade development, COMESA has undertaken such activities as demand–supply surveys and buyer–seller meetings; the holding of seminars for private entrepreneurs on 'Doing Business in COMESA', and other similar business events such as the COMESA trade fairs, the last of which took place in Lusaka, Zambia and coincided with the launching of the COMESA Free Trade Area.

Recognising that the African entrepreneur has a high propensity to import from outside the COMESA region because exporters from non-African sources usually have trade finance facilities such as the 90-day credit, COMESA established the Eastern and Southern African Trade and Development Bank to provide trade and development finance for intra-regional trade as well as national and regional projects.

Over the years, COMESA has recognised that the volume of its intra-regional trade has been low because of a lack of adequate information about the availability, pricing and sourcing of products. To deal with this problem, COMESA has introduced its Trade Information Network project, a software programme and database to provide relevant trade information to entrepreneurs through their respective Chambers of Commerce. Beyond this, COMESA has also provided other forms of trade information to the private sector through COMESA's website.

In the area of investment, COMESA initiated an 'investors' roadmap' to identify all difficulties that investors encounter in trying to invest in each of the member states and in the region in general. Steps are being taken to declare COMESA a single investment region, with a harmonised investment code endorsed by the participating countries. COMESA has also initiated the Standard, Quality, Meterology and Testing programme to assist member states to improve the quality of their products, and embarked on a comprehensive monetary and financial cooperation programme. Indeed, it has been the first African REC to introduce its own travellers' cheques and its member states have been able to use their national currencies for the settlement of intra-COMESA trade transactions through a clearing house. Clearly then, the volume of trade has been on the up.

As a result of the adoption of SAPs by its members, however, the orientation of this subregional economic grouping has suffered a change of direction. One aspect of this has been resort to the use of foreign currencies for intra-COMESA transactions; also, difficulties arose that caused the COMESA travellers' cheques to be withdrawn from circulation. Because of these developments, COMESA has decided to restructure its clearing house to make it more commercially oriented. It has taken steps to establish a Regional Trade Facilitation Project, which is a political risk guarantee facility, and another instrument called the COMESA Payment and Settlement System. The latter is aimed at overcoming the identified problem of a lack of information for borrowers that results in higher transaction costs. It would also ensure higher certainty and speed of payments and a reduction of risks associated with currency convertibility. The effect of these measures should be to boost the volume of intra-regional trade.

IGAD

The Inter-Governmental Authority on Development (IGAD) is one of the regional integration initiatives of this subregion. It was created in 1996 to supersede the Intergovernmental Authority on Drought and Development (IGADD), which was founded in 1986. Its creation was aimed at revitalising its mandate and expanding its sphere of activity to deal with priority areas of economic cooperation, political and humanitarian affairs, food security and environment protection. Its member States are Djibouti, Eritrea, Ethiopia, Kenya, Somalia, Sudan and Uganda.

IGAD's mission includes subregional integration through promotion of food security, sustainable environmental management, peace and security, intra-regional trade and the development of improved communications infrastructure. To that end, IGAD has agreed to cooperate in key economic priority programmes/projects such as trade, industry, tourism, communications and telecommunications. Important projects include the construction of missing links on the Trans-African Highway and the Pan African Telecommunications Network (PANAFTEL); the removal of physical and non-physical barriers to interstate trade; the improvement of ports and inland container terminals; the modernisation of railways and telecommunications services; and training in grain marketing.

Other projects in the area of food security include such priority programmes as the establishment of a regional integrated information system; enhancing the remote sensing capacity of member states; establishing a marketing information system; promotion of the sustainable production of drought-tolerant, high-yielding crop varieties; improved livestock production; capacity building in integrated water resources management; and the implementation of international conventions to combat desertification.

In the context of the rather delicate political and security situation in the Horn of Africa, IGAD has two important medium-term projects under execution. These are capacity building in the areas of conflict prevention and alleviation and the mitigation of humanitarian crises. The countries of this subregional economic community can be said to have abundant resources, which, when properly developed and tapped, could propel its people to economic prosperity. In particular, mention must be made of the rich endowment of rivers, lakes and forests; abundance of livestock; and a high agricultural potential.

East African Cooperation Commission (EACC)
In their effort to revive the defunct East African Community, the governments of Kenya, Uganda and Tanzania signed an agreement for the establishment of a Permanent Tripartite Commission for East African Cooperation. Bearing in mind their regional and international commitments, such as the Abuja Treaty establishing the African Economic Community, the East African Cooperation countries have decided to cooperate in certain trade, investment, tourism, culture, foreign policy and diplomatic areas as indicated in the East African Cooperation Development Strategy (1997–2000). Indeed, the objective has been to use the three countries as the 'fast track' of the regional integration process in East and Southern Africa. Hence the countries are expected to be in the vanguard of accelerated implementation of trade liberalisation and currency convertibility.

SADC
The Southern African Development Community (SADC), with a few exceptions, has a membership overlapping with that of COMESA. It was transformed from the Southern Africa Development Coordination Conference (SADCC) established in 1980, to a Development Community in 1992. Its present membership is 14 and it has a combined GDP of US$170 billion. The primary objective of SADC is economic cooperation and integrated development and it has over 407 projects with a total value of US$809 billion. Half of this amount was mobilised from external sources and 75 per cent was allocated to the development of transport and communications. In fact, this is one of the sectors where SADC has made the greatest impact. Of late, it has begun a serious trade liberalisation and development programme. The community has the objective of establishing a free trade area within eight years of the ratification of its trade protocol.

SACU

The existence and importance in Southern Africa of the Southern African Customs Union (SACU) cannot be overlooked. Within SACU, all tariff and non-tariff barriers have been eliminated. The SACU dates back to 1910 and links Botswana, Swaziland, Lesotho, Namibia and South Africa. Under the SACU agreement, the participating countries long ago constituted a common external tariff against non-SACU countries and established their own uniform excise and consumption taxes.

Central African Region

ECCAS was established in 1983 when the Heads of State and Government of the region decided to expand on the membership of the then UDEAC, and to create an economic community. The objective of ECCAS has been to establish a customs union through the elimination among their member states of duties, quota restrictions, prohibitions and administrative trade barriers, and the adoption of a common external tariff. Like all the other African RECs, ECCAS envisages the various stages of subregional economic integration, including the creation of a free trade area and the establishment of a customs union. Regrettably, one can only say that since its creation, the organisation has faced critical resource constraints and political problems. Meanwhile UDEAC, with a membership that can be considered a subgroup of ECCAS, has been revived with massive donor support and resources, enabling it to launch various programme initiatives, particularly in the transport sector. It should be noted that this subregion is still embroiled in serious conflict.

The North African Region

The Arab Mahgreb Union (AMU) was reactivated by a declaration signed on 17 February 1989 in Marrakesh, Morocco. Its member states are Tunisia, Algeria, Libya, Mauritania and Morocco. According to its legislative instruments, the AMU was expected to establish its free trade area before 1992. In principle, the customs union was to have been accomplished before the end of 1995 and the Mahgreb Common Market was envisaged for the year 2000. Unfortunately, owing to political problems, the AMU has not been in a position to develop any type of functional linkage between itself and the African Economic Community.

Current Issues and Problems in African Integration

The most basic problem in the promotion of continental integration in the context of the Abuja Treaty is that on the whole the programmes of the RECs and those of other existing groupings have not been formulated with the AEC in view. However, it must be recognised that COMESA and ECOWAS have made efforts to take the AEC provisions into account when revising their treaties and protocols: to avoid the compartmentalisation of programmes and establish linkages between the AEC and RECs, these two organisations have endeavoured to cooperate with the OAU in taking timely and appropriate actions.

The problem of overlapping membership of the RECs arises from the failure of all the regional groupings to focus on Africa's continental integration as a final objective of all regional/subregional efforts. Conflicts in scheduling meetings and wasteful duplication and competition are a direct result of this lack of clear purpose.

Another problem is the institutional weakness in the RECs and in the AEC, particularly with regard to the capacity to formulate and monitor programmes. In this regard, it is observed that these institutions are embarking on too many programmes simultaneously, without establishing priorities that would take account of their limited capacities and available financial and other resources. This situation creates external dependence in terms of resources and expertise and, above all, leads to apathy on the part of member states which fail to see the real benefits from the activities and programmes of regional groupings.

There are also various types of political problems arising from the real or imagined fears of some members about domination, external interference and armed conflict. The break-up of integration groupings or the regression to smaller groupings is often a direct result of these problems, and usually linked to government attitudes regarding integration – in many cases, still seen as a matter of convenience rather than necessity. This attitude is fast changing in the light of the realities of globalisation.

A danger therefore lies in the proliferation of regional economic organisations, competing for the same economic space and engaged in wasteful duplication of effort. Many countries are seeking concurrent membership in more than one REC. For example, COMESA member countries are increasingly becoming members of SADC; ECCAS countries also are becoming members of SADC and /or COMESA; and almost all members of IGAD are also members of COMESA. All this makes horizontal coordination difficult as the same country progresses at different paces in the different RECs it joins. The inability to stabilise membership of the RECs renders them unsustainable, and their operations are wasteful and expensive for the countries involved. The regional organisations can ill afford to indulge in unplanned and unchartered courses of development to which they are constantly subjected by the ever-changing political kaleidoscope.

The regional integration process in Africa is being slowed by the perception that there is a conflict between the national development objectives of the member countries and the cooperation and integration objectives of the RECs. Hence, when the countries adopt regional policy decisions, they seldom back them up with national legislation necessary for their implementation. In principle, the national and REC programmes should be harmonised and made to complement each other. When they do not, as is often the case, there is a tendency for REC member states to overlook their financial obligations and other commitments to the subregional and regional organisations.

Another apparent conflict relates to the relationship between the RECs and the subgroups within the RECs: UEMOA in ECOWAS, CEMAC in ECCAS, and the SADC and the EACC in COMESA. If we accept the principle of *variable geometry* whereby these sub-groups seem to be aiming at a closer and faster pace of association than is applicable for the general REC membership, then the fact that some members are attempting to move faster should not be a constraining factor on others; in fact the reverse should be the case.

The financial problems faced by the RECs are grave when one considers their full implications for the establishment of the AEC in the long term. At the moment, many RECs do not depend totally on membership contributions to run their programmes. A reasonable portion of the recurrent costs is covered from membership contributions, but as for capital expenditures, these hardly go beyond office buildings for the REC secretariat. Invariably, development activities are funded by foreign aid. All the RECs face serious financial problems and have been floating the idea of devising self-financing mechanisms to generate financial resources for their running costs. Indeed, some RECs have succeeded in formulating and applying such mechanisms. In this connection, the UEMOA secretariat provided its members with tax options and the formalisation of the transfer of these tax revenues to the coffers of the Union. CEMAC has also been exploring the prospects of undertaking a similar study with a view to strengthening its budgetary base. Thus, as the RECs are on an irreversible course of development (through the establishment of many supporting institutions, the development of programmes and the undertaking of capacity building activities), and as member states are increasingly committed to regional development (which is owned and managed by themselves), many of the problems and difficulties raised here will need to be resolved in building the future.

African countries stand to benefit from regional integration, which creates propitious conditions whereby they would no longer spend disproportionately large sums of money to fight border wars and contain internal insurgency. With regional integration, fears of territorial loss which neighbouring countries entertain would be reduced, since countries formerly in conflict would belong to the same economic community. The development of the border areas in Africa, which until now have been sources of conflict over shared resources, would be greatly enhanced by regional cooperation and integration.

In connection with the above, we note that many countries share the water resources of the Nile, the Zambezi, the Congo and the Niger rivers. But riparian cooperation is not effective: many states are competing for control of the use of these water resources. Here again, a lasting solution to the problems of development and trans-boundary resource management is provided by regional cooperation and integration.

The AEC will encourage the RECs to address the problem of the equitable distribution of economic benefits in regional integration arrangements. Since there is a tendency for wealth and population to gravitate to points where there are benefits of economies of scale, it is hypothesised that its consequences will leave some of the former relatively underdeveloped states marginalised. But this is a problem that can be corrected by sound industrial and fiscal policies based on a judicious determination of industrial locations in a region and compensatory finance. Recognising this as a thorny issue, ECOWAS has commissioned a study with a view to establishing inter-state industrial zones in the region.

The SADC has also foreseen the problem and has made adequate provision in its treaty for the establishment and equitable distribution of institutions and development projects in all areas of cooperation, including industry, investment and finance, infrastructure and trade. Similarly, COMESA institutions are being established in member countries with a view to ensuring that such institutions and the benefits from the establishment and development of industrial projects are equitably distributed in the Community.

In July 2000 in Lome, Togo, the OAU Heads of State and Government adopted and signed the Constitutive Act of the African Union. The Act came into force in July 2001 when two-thirds of the OAU member states had ratified it and the Union formally replaced the OAU in July 2002 in Durban, South Africa, where the Union was launched with great fanfare the day after the OAU was finally buried. In the theory of regional economic integration, political union is the highest stage of the integration process: what inauguration of the AU means, therefore, is that the necessary political and institutional framework is being provided for the economic, political, social and cultural integration processes to proceed concurrently.

An important fact to underscore is that within the framework of the African Union the functions of the Executive Council will be essentially socio-economic. They will cover such fields as foreign trade; energy, industry and mineral resources; food, agriculture, animal resources and livestock production; forestry, water resources and irrigation; environmental protection; humanitarian action and disaster response and relief; transport and communications; education, culture, health and human resources development; science and technology; nationality, residency and immigration matters; social security, including the formulation of mother and child care policies, and policies relating to the disabled and handi-capped; and the establishment of a system of African awards, medals and prizes.

Conclusion: the Way Forward

There is no doubt that regional integration is the best paradigm for responding to the challenges of development and transformation. This view is based on a number of factors: 15 African countries are landlocked and transport and communication links on the continent as a whole are still rudimentary. Only five African states have a population of more than 30 million; eight countries have a population of less than 1 million each; and 14 countries have a population between 1 and 4 million. It shows that the national markets of Africa's 53 states are not only too small to attract significant investment flows but are also too balkanised to generate meaningful economies of scale in diversification efforts.

On the other hand, considered as a single economic space, the African continent has a potential market of over 600 million people, a natural resource base of huge dimensions and a diversity unsurpassed by any other continent on the planet. Therefore, geography, small country markets and the extreme balkanisation of the continent have continued to make regional cooperation and economic integration an essential and indispensable part of the strategic policy approach to development in Africa. The small countries' economies, hamstrung in terms of transport, communication and production capacities, are just not viable in an increasingly integrated world economy. And retreating into isolation behind high tariff barriers is no longer an option in view of the commitments demanded by the multilateral trading disciplines of the WTO, and given the need for access to finance and investment for fast-changing technologies, new production methods and export markets.

The regionalisation of economic activities will enable national economies to build capacities in all critical areas, from the absorption and generation of new technologies to production and marketing as a springboard for more meaningful participation in the world economy. As our entrepreneurs – in partnership with foreign investors from the traditional countries in Europe and North America, and from the advancing countries of the South – respond to the free movement of goods, capital and services within Africa's regions, and develop their supply capacity (productivity, scale and scope of production, marketing), increasingly they will be able to exploit global opportunities in the gradual step-by-step process of integration into the world economy. To this extent, therefore, the present *status quo* of policy reform without strategic direction in most member states cannot be accepted as appropriate for meeting the challenges of the global economy of the 21st century.

While the foundation for regional economic cooperation and integration in Africa has been well laid through the establishment of the AEC, the RECs should continue to build their capacities, harmonise and coordinate their activities, build support institutions, improve performance and avoid wasteful duplication of effort. This will include the harmonisation of national reconstruction programmes of the member states with those of the RECs, in such a way that one can complement the other. The same should hold true regarding relationships between the RECs, the AEC, the multilateral organisations and the African Union.

16

Transfrontier Regionalism: the European Union and Post-Colonial Africa

A. I. Asiwaju

Transfrontier regionalism is a reference to a novel category of internationalism, forced on territorially adjacent sovereign states. Such states are compelled to interact for reasons not only of common interest in the human and natural resources straddling a shared international boundary, but also of common concern about the cross-border environmental impacts of human activities and/or acts of God. Although the aspect of a transfrontier region specifically focused in this presentation is the one relating to artificially partitioned ethnic groups, giving rise to the global phenomenon of peoples of identical languages and cultures being found across international boundaries, it is essential to bear in mind the other closely interrelated manifestations of transfrontier regions: namely, the wide spectrum of transboundary natural resources ranging from land, water (surface and underground) and air to liquid and solid minerals, as well as the flora, fauna, the inherently indivisible environment and the ecosystem.

Depending on the policy pursued by one or the other state *vis-à-vis* its geographically contiguous neighbour(s), the international interactions generated by such transboundary human and natural resources may be one of conflict and war, or of cooperation and peace. While the conflictual has been the dominant perspective, the cooperation option has always remained conceptually open and feasible.

In Europe since the end of the Second World War, the policy emphasis has significantly shifted from a disposition to war to an ever-increasing commitment to the exploration and systematic utilisation of the peaceful and cooperative potentials of international boundaries and shared borderlands. Beginning as uncoordinated informal local initiatives based on the spontaneous reactions of transborder peoples and vivisected ethnic groups across several of the international boundaries in Western Europe, the Organisation of European Regions or 'Euregios' (regions that although traversed by international borders nevertheless constitute a unit)[1] has evolved from the status of powerlessness to that of a well coordinated 'power house of European integration'.[2] From their original positions as informal, if not parallel or illegal organisations, Euregios now operate everywhere in the region as formal institutions recognised by both domestic and international laws. They have also become effectively coordinated at both regional and sub-regional levels.

So successful has been the practice of transborder cooperation and so manifest is its contribution to the spectacular achievement of European integration, that it has attracted policy makers outside the primary diffusion centre in Western Europe. As well as becoming the standard practice in Northern Europe – notably in the Scandinavian countries – the post-1945 development in Western Europe has been adopted as the model in Central and Eastern Europe since the demolition of the Berlin Wall and the collapse of socialist regimes. It is also being actively canvassed and replicated outside Europe – notably in North and Latin America, as well as in Asia.[3] The centenary of the Anglo-French partition of Borgu, one of the several prospective African Regions or 'Afregios' created in consequence of the European partition and the subsequent emergence of dependent African states, provides the opportunity for a renewed reflection on the whole range of African potentials, begging for policy exploration and application.[4]

The European Model

In Europe, transfrontier regionalism is known to have started and developed as a companion movement to the evolution of European integration. Indeed, the aim of transfrontier regionalism is the achievement of transfrontier micro-integration that would dovetail into the European macro-integration. Originally promoted by the Council of Europe (founded in 1949, and still the prime mover), transfrontier regionalism was exceptionally boosted in the 1980s by the adoption of a regional approach to planning and development by the better-resourced European Economic Community, now the European Union, and the systematic promotion of the concept of a new *Europe of the regions* in contradistinction to that of the old Europe of the nation states. In the rather instructive words of Giuseppe Vedovato, an Italian expert,

> The starting point for the development of transfrontier regions can be situated in the immediate aftermath of the Second World War, when the insurmountable political and ideological barriers that had descended on Europe, and the serious problems of reconstruction made it necessary to look to new openings and new territorial co-operation 'models'. It was a time that saw the almost spontaneous establishment of contact between local communities that were to render frontiers more 'permeable' and give rise to a variety of different organisational forms.[5]

By 1986, when the European Single Act was initiated to anticipate the primacy of regions as choice units for planning and development in the European Com-munity, Euregios and associated transfrontier cooperative initiatives had become permanent features of life in member states of the Council of Europe and the European Economic Community. The European Charter on Frontiers and Transfrontier Regions, adopted by the Association of European Border Regions (AEBR) with headquarters in Bonn, contains a list of 46 such regions and associations located all over Western and Northern Europe, but concentrated on the Rhine (known as the Waal in the Netherlands), Europe's main river of unity, which serves as the international boundary between Germany and France and between Germany and the Netherlands.[6]

Among typical examples of organised Euregios are the Regio Basiliensi created definitively in 1963 around the Swiss-French-German trinational conurbation of Basel as the nucleus of a larger transfrontier region that embraced the Swiss Jura, the German Black Forest and the French Vosges, a region of about 2 million inhabitants, who commonly speak a local German dialect. Then there is the Rhine–Waal Euregio, launched in 1970 to promote German-Dutch cooperation in the area along and across the binational boundary. The Arge Alp, the Alpe Adria and the Cotrao – regional organisations of the Central, Eastern and Western Alpine regions respectively – connect Italy with Alpine neighbouring countries, including former Yugoslavia in the case of the Alpe Adria in the heyday of the iron curtain. In Northern Europe, where the Scandinavian countries (Denmark, Finland, Norway and Sweden) have developed a series of bilateral and multilateral agreements to curb activities that could lead to the pollution of the air, soil, fresh water and the sea, the regions that are most advanced in the promotion of transfrontier cooperation include the North Calotte Area, the West Nordic Region Archipelago, ARKO, Østfold-Bohuslän/Dalsland, Orsund Canal and the Bornhoim/Southeastern Skane.

The organisations of the individual transfrontier regions draw considerable strength from their multi-sectoral nature, each combining social, economic, environmental and other interests and thus involving a large number of stake-holders. Also advantageous is their disposition to form bigger and stronger regional formations such as the Committee for the Promotion of the Alpine Region with headquarters in Turin, (Italy) and the Conference of the Upper Rhine Valley Planners. Other transfrontier cooperation models which emphasise specialised functions include the Euregios of the Cities, such as the one involving several municipalities in the Meuse–Rhine Euregio; the Euregio of the Chambers of Commerce; the Cooperation Agreement between Vice-Chancellors of the Universities of Liège (France), Maastricht (Netherlands) and Aix-la-Chapelle (Germany), and the more imaginative international Scheidt Faculty linking higher education and applied research in Zeeland and Flanders.

Over the years, especially since the late 1970s, transfrontier regionalism in Europe has gained tremendously in lobbying power and political influence. This significant growth has been achieved by the capacity for self-empowerment exhibited by European borderlanders who exploited to the fullest the advantages of a wider political environment, characterised by the post-1945 embrace of democracy and commitment to respecting fundamental human rights. This capacity was exhibited in the building of certain strategic institutions which won recognition and support for transfrontier regionalism at national and, more especially, international levels in Europe. First came the establishment in the early 1980s of the AEBR, which has since functioned as the common front at continental level. Next was the creation of the Liaison Office of the European Regional Organisations, anchored on the AEBR as its core and strategically located in Strasbourg, seat also of the Council of Europe and the European Parliament, both of which obviously constitute the target European institutions.

Part of a wider array of evidence of the tremendous influence which transfrontier regionalism came to wield on the European institutions in Strasbourg are (1) the adoption, not only of the European Outline Convention on Transfrontier Cooperation between Territorial Authorities and Communities, but also of the Additional Protocols to the Outline Convention by the Council of Europe in 1980 and 1993 respectively; (2) the creation within the Council's secretariat of a specialised Office for Local and Regional Authorities in 1984; and (3) the institutionalisation of the Conference of Ministers Responsible for Regional Planning.

With regard to the European Economic Community and the European Commission in Brussels, proof of an equally effective penetration by transfrontier regionalism is provided by the coming into effect of the Single European Act and the enthronement therein of regions as the primary planning and development units in Community Europe. Border regions, which constitute the heart and the bulk of the so-called 'transregional' category (regions in different states especially those on both sides of borders between members states) recognised in the Act, have been the main beneficiaries of the European Region Development Fund created by the European Commission and disbursed under the so-called INTERREG Programme.

With the widespread collapse of socialist regimes in the early 1990s and the subsequent establishment of democratic, political and economic pluralism in Central and Eastern Europe, events that have raised the unabating prospects for the ultimate admission of former socialist Europe into the European Union, transfrontier regionalism has spread its influence into Central and Eastern Europe.[7] Many and varied proofs point to a wide range of illustrative projects as between the former socialist economies themselves. In the first subcategory is the Euregio Egrensis, consisting of local authorities of the Czech Republic and the German *länder* of Eastern Upper Franconia, the Northern Upper Palatinate and the Saxon Vogtland. A similar observation holds for the Pomeranian Euregio, astride the Oder–Neisse border between Poland and Germany. A more direct evidence of the link between the transborder cooperation initiative in Central and Eastern Europe and their Western European precedents is in Poland's ratification of the European Outline Convention on Transfrontier Cooperation between Territorial Authorities and Communities in 1993 and the frequent citation of its provisions as antecedents for Poland's several transborder cooperation agreements with neighbouring countries both in Western as well as in Eastern and Central Europe.

The other subcategory of actively organised transfrontier regions in Central and Eastern Europe, linking the former socialist states directly with each other, may be illustrated by the Carpathian Euregio project, initiated in 1992 and formally established in early 1993. The project covers approximately 118,000 square kilometres of land and about 12.5 million people, made up of the adjacent borderlands of Poland, Hungary, Slovakia and Ukraine, with Romania participating as an observer on account of her two proximate provinces in Northern Transylvania. It is assisted by the Institute for East–West Studies in Atlanta, with funding support from an American foundation and the Sasakawa Peace Foundation of Japan. The contributions from outside are made to a specially created Foundation for the Development of the Carpathian Euregio. As with the older transfrontier regional development projects in the West, the new transborder regional development initiatives in Eastern and Central Europe are also supported by the European Region Development Fund, especially under its so-called PHARE Programme.

African Comparability

Overview

The point may no longer bear repetition in detail because it has been made so frequently in several of the writer's published works that, contrary to popular belief, state territories and boundaries in post-colonial Africa are structurally and functionally not so different from those found elsewhere in the wider world of the nation states created in consequence of preceding centuries of imperialist expansion and colonial domination by erstwhile metropolitan powers, now core member states of the Council of Europe and the European Union.[8]

While not denying important difference in the details of history and geography, significant similarities have been identified between Africa and Europe with special regard to local peoples' perception of the arbitrariness of the processes and overall artificiality of the partition effects. Comparative studies of the localised impact of the boundaries in Africa and Europe point more to similarities than differences. Traditional lamentations about Africa often ignore these crucial similarities and block clearer vision of the vital lessons which Africa can learn from the European historical experience.

It is generally lamented, for example, that Africa was badly partitioned: that African boundaries are artificial, often arbitrarily drawn with little or no regard for pre-existing socio-economic patterns and networks on the ground; that the boundaries have erratically split unified culture areas and mindlessly fragmented coherent natural planning regions and ecosystems; that a good many of Africa's contemporary economic problems have stemmed from the fact of territorial division into such a large number of competitive rather than complementary national economies; and, finally, that many of the continent's current political problems have their origins in the arbitrary nature of the colonial boundaries that (among other things) artificially juxtaposed incompatible or antagonistic groups.

However, none of these claims, pointing to Africa as unique, has been sustained by findings of focused comparisons with Europe. If anything, the comparative assessments, based on detailed case studies, have demonstrated a replication of the quintessence of the European experience in Africa. In Europe, as in Africa, neighbouring border regions represent areas of opposing official languages, national cultures and histories as well as differing economic systems, disharmonious legal regimes and parallel administrative traditions, all superimposed upon invariably distinct local indigenous cultures straddling inter-sovereignty boundaries.

Hence the extremely close similarities that have been found in respect of – on one hand – the Catalans, 'an ethnic group neither French nor Spanish' in the Cerdanya valley of the Eastern Pyrénées, split into two by the Franco–Spanish border,[9] and – on the other – the western Yoruba and the Hausa, ethnic groups that are neither French nor British, and each of which came to be split into the officially different worlds of the French and the British by the present-day Nigeria–Benin and Nigeria–Niger borders respectively.[10] Needless to further state that the Catalans in Europe and the Yoruba and Hausa in Africa are but a few of the more numerous vivisected ethnic groups or transborder peoples found across virtually all state frontiers in the two continents.

Partitioned Europe and partitioned Africa are, by more or less the same processes, continents of excessive multiplicity of state territories and state frontiers, Europe palpably more so than Africa. Quite apart from the obviously larger number of states, considering the relatively smaller territorial size of Europe vis-à-vis Africa, there is also the fact of greater instability of the nation-state territorial framework in Europe. This contrast shows best in the paradoxically limited effect that post-colonial Africa's widespread and ever deepening political crises have produced on state territories and boundaries in the continent, on one hand, and, on the other, the widespread and fundamental cartographic revisions that have taken place in Europe in consequence of contemporary European crises. It has been estimated, for example, that 'more than 60 per cent of [Europe's] present borders [were] drawn during the twentieth century' and that no less than '8,000 miles of new political lines' have been drawn to frame present-day Central and Eastern European countries as a result of the crises that have come over Europe in the aftermath of the collapse of socialist regimes in the late 1980s and early 1990s, with the resultant dissolution of certain existing states and the creation of new ones.[11]

In Europe, as in Africa impacted by Europe, state territories and boundaries have been found to share the characteristics of essentially arbitrary creation and locally perceived artificiality. From the modern state formation processes in the two continents, similar forms of territorial absurdity have resulted, as is evident in the ludicrous shapes and sizes of state territories and the comparable incidence of inherently dependent entities such as landlocked states and enclaves. There have also been similar experiences with artificially partitioned natural regions (seas, lakes, rivers, mountains, valleys, forests, deserts, and so on) and, more gravely, coherent ethnic groups and culture areas. The latter feature has proved to be extremely productive of ethnic or national minorities and the associated questions of irredentism and the horrific practice of 'ethnic cleansing'. Both in Europe and post-colonial Africa, state frontiers are notorious for their roles as irritants of disputes within and, more especially, between the states.

These and other similarities in the structures and problems of state territories and boundaries in Europe and Africa ought not to have been a surprise, since the boundaries in the one continent have remained more or less as created by imperialists from the other continent, who drew and managed them on the model of the borders in their own respective metropolitan countries. It has been argued in detail elsewhere that, in Europe as in Africa, the boundary-making processes as well as the structures and functions of the resultant state frontiers are more similar than dissimilar. The same observation goes for the types of legal instruments and political engineering that have the same pattern of diplomacy. The point then is that, given these essential similarities, lessons of experience in the one continent cannot and must not be lost on the other.

Transfrontier regionalist pressure in Africa

There are in Africa similar kinds of pressures of local history and geopolitics for transborder cooperation and wider regional integration as are known to have operated in Europe since the Second World War and up to the present. With regard to transborder cooperation, the focus of this presentation, it is pertinent to draw attention to the widespread presence of vibrant transfrontier regions awaiting appropriate policy adjustments to mature them into formidable transfrontier regional organisations, capable in turn of galvanising the various fledgeling subcontinental organisations and transforming these into the African regional organisation envisioned in the African Economic Community Treaty adopted in 1991 on the model of the European Economic Community Treaty of 1957.

Much as in Europe, the prospects for transfrontier regionalism in Africa appear irresistibly driven by four interlocking forces: the local populations; border economies; natural resources and the environment; and the widely recognised necessity to ground African regional/subregional integration projects on the realities of local African history and culture. In fact, as we have argued elsewhere (Asiwaju, 1992), the continuous operation of these factors has led to various micro-integration formations across Africa's international boundaries, each begging to be formalised and thereafter used as a cornerstone of the wider regional integration projects being pursued by states in the various subregions of the continent.

The first and most fundamental of the four forces compelling transfrontier regionalism in Africa is the commanding presence everywhere of vivisected or partitioned ethnic groups and culture areas. The continent-wide operation of this exceptionally vibrant factor has ensured a systematic and sustained contradiction and obliteration of the normal separation or barrier functions and effects of the inter-sovereignty boundaries. This effacing impact of Africa's 'transborder peoples' is produced by the operation across the borders of the stronger networks of cultural, socio-economic and even political interactions between borderlanders astride specific segments of every border. They speak identical indigenous languages and share related cultural identities – such as the traditional region, memories of common ancestral origin, and identical socio-economic and political institutions – as well as, in many instances, very close kinship ties.

In situations such as those of the Shona across the Manica sector of the Zimbabwe–Mozambique border, the Ketu-Yoruba astride the Nigeria–Benin border or, as we will shortly see, the Baatonu of the Nikki Kingdom of Borgu, who likewise straddle the Nigeria–Benin border, memories of common allegiance to the same pre-colonial state are often retained to strengthen the feeling of solidarity that binds territorial communities on both sides of African boundaries. The significance of this ethnic dimension of transfrontier solidarity in Africa is underscored by a ubiquity which has been solidly documented in the writer's book, *Partitioned Africans: Ethnic Relations across Africa's International Boundaries, 1884–1984.*

The second interrelated factor forging transfrontier regional coherence is *cross-border trade*. It is a good measure of the significance of this factor that after decades of being ignored, it has become a focus of attention by researchers and consultants working mostly for international development and donor agencies, including such high-profile ones as the World Bank, the United States Agency for International Development (USAID) and the Paris-based Club du Sahel of the Organisation for Economic Cooperation and Development (OECD). The widely circulated studies, reports and publications that have resulted from these endeavours leave nobody in any further doubt about the dominance of the mostly unofficial forms of inter-African business transaction *vis-à-vis* the recorded aspects. The continent-wide spread of the phenomenon is indicated by such publications as those by Janet MacGaffee *et al.*, focusing on former Zaïre as a typical Central African case; Chris Ackello-Ogutu and P. N. Echessah on Eastern Africa, funded by USAID; and Johnny Egg and John Igue in respect of the West African subregion, funded separately and severally by the French Ministry of Cooperation and the Club du Sahel of the OECD in Paris.[12]

Realisation of the magnitude of the cross-border trade flow and the truly regional character of the operational dynamics has led the authors of expert West African studies to appreciate and support the need for a radical reorientation of current approach to regional integration in favour of a new strategy which they have called market-driven integration.[13] The essence of this suggestion is that instead of continuing to pursue the model of traditional international organisations, regional integration in Africa should be rooted in the alternative realities of transnational interactions as so strongly manifested in cross-border trade.

ECOWAS, therefore, has been conceptually reorganised into three separate sub-groupings or ecumenes based on the degree of intensity of the economic interactions across the borders of the states so grouped. The suggested restructuring of the West African subcontinent has thus resulted in the identification of three overlapping units:[14] West, embracing the wider Senegambia region comprising The Gambia, Senegal, Mauritania, Mali, Guinea, Guinea-Bissau and Cape Verde; Centre–West, made up of Côte d'Ivoire, Ghana, Burkina Faso, Liberia and Sierra Leone; and East–West, consisting of Nigeria and the neighbouring states of Benin, Togo and Niger. A similar suggestion is possible for the identification of Tanzania and her neighbours; the Republic of South Africa and the territorially adjacent countries; and the Democratic Republic of Congo (former Zaïre) and its immediate neighbours.

The third factor in cross-border pull in Africa is the irresistible force imposed by the wide array of transborder natural resources, including natural habitats and ecosystems. The importance of this crucial factor is especially emphasised, not only by the high incidence in the use that has been made of *rivers* (such as the Zambezi, the Limpopo and the Mano), *lakes* (such as the Chad, Victoria and Malawi) and *mountains,* (such as Cameroon, Adamawa and Kilimanjaro) as boundaries but also commonplace characteristics of such transnational rivers as the Nile, the Niger, the Senegal and the Orange as Africa's rivers of unity.

Potential as strong stimulants of transborder cooperation in planning, development and joint management has also been demonstrated, paradoxically, by transboundary strategic resources better known for the roles they have actually played as irritants of international conflicts: the off-shore hydrocarbon deposits in the Gulf of Guinea that have provoked a prolonged border dispute and recently triggered off armed conflict and aggressive litigation between Nigeria and Cameroon; the earlier Libya–Chad and Mali–Burkina Faso border conflicts and international litigation over shared boundary stretches suspected to be rich in solid minerals (the Aouzur strip in the one case and the Agacher corridor in the other). Cross-border floral and fauna, critical to the all-important tourist industries of most Eastern and Southern African countries, can also boost transfrontier regional solidarity, even though they have proved they can be factors of conflict in equal measure.

The fourth and final indication of prospects for transfrontier regionalism in Africa is the evidence of an ever-increasing number of advocacies. To arguments about a reorientation of regional integration projects on the more solid foundations of local African cultures, inspired by known affinities of history and traditions of the people,[15] has been added the advocacy for a market-driven perspective, informed by scientific data collection and analysis regarding transborder business transactions and their wider regional dynamic and networks. Add these arguments to the spontaneous popular support for and grassroots participation in the transborder cooperation policy consultative meetings that had been held in 1988–92 between Nigeria and her neighbours[16] and in Zimbabwe in 1995 and 1996 in the context of an ongoing research project on the development of border regions in Eastern and Southern Africa, initiated by the Nairobi-based United Nations Centre for Regional Development (UNCRD) Africa Office.[17] One final factor that has stimulated an ever-increasing awareness of the imperative for transborder cooperation is the deepening African crisis that, as in the Great Lakes Region, the Horn, West Africa (notably Sierra Leone, Liberia and Guinea-Bissau) and Angola has produced such dramatic effects as spectacular refugee movements and cross-border spillovers of armed rebellions in adjacent states.

There are reliable indicators of the existence in most African border locations, of potential regional group(s) made up of local political figures, experts in economic and social affairs and scientists to devise most appropriate scenarios – groups like those that have played critical roles in European transfrontier regionalist organisations. There are chances for the African regional groups to transform into transborder cooperation pressure groups, if the current tempo for democratisation in Africa is maintained. We shall return to this point in the final sections of this chapter.

The Borgu Case Study

Borgu exemplifies Africa's potential transfrontier regions, characterised by a vibrant indigenous transborder population of identical ethnic and linguistic compositions and alignments. Borgu is especially distinguished by the extraordinary feeling of allegiance on the part of the admittedly diverse constituent communities, who are known throughout their remembered history to jealously guard and collectively defend their territorial integrity. Situated on the right bank of the River Niger and enclosed by the ninth and twelfth parallels of latitude and the first and fourth meridians of east longitude,[18] historic Borgu has been estimated to cover a territory of approximately 70,000 square kilometres and about 2 million inhabitants.[19] As will be made clear presently, the hallmark of history is the unity in the diversity of ethnicity, culture and polities.

Since the Anglo-French partition of 1898 and the installation of two adjacent colonial regimes, which lasted until August and October 1960 in the French and British parts, respectively, Borgu has consisted of the two distinct parts. The communities to the west of the border, incorporated into the former French colony of Dahomey (present-day Republic of Benin), embraces such principal settlements as Nikki, Parakou, Djougou, Kouade, Kandi and Bembereke. In the east, the Nigerian Borgu, formerly administered as part of the British Protectorate of Northern Nigeria, comprises settlements and chiefdoms such as Bussa, Illo, Kaoje, Kenji, Agawara, Rofia and Aliyara (Babana) and Wawa in the north, and, in the south, Kaima, Kanu, Okuta, Ilesha, Gwanara and Yashekera.

To date, Borgu has remained divided into the two main official blocs of francophone (Benin) and anglophone (Nigeria). Each of the different parts of this historic land has been further 'scattered' by reason of the vicissitudes of the territorial arrangements effected on each side during both the colonial and post-colonial eras. On the Nigerian side of the border,[20] for example, the pre-colonial sensitivity about the overall integrity of Borgu was completely ignored, first, by a restructuring into two aggressively competing emirates of Kaima in the south and Bussa in the north. Then there were the series of territorial excisions and restorations especially in northern Borgu. Thus, in 1905, Illo, Kaoje, Lefaru and Gendenni in the north-east were merged with Gwandu Emirate to compensate Sokoto Caliphate for parts of its territory which the British had conceded to the French. Although Agawara and Rofia were eventually restored to Borgu, Illo, Kaoje and Kenji remained in the Gwandu Emirate, now part of the Benin Kebbi State created in 1991. In the colonial period, Borgu's distinctiveness was further disturbed by attachments at different times to such other larger provinces as Yauri, Kontagora and, finally, Ilorin. Nigerian Borgu ended up being organised into four or so distinct local government areas, 'scattered' across the boundaries of three adjacent states of Kwara, Niger and Birnin Kebbi.

A similar experience of internal territorial dismemberment has been recorded for the French portion of Borgu. Apart from a characteristic division into smaller territorial units, explicitly for administrative convenience, and not out of regard for any historical antecedents, there is the mindless merging of the Barba – the people of Borgu – with non-Barba in such new administrative units as Gourma and Middle Niger, two of the four *cercles* into which the French initially organised their portion of Borgu. The other two, predominantly Barba in population, were the *cercles* of Borgu and Djougou-Kouande. Eventually, French Borgu was organised into two main *cercles* – Parakou, comprising the subdivisions of Kandi, Malaville (predominately Dendi in population) and Kouande. The location of the headquarters of the Kandi *cercle* in Nattingou in Somba country, outside historic Borgu, was as culturally irritating to the Barba in the French sphere as the merger of Illo with Gwandu has been to their kinsmen in Nigerian Borgu. Today, the Beninese portion of historic Borgu is embraced in the départements (equivalents of states in Nigeria) of Borgu and Atacora and their constituent *sous-préfectures* (equivalents of local governments in Nigeria).

These colonial and post-colonial territorial arrangements and the accompanying administrative practices were viewed as unacceptable by the vast majority of the Borgawa, the collective reference to the peoples of Borgu by their Hausa neighbours, who came to see the developments as unpardonable effrontery, insulting to their age-old perception of both the larger culture area and the specific state territories within it as sacred and inviolable. This point is extremely vital to a proper understanding of the systematic and sustained reactions against the European imperialist partition and colonial rule, reactions that were continued, even if subtly, into the post-colonial era. Since the details of history are so well known, it will suffice simply to emphasise that the most central theme in the history and culture of Borgu is unity in diversity of ethnicity, language, religion, politics and economy. This unique quality has not only permitted the people's own perception of themselves as Barba, but also justified the objective identification of Borgu as a definable culture area.

It is remarkable that, in spite of the internal differentiation into several distinct ethnic and linguistic groups and subgroups of which the most dominant are the Baatonu and the Boko (the majority and the ruling élite respectively), the Borgawa view themselves as 'one people' and relate to Borgu as 'our country', an indivisible common patrimony in spite of traditional organisation into numerous, often competing kingdoms with three main power blocs centred on Bussa, Nikki and Illo. Anene's observation is especially instructive, for, in spite of the overall emphasis which his study places on fission rather than fusion of the culture areas through which the boundaries of Nigeria were drawn, he has to acknowledge even if reluctantly that 'Borgu was from its undefined "ancient" beginning a distinct political area, the integrity of which the Borgawa [Baatonu or Boko; Nikki or Illo] were determined to defend with their blood.'[21]

This extraordinary sense of collective allegiance to Borgu as the 'patrie' of all Borgawa was demonstrated throughout their known history. There was a patriotic response by all and sundry to the call of duty in defence of the entire land whenever the territorial integrity of Borgu was threatened either from within – in times, for example, when any of the constituent states singly or in combination engaged in actions capable of disturbing the delicate balance between all the groups – or more often from without, when powers outside Borgu threatened the safety and security of the corporate area. As Anene once again acknowledges, the Borgawa proudly claim that 'until the partition of their country by the Europeans they had never yielded to alien domination'.[22] The Borgawa were known to have collectively fought and successfully warded off the invasions of Songhai under the Askias in the sixteenth and seventeenth centuries, the Habe or Hausa states in the 18th century and the Fulani jihadists in the first half of the 19th century. It is probably the fact of these collective defence actions that leads Kenneth Lupton (1984) to categorise the political system of the Borgawa as one of a 'standing alliance'.

Apart from the collective claim of the Borgawa on Borgu as a common patrimony, there is other historical evidence that buttresses the argument for the identification of the area as a coherent region. One such indication, flowing from the issue of collective allegiance and the history of the culture area as 'a defended area', is the unmistakable evidence of the clarity of people's notions of territory and boundary. However, as elsewhere in pre-colonial Africa and as is still manifest in most indigenous African societies, the concept of boundaries understood among the Borgawa is not compatible with the inflexible lines of territorial demarcation that nation-state Europeans later came to establish to separate respective areas of territorial jurisdiction. Whether between states within Borgu or between Borgu and adjacent lands such as those of the Yoruba (Oyo and Sabe) to the south and south-east, the Nupe and the Somba to the east and the Hausa to the north, the notion of boundary entertained by the Borgawa was significantly one of mutual inclusion, not exclusion.

Indeed, as Obare Bagodo has explained, boundaries as expressed in Baatonu (the language of the largest single ethnic group in Borgu) are references to 'zones of contact and convergence of interests', points of meeting and interaction rather than those of separation, *tem yina yeru* rather than *tem bonu yeru*.[23] Politically, for example, Borgu has been variously described as some sort of 'confederation' or, as we have already noted, 'a standing alliance'. While each of the constituent states maintained its own autonomy – Bussa, Nikki, Illo, Wawa and Kaima, the actual number varying in accordance with the changing fortunes of the various power centres – they were interconnected by several factors: common foundations on identical strata of aboriginal culture; derivation of the ruling dynasties from the same culture hero, Kisra; exchange of gifts among the rulers, especially at the ascension of each; participation in one another's traditional festivals, such as the *gani;* and the use of identical ritual and ceremonial instruments such as the *kakaki* or trumpets.

The emphasis on boundaries as points of contact and mutual interaction is found to have been even more widely applied to the overall benefit of the evolution of Borgu as a significantly integrated region and one with a disposition to form alliances with tested states and societies outside Borgu. The notion of boundary culturally entertained by the Borgawa is also known to have consolidated the tradition of a symbiotic relationship between the distinct ethnic and linguistic groups and subgroups such as those of the Baatonu and the Boko, and advanced the process of a continuous fusion of the otherwise distinct cultures and sub-cultures. While the preservation of the integrity of Borgu remained the constant concern of all Borgawa, military alliances such as the one which the kingdoms of Borgu were known to have forged with the ancient Yoruba state of Oyo to check the advance of the Fulani *jihad* pointed to the extent to which the Borgawa were prepared to permit the permeability of the external boundary of their collective homeland if such a concession would enhance the safety and security of the patrimony. Although the Eleduwe War of 1835, collectively fought by the Borgawa and the Yoruba against the Fulani, brought defeat rather than victory to the allies and was particularly disastrous for the Borgawa states of Nikki and Wawa, whose rulers and other valiant soldiers perished at the battle, the corporate existence of Borgu was preserved.

The flurry of activities, especially the mass movements of supporters of contesting princes from the Nigerian side (notably Yashekera and Aliyara) to Nikki that took place as a result of the successive succession struggles in the colonial era,[24] were constant reminders that the local people have not quite accepted the fact of the Anglo-French partition, including the separation roles and functions of the inter-state frontier negotiated by the European authorities. Other factors blurring the separation functions and effects of the boundary included the series of protest migrations that took place from time to time when there were police or administrative problems on either side of the border; cross-border trade with special reference to smuggling; and the essentially indeterminate character of the border, arising from its controversial delimitation and the totally unsatisfactory demarcation of the segment of the Nigeria–Benin border in the Borgu.[25] The last factor has led to a situation where farmers from either side cleared the lands with little or no regard for the position of the boundary.

Comparable to Borgu are such adjacent transborder culture areas as 'Hausaland Divided'[26] between anglophone Nigeria and francophone Niger, to the immediate North and, to the immediate South, Western Yorubaland. The similarity has been instructively illustrated by case studies of the Ketu and Sabe subgroups who, like the Borgawa, have straddled the Nigeria–Benin border.[27] The existence of other African examples has been solidly documented by the writer's regional survey study, published as *Partitioned Africans*.

Policy Reflections

If, then, as we have tried to show, there are in post-colonial Africa as many potentials and even pressures for transfrontier regionalism as in post-war Europe, why has the actualisation in Africa lagged so much behind the events and developments in Europe? What are the obstacles in Africa, and what hopes for the future?

These questions, like the preceding argument itself, are not new. However, the centenary of the Anglo-French partition of Borgu, an act that completed the admittedly problematic delimitation of the present-day Nigeria–Benin border, provides a golden opportunity for a renewed discussion and necessary update on transborder cooperation policy promotion as a cornerstone of regional integration endeavours in Africa. Finding satisfactory answers to these essential policy questions must engage attention, in view of their obvious relevance to the realisation of a future widely viewed as lying not in an Africa of the nation state, but in a continent of regions and peoples on the model of the European Union.

With regard to the obstacles, the often-made point must bear repetition that the most crucial of these, and the ones that must be specially targeted, are the entrenchment of the nation-state structure and the failure to embrace the principles and practice of democratic governance. The first task is to loosen the grip of the nation-state structure and its interrelated negative features, such as unbridled assertions of territorial sovereignty and what has been called 'state nationalism'. The absorption of these features by the Western-educated élites who provided the leadership at all levels for the new sovereign states in post-colonial Africa has magnified this task, which needs to be addressed as much at the core as in the border areas of the new states.

In the particular case of the new élites in the border areas, who must now be converted into active membership of regional groups, assimilation into contrasting European cultures has given rise to a mindset that in turn has produced the familiar back-to-back, rather than the more desirable face-to-face, relationships across the borders. The effect has been especially dramatic in the several cases in Africa where the élites on the different sides are also products of the same indigenous culture.[28] While their non-literate parents and relations on both sides of the borders have persisted in the maintenance of cherished kinship and other socio-cultural ties, or the exploitation of the business advantages of the border locations, educated élites among 'partitioned Africans' seldom develop relationships across the borders as they do with their peers inside the nation state, even when, as is often the case, such peers belong to other indigenous cultures.

There is a very interesting irony in the history of post-colonial Africa vis-à-vis the history of contemporary Europe: that it was precisely at the time when Europeans – in the immediate aftermath of the last and most tragic of the wars brought about by the state nationalisms of the preceding three centuries – embarked on a systematic conversion from a nationalist to a regionalist ideology that the state nations of Africa reared their ugly heads. Thus, while in Europe the upward swing since 1945 has been towards the achievement of a trans- and supra-national 'integration' and the 'defunctionalising', 'devaluating' and 'overcoming' of 'national boundaries', in Africa and the wider world of former European colonies, the boundaries 'traced by (erstwhile) European colonial powers' became 'utterly sacred and one of the main political concerns is to demarcate, sharpen, strengthen and harden them'.[29]

In Europe, finally, while one frequently hears and reads about popular criticisms of the nation state as an 'obsolete' mode of societal organisation, of the need to 'efface [this mode] toward higher levels (European Union) and lower levels (local regional communities) … and of borderlands communities as miniature exemplars of new, United Europe',[30] in Africa the contemporary state nations remain firmly grounded on the doctrine and practice of territorial sovereignty, and regional integration projects are pursued on the model of classical international organisations. In Africa, international boundaries and borderlands are held and treated more as points of discontinuity than continuity, and as barriers rather than bridges between the state nations, or cornerstones for wider regional integration. In Community Europe, the emphasis is on decentralisation of territorial administration and decision-making process; in post-colonial Africa, the trend is ever increasing centralisation of control.

The ruling élites of post-colonial Africa are prepared to continue to draw their inspirations from a pre-war Europe that contemporary Europeans themselves are determined to forget. But, lamentably, they seem to turn their backs on their own ancestral pasts characterised, as Basil Davidson has aptly pointed out and as we have amply demonstrated in the Borgu case study, by 'a genius ... for integration ... by conquest ... [and] also by an ever-fruitful mingling and migration' and an inherent impatience with exclusive boundaries.[31]

The sharp contrast in the two histories, Africa and Europe since 1945, goes beyond the question of the ideology of nationalism on one hand and regionalism on the other. While post-war Europe represents a conversion not only from nationalist into regionalist political ideology but also from militarism and totalitarianism into full-fledged democracy and total commitment to the defence and preservation of human rights and fundamental freedoms, contemporary Africa saw a progressive degeneration into an era of undemocratic governance, the popularisation of repressive authoritarian regimes, unbridled human rights abuses, massive official corruption, a total lack of transparency and accountability of the leadership in most of the states, and ever-increasing and worsening political crises that have turned Africa into a continent that is ahead of all others in the number of civil and inter-state wars fought since the end of the Second World War.

The difference between Africa and Europe must be viewed as the gauge for measuring the gap that has to be bridged if development in today's Africa of the state nation is to be redirected to achieve a future Africa of the regions and the peoples on the model of the European Union. This has to be firmly grounded on the active and systematic practice of transfrontier regionalism and nourished by a region-wide embrace of the principles and practice of democratic governance, administrative decentralisation and accountability, plus a total commitment to the respect for human rights and fundamental freedoms. It was, no doubt, the deep resentments which post-war Europeans came to nurse against state nationalism, militarism and authoritarianism, and their warm embrace of democracy, transparency, accountability and respect for fundamental human rights and freedoms that gave border communities, hitherto thoroughly suppressed and downtrodden in nation-state Europe, the chance to organise themselves into the ever-thriving transfrontier territorial communities and authorities that have become the cornerstones for the realisation of Community Europe. Similar socio-political conditions must be created and nourished if Africa is to become like the Europe that has long replaced the older entity that created its colonial and neocolonial states.

While not doubting 'that the European experience in the field of overcoming state nationalism and alleviating the problems of border peoples can be some inspiration elsewhere', notably in Africa, Raimondo Strassoldo, whose works on Europe have been so complementary to the writer's on Africa, has expressed the hope that 'transnational unions in other continents will be grounded on other bases than the immense heaps of rubble and corpses we had in Europe'.[32] He has also expressed the wish 'that European horrors would not be replicated' elsewhere.[33] The facts in Africa have not matched Strassoldo's hopes and wishes. The details have not been and cannot be the same in Africa as in Europe; but the horrors generated by malfunctions of Africa's post-colonial states have not been less terrifying than those of pre-1945 Europe. Records of Africa's ever-worsening socio-political crises point to an African equivalent of the 'heaps of rubble and corpses' of European history. Witness, for example, the genocides, mass killings and mass graves as well as the wanton destruction of property and infrastructure that have accompanied the several cases of armed conflict in Congo (Kinshasa), Nigeria, Angola, Mozambique, Zimbabwe, South Africa, Namibia, Uganda, Rwanda, Burundi, Congo (Brazzaville), Somalia, Sudan, Liberia, Sierra Leone, Algeria, Morocco, Somalia, Cameroon, Ethiopia and Eritrea. To the man-made crises must be added the several instances of acts of God, notably the droughts and famines in the entire Sahelian zone, from Senegal in the west to Djibouti in the east, in the mid-1970s and mid-1980s.

Yet, in all their variety, what the African crises demonstrate is the inherent ineffectiveness of the individual state acting in isolation, and the imperative of transborder cooperation and regional integration as more valuable strategies for the resolution of crisis. Consider manifestations such as the massive movements of refugees across boundaries of many a troubled state nation on the continent, or the high incidence of cross-border spillover of armed revolt, including the many instances of secessionist wars. It is quite instructive, for example, that one of the great thoughts that the crises in the Great Lakes Region have provoked is the innovative suggestion to turn the area into a platform for a new subregional organisation. If and when this happens, the initiative can draw its main inspiration from such existing establishments as the Inter-State Commission for the Campaign against Drought in the Sahel and IGAD, based in Ouagadougou and Djibouti respectively, and both created in response to the environmental disaster sequel to the Sahelian droughts and famines of the 1970s and 1980s.

There is no doubt that in Africa we still have a long way to go, judging from the gaps that must be bridged in order to attain Europe's level of regional development. But the future is predictably one of a steady gravitation towards an ever-increasing appreciation of institutionalised transfrontier cooperation as an indispensable cornerstone for the realisation of durable regional integration projects. Although the relevant developments in the various subregions are still largely owing to state initiatives, their obvious alignment with realities of cross-border socio-economic interactions and networks are likely to result in ultimate inter-connections and interdigitations, leading to genuinely empowered and popular cross-border regional organisations that are capable of providing the needed support for wider regional integration projects.

In the Mahgreb, the relevant developments relate to the emphasis placed on co- or joint development of shared border regions in such bilateral instruments as the Algeria–Tunisia Friendship Treaty of 19 March 1988 and the Morocco–Algeria Agreements of 29 May 1991. Of similar significance was the Libya–Tunisia Agreement of 1988 which ended the dispute over the continental shelf in and around the Mediterranean Gulf of Gabes and established, instead, a joint venture for the cooperative development and exploitation of the transborder hydrocarbon resources. In the Mahgreb, these cross-border cooperative policy initiatives provide a secure foundation for a larger regional integration architecture with wider subregional networks of infrastructure and services such as the large-scale distribution of Libyan and Algerian petroleum products and gas to Tunisia and Morocco, and through them to Southern Europe and beyond.

In the adjoining areas of the ECOWAS and ECCAS, the prospects for transfrontier regionalism would also appear to have been significantly boosted by policy initiatives and actual developments, including:

- Nigeria's high-profile transborder cooperation policy promotion which, in 1988–92, involved a series of highly successful bilateral consultative workshops with Benin in Topo, Badagry, in May 1988; with Niger in Kano in July 1989; with Cameroon in Yola in July 1992, and with Equatorial Guinea in Calabar in November 1992;
- the creation of such imaginative bilateral and multilateral institutions as the Nigeria–Niger Joint Commission for Cooperation and the Lake Chad Basin Commission with impressive permanent secretariats in Niamey and N'Djamena respectively; and more recently, the Gulf of Guinea Commission;
- the provision in Chapter 58 of the 1993 ECOWAS Revised Treaty for the creation of 'national border authorities' on the model of Nigeria's National Boundary Commission (1987), to ensure peaceful settlement of conflicts, promote cross-border cooperation, and stimulate a special development focus on habitually neglected border regions both within and between member states;
- the adoption of a strategy, as articulated in ECOWAS's subregional Industrial Cooperation Policy of 1983, to open up economic pathways within the Community itself, leading in 1994 to a study for the establishment of inter-state industrial zones across certain designated transborder subregions linking land-locked with coastal member states;
- the exceptional performance of the Liptako–Gouma Integrated Development Authority (headquarters in Ouagadougou, Burkina Faso), created in 1970 to reverse the double marginalisation or peripheralisation of the adjoining border regions of the landlocked states of Burkina Faso, Mali and Niger; and,
- the market-driven approach to West African integration, suggested by the

findings of a research programme on cross-border trade funded by the OECD's Club du Sahel in Paris.

Finally, there is the ongoing research project on the development of border regions in Eastern and Southern Africa, initiated in 1992 by the United Nations Centre for Regional Development's Africa Office in Nairobi, Kenya. This laudable project has featured two highly successful international workshops: one in Kariba, Zimbabwe, on the border with Zambia in August 1995; and the other in Mutare, also in Zimbabwe, on the border with Mozambique. Among the credits which this project can claim are cross-border cooperative or linkage initiatives, including the launching in 1996 of a progressive local periodical, *Bridging the Borders: Kariba–Siavonga Newsletter*, published twice yearly and very well received on both sides of the Zimbabwe–Zambia border. On the same border sector a bilateral steering committee has been established to accelerate the process of interaction between the local élites and the authorities on both sides of the border.

One recent intervention that is bound to have some positive, even if unintended, effect on transfrontier regional integration in Southern Africa is the Spatial Development Initiatives (SDIs). Funded by Northern entrepreneurs sourced by the World Bank, the SDIs are concerned with the development and upgrading of infrastructure facilities, notably toll roads and railways linking several SADC countries, for the benefit of investments in ports, tourism, mining and major industrial projects. Three toll-road axes deserve particular mention: the Maputo corridor linking Maputo with Durban in South Africa along the coast and through Pretoria to Gaborone in Botswana and Windhoek and Walvis Bay in Namibia; the Nicagala corridor linking the ports of Nicagala and Beira on the Mozambican coast with Lilongwe in Malawi in the north and Harare in Zimbabwe in the south; and the Taraza corridor linking Dar-es-Salaam in Tanzania with Lusaka (Zambia), Lumumbashi (Democratic Republic of Congo), and Lobito and Benguela in Angola. The road networks apart, there is also the Kgalagadi Peace Park project twinning South Africa's Kalahari Gemsbok Park and Botswana's Gemsbok National Park into a single cross-border tourist authority. While the intentions were not to boost southern developments as such, there is a coincidence of interests that is bound ultimately to impact positively on concerns for subregional integration and transfrontier regional cooperation in the SADC.

Policy Conclusions and Recommendations

To sustain these admittedly modest developments and ensure their acceleration and spread, there is a need for a radical reorientation of the mindset of post-colonial Africa's so-called 'inheritance élite'. This calls for three interrelated recommendations:

• an urgent action plan on the part of policy makers in Africa;

- a rededication of support on the part of African and Africanist research communities in and outside Africa; and
- appropriate assistance from donor organisations and communities, especially friends of Africa in the European Union and the North American Free Trade Area (NAFTA).

In the search for helpful policy decisions, the African Union must be specially targeted. Having so wisely resolved (as the OAU) through its Charter of 1963 and the Cairo Declaration of 1964 to legitimise the inherited colonial boundaries in the interests of continental peace and stability, it must not permit itself to go too far into the 21st century without taking the long-overdue next logical step: that of ensuring the conversion of the inherited borders from barriers into bridges between the member states. In doing so, the organisation stands to profit from the experience of Europe, erstwhile coloniser of Africa, where border problems similar to those in post-colonial Africa have been and are still being tackled with noticeable success. Especially recommended is the adoption of instruments of a continent-wide application on the model of the European Outline Convention on Transfrontier Cooperation between Territorial Authorities and Communities, which took effect in 1984 and has since been ratified and adopted by an ever-increasing number of European states, including those like Poland in the recently decolonised subregions of Central and Eastern Europe. The AU, possibly through the African Development Bank (ADB), should create an African regional development fund similar to the European Region Development Fund and for purposes analogous to the INTERREG Programme in Community Europe.

Second, African and Africanist researchers must shift emphasis from the traditional statist and therefore predominantly conflictual perspective and refocus on projects that explore further the potential for peace and the cooperative and regional integration of African boundaries. African research institutions outside the continent, such as the imaginative, border-focused Program on International Co-operation in Africa (PICA) inaugurated at Northwestern University, Illinois, in 1989, must collaborate actively with parallel institutions within Africa such as the Centre for African Regional and Border Studies recently established at the University of Lagos under the distinguished chairmanship of Professor Adebayo Adedeji to focus permanently on the factor of boundaries in regional integration, particularly in Africa.

The third and final policy recommendation relates to the role expected of the wider international community, especially the European Union, which embraces the erstwhile imperial and colonial powers that partitioned Africa, including Borgu, at the turn of the last century. The Borgu centenary offered a rare opportunity for post-war Europe to be specially sensitised not only to the wrongs done and the debts owed to formerly colonised Africa, but also to the compelling moral duty to make necessary amends through appropriate programmes of assistance.

In this regard the following specific recommendations are offered:

- radical adjustment of the current IMF and World Bank practice of supporting only nationally based projects: this lending policy, which has tended to accord favourable attention to the nation-state territorial structure, must be blended with increased support for regional development initiatives;
- active support by developed countries, especially those of the European Union and NAFTA, for the repatriation of ill-gotten wealth invested by corrupt African leaders and government officials in their economies, especially the money markets and real estate sectors. This will boost transparency, a major component of democratic governance and a requirement for the realisation of transfrontier regionalism in Africa;
- the extension to Africa by the European Union, especially the European Commission, of the same kind of funding support which it has extended to Eastern and Central Europe *vis-à-vis* transfrontier regional programmes;
- the twinning of exemplary Euregios (for example, the Region Baschensi) with prospective African transfrontier regions such as Borgu.

With this last prospect in mind, this chapter concludes with a call to the governments and peoples of Britain, France and Germany[34] – European nation states whose nationals were responsible wholly or in part for the arbitrary partition of Borgu – to make contributions that would accelerate its evolution as an exemplary Afregio on the model of the Euregios that since the 1950s have been painstakingly nurtured across the borders of the erstwhile European metropolitan states, especially those of France and Germany, the emerging 'Framany' of the European Union.

Notes

Original research for this chapter was supported by a grant from IFRA–Ibadan (French Institute for Research in Africa, based at the University of Ibadan Institute of African Studies) in 1998 and a supplementary scholarship from the CIES, Paris, in 1999, also facilitated by IFRA–Ibadan. Earlier versions of the chapter have been presented and partially published in proceedings of seminars at IFRA–Ibadan, November 1998, the Centennial Colloquium on the Anglo-French Partition of Borgu, Parakou and Nikki, April 1999, and, most recently, the 19th Congress of the International Committee of the Historical Sciences, Oslo, Norway, August 2000. The author gratefully acknowledges research funding support as well as criticisms and suggestions for improvement.

1 Vedovato, 1995: 2. See also Council of Europe, 1995; Ricq, 1996.
2 Vedovato, 1995: 3.
3 For sample essays on North America and Latin America, see Liambi, 1989; Ganster, 1990; Hassan, 1983. For transfrontier regionalism in Asia, see Gooneratne and Mosselman, 1996: 148–9.

4 For the writer's previous work on the subject of African potentials for transfrontier regionalism, see Asiwaju, 1984; and Asiwaju, 1992.

5 Vedovato, 1995: 3. Older historical accounts are contained in von Malchus, 1975; Strassoldo, 1973; and Tagil, 1982.

6 AEBR, 1994.

7 Vedovato, 1995: 9–13.

8 See, in particular, Asiwaju, 1996a.

9 Sahlin, 1989.

10 Asiwaju, 1976; Miles, 1994.

11 Foucher, 1998: 235.

12 MacGaffee *et al.*, 1991; Ackello-Ogutu and Echessah, 1997; Egg and Igue, 1993.

13 Egg and Igue, 1993.

14 *Ibid.*

15 Asiwaju, 1985; Adotevi, 1997.

16 The bilateral series of consultative workshops between Nigeria and each of its neighbours has been documented in the published proceedings: Asiwaju and Barkindo, 1993; Asiwaju and Igue, 1994; Asiwaju, Barkindo and Mabale, 1996.

17 For the UNCRD initiative for Eastern and Southern Africa, see the special issue of *Regional Development Dialogue*, 17, 2 (1996), especially the subsection titled 'Regional Development beyond Borders', pp. 136–215; and Asiwaju and de Leeuw, 1998.

18 Anene, 1970: 194.

19 This estimate is owed, at least in part, to Bagodo, 1994: 63.

20 Relevant studies include Crowder, 1974; Stewart, 1984; and Lupton, 1984.

21 Anene, 1970: 198.

22 *Ibid.*

23 Bagodo, 1994: 67.

24 This kind of protest migration took place in 1907 when Woru Taru, the dethroned Sarkin Yashekera, migrated with virtually the entire population of Yashekera to Nikki, where he eventually succeeded to the throne as the Sina Boko in 1917. Similar migrations took place from Kenu, Ilesha and Aliyara (Babana) to protest against British colonial arrangements that forced chiefdoms formerly under Nikki to be subjected to new territorial authorities, especially that of Kaima.

25 To date, there are two conflicting definitions of delimitation instruments for this sector of the boundary: the Anglo-French agreement of 1906 and the modification reached in 1960 as a result of two preceding years of meetings of the Surveyors-General of Nigeria and Dahomey, authorised by the two central governments. The demarcation of this sector of the boundary, based on the 1960 description, was initially contested by Dahomey and has remained controversial (see MacEwen, 1991).

26 For a fascinating case study, see Miles, 1995.

27 For the Western Yoruba case studies, see Asiwaju, 1970; 1973; and 1976.

28 For a detailed case study, see A. I. Asiwaju, 1975: 227–47.

29 Strassoldo, 1989a: 392. For a more systematic comparison of Africa and Europe, see Asiwaju, 1996a.

30 Strasssoldo, 1989a: 392.

31 Basil Davidson, quoted by Anene, 1970: 2.

32 Strassoldo, 1989a: 392.

33 *Ibid.*

34 All three colonial powers showed interest in Borgu: Germany conceded the area to France as a result of the bilateral convention of 23 July 1897 whereby France, in return,

ceded Kirikiri, Bafilo and the so-called 'Mono triangle' to German Togo. The Anglo-French convention of 14 June 1898 settled the conflicting interest through a bilateral partition.

Bibliography

Ackello-Ogutu, C. and P. N. Echessah (1997) *Unrecorded Cross-Border Trade between Tanzania and Her Neighbours: Implications for Food Security*, Nairobi: USAID Regional Economic Development Support Office.

Adotevi, S. (1997) 'Cultural Dimension of Economic and Political Integration in Africa', in R. Laverge (ed.), *Regional Integration and Cooperation in West Africa*, Trenton, New Jersey: Africa World Press; and Ottawa: International Development Research Centre.

Akiwunmi, M. and M. Anderson (eds) (1982) *Frontier Regions in Western Europe* (special issue of *European Politics*, 5, 4).

Anderson, M. and E. Borts (eds.) (1998) *The Frontiers of Europe*, London: Frances Pinter.

Anene, J. C. (1970) *The International Boundaries of Nigeria: the Framework of an Emergent African Nation*, London: Longman.

Asiwaju, A. I. (1970) 'The Alaketu of Ketu and the Onimeko of Imeko: the Changing Status of Two Yoruba Rulers under French and British Colonialism', in M. Crowder and O. Ikime (eds.), *West African Chiefs: Their Changing Status under Colonialism and Independence*, Ile-Ife: University of Ife Press, pp. 134–60.

—— (1973) 'A Note on the History of Sabe: an Ancient Yoruba Kingdom in Dahomey', *Lagos Notes and Records*, 17–29.

—— (1975) 'Formal Education in Western Yorubaland, 1889–1960: a Comparison of the French and British Colonial Systems', *Comparative Education Review*, 19, 3: 434–50.

—— (1976) *Western Yorubaland under European Rule, 1889–1945: a Comparative Analysis of French and British Colonialism*, London: Longman.

—— (1984) *Artificial Boundaries*. Lagos: University of Lagos Press, Inaugural Lecture series.

—— (1985) *Partitioned Africans: Ethnic Relations across Africa's International Boundaries, 1884–1984*, London: C. Hurst and Co.; New York: St Martins Press.

—— (1992) 'Border and Borderlands as Linchpins for Regional Integration in Africa: Lessons of the European Experience', *Africa Development*, 17, 2: 345–63.

—— (1996a) 'Public Policy for Overcoming Marginalisation: Borderlands in Africa, North America and Western Europe' in Sam Nolutshungu (ed.), *Margins of Insecurity: Minorities and International Security*, New York: University of Rochester Press, pp. 251–84.

—— (1996b) 'Borderlands in Africa: a Comparative Research Perspective with Particular Reference to Western Europe', in Paul Nugent and A. I. Asiwaju (eds.), *African Boundaries: Barriers, Conduits and Opportunities*, London: Frances Pinter, pp. 253–65.

—— (2000) 'Fragmentation or Integration: What Future for African Boundaries?', in M. A. Pratt and J. A. Brown (eds.), *Borderlands under Stress*, London: Kluwer Law International, pp. 199–209. An earlier version was published as 'Territorial Disaggregation or Regional Integration: What Future for African Boundaries'? in *Interrregiones* (Institute for European Regional Research, Siegen, Germany) 7 (1998): 45–67.

Asiwaju, A. I. and P. O. Adeniyi (eds.) (1989) *Borderlands in Africa: a Multidisciplinary and Comparative Focus on Nigeria and West Africa*, Lagos: University of Lagos Press.

Asiwaju, A. I. and B. M. Barkindo (eds.) (1993) *The Nigeria–Niger Transborder Cooperation*, Proceedings of a Bilateral Workshop, Kano, July 1989, Lagos: Malthouse Press.

Asiwaju, A. I., B. M. Barkindo and R. E. Mabale (eds.) (1996) *The Nigeria–Equatorial Guinea Transborder Cooperation*, Proceedings of a Workshop Held in Calabar,

November 1992, Lagos: National Boundary Commission.

Asiwaju, A. I. and M. de Leeuw (eds.) (1998) *Border Regions Development in Africa: Focus on Eastern Southern Subregions,* Nagoya, Japan: UN Centre for Regional Development Research Publications Series.

Asiwaju, A. I. and O. J. Igue (eds.) (1994) *The Nigeria–Benin Transborder Cooperation,* Proceedings of a Bilateral Workshop, Togo, Badagry, May 1988, Lagos: University of Lagos Press.

Association of European Border Regions (AEBR) 1994 *European Charter on Frontier and Transborder Regions: Aims and Tasks of the Association of European Border Regions,* Bonn: AEBR.

Bagodo, A. I. (1994) 'Liens Ethniques et système de chefferie traditionelle comme élément de coopération transfrontalière: exemple des Bariba' in Asiwaju and Igue, 1994: 61–79.

Briner, H. J. (1986) 'Regional Planning and Transfrontier Cooperation: the Regio Basilliensi', in Martinez, 1986: 45–56.

Crowder, M. (1974) *Revolt in Bussa: a Study of British 'Native' Administration in Nigeria Borgu,* 1902–1934, London: Faber and Faber.

Council of Europe (1995) *Examples of Good Practice of Transfrontier Cooperation Concerning Members of Ethnic Groups Residing on the Territory of Several States,* Strasbourg: Transfrontier Cooperation in Europe Series, No. 5.

Egg, J. and J. Igue (1993) *Market-Driven Integration in the Eastern Subregions [of West Africa]: Nigeria's Impact on its Immediate Neighbours,* Paris: Club du Sahel.

Foucher, M. (1998) 'The Geopolitics of European Frontiers' in Anderson and Borts, 1998: 235–50.

Ganster, P. (1990) 'The Andean Border Integration: Report on a Seminar in Lima, Peru, 3–6 July 1989', *Journal of Borderlands Studies,* 5, 1: 95–110.

Gooneratne, W. and E. Mosselman (1996) 'Planning across the Border: Border Regions in Eastern and Southern Europe', *Regional Development Dialogue,* 17, 2: 136–55.

Hassan, N. (1983) 'European Transboundary Cooperation and its Relevance to the United States–Mexico Border', *Journal of the American Institute of Planners,* 49, 3: 336–43.

Liambi, L. (1989) 'The Venezuela–Colombia Borderlands: a Regional and Historical Perspective', *Journal of Borderlands Studies,* 4, 1: 1–38.

Laverge, R. (ed.) (1997) *Regional Integration and Cooperation in West Africa,* Trenton, New Jersey: Africa World Press.

Lupton, K. (1984) 'The Partitioning of Borgu in 1898 and the French Enclaves in Nigeria', *Journal of the Historical Society of Nigeria,* 12, 3–4 (1984–5): 77–94.

MacEwen, A. C. (1991) 'The Establishment of the Nigeria/Benin Boundary, 1889–1989', *Geographic Journal,* 157, 1: 62–70.

MacGaffee, J. *et al.* (1991) *The Real Economy of Zaïre: Contributions of Smuggling and Other Unofficial Activities to Wealth,* Philadelphia: University of Pennsylvania Press.

Martinez, O. J. (ed.) (1986) *Across Boundaries: Transborder Interaction in Comparative Perspective,* El Paso: Western Texas Press.

Miles, W. F. S. (1995) *Hausaland Divided: Colonialism and Independence in Nigeria and Niger,* Ithaca: Cornell University Press.

Nugent, P. and A. I. Asiwaju (eds.) (1996) *African Boundaries: Conduits and Opportunities,* London: Frances Pinter.

Nolutshungu, Sam (ed.) (1996) *Margins of Insecurity: Minorities and International Security,* New York: University of Rochester Press.

Ricq, C. (1996) *Handbook on Transfrontier Cooperation for Local Regional Authorities in Europe,* Strasbourg: Council of Europe.

Sahlin, P. (1989) *Boundaries: the Making of France and Spain in the Pyrenees*, Berkeley: University of California Press.

Strassoldo, R. (1973) *Frontier Regions: an Analytical Study*, Strasbourg: Council of Europe.

—— (1989a) 'Border Studies: the State of the Arts in Europe', in Asiwaju and Adeniyi, *Borderlands*: 383–95.

—— (1989b) 'Perspective on Frontiers: the Case of Alpe Adria', in Anderson and Borts, *The Frontiers of Europe*: 75–90.

Stewart, M. H. (1984) 'The Borgu People of Nigeria and Benin: the Disruptive Effect of Partition on Traditional Political and Economic Relations', *Journal of the Historical Society of Nigeria*, 12, 3–4: 95–119.

Tagil, S. (1982) 'The Question of Regions in Western Europe: an Historical Background', in Anderson (ed.), *Frontier Regions*: 18–33.

Vedovato, G. (1995) *Transfrontier Cooperation and the Europe of Tomorrow,* Strasbourg: Council of Europe.

von Malchus, Viktor (1975) *The Cooperation of European Frontier Regions: States of the Question and Recent Developments*, Strasbourg: Council of Europe.

Epilogue

The New Partnership for Africa's Development (NEPAD)

NEPAD: Yet Another Plan, Another Initiative and New Partnership?

From the contributions of the sixteen scholars, policy makers, civil society leaders and international civil servants contained in this book, it is clear that the way forward lies not in preparing a new development strategy for Africa but in strategising as to how to operationalise the ones that have been prepared in the 1980s and 1990s on the basis of the four cardinal principles that were agreed upon by the African governments and people as the cornerstones of the socio-economic and political development and transformation of their respective countries and of their continent. These four fundamental principles are self-reliance – national and collective – self-sustainment, democracy and sustainable human development. Over the past three decades, the consensus of informed African opinion is that the actualisation of these principles will facilitate the democratisation of the development process as well as ensure equity and justice in the distribution of resources and the fruit of development through the progressive eradication of unemployment and mass poverty.

The process of self-reliance involves:

- the internalisation of the forces of demand which determine the direction of development, the economic growth process and patterns of output;
- increasing substitution of domestic factor inputs for external factor inputs;
- increasing participation of the mass of the people in the production and consumption of the social product; and,
- increasing self-sustainment through the promotion of the patterns and process of a holistic, sustainable human development in which the different sectors, subsectors, programmes and activities mutually support and reinforce each other, so that when they are related to the internalisation of the forces determining demand and supply, the whole economic, social and political system develops its own internal dynamics (Adedeji, 1989).

From the concepts of self-reliance and self-sustainment have emerged the following preconditions for socio-economic development and transformation:

- a thorough knowledge of natural and human resources at country, subregional and regional levels if meaningful development and economic growth is to be generated;
- a full understanding of the types of goods and services to be produced and of the skills to be developed to produce them;
- the appropriate type of technology to be developed and imported;
- the appropriate development institutions to be established.

In other words, in the context of self-reliance (both national and collective) and self-sustainment, the supply of natural resources expected to be available for development and the choices of commodity and service composition of output would determine the pattern of skills and the type of technologies to be developed locally (and the pattern of equipment to be imported and subsequently produced at home), as well as the institutional capabilities and capacities that will be needed.

The imperative of collective self-reliance through regionalisation has been with the African countries even before they gained their political independence. Pan-Africanism was the rallying point for African leaders in their agitation for independence as it was perceived as the only way that economic decolonisation could supplement political independence and give it meaning. Indeed, the vision of regionalism, and especially of Pan-Africanism, has always been popular among Africans.

Even during the colonial era, regionalism was encouraged by the colonial governments not out of any idealism but principally because of the need to exploit the potential of the economies of scale. Thus, the French colonial administration did establish two federations – Afrique Occidentale Française (AOF) and Afrique Equatoriale Française (AEF). Eight colonies – Mauritania, Senegal, French Sudan (now Mali), French Guinea, Dahomey (now Benin), Niger, Côte d'Ivoire and Upper Volta (now Burkina Faso) – constituted the federation of French West Africa. The French Equatorial Federation was made up of what became the Central African Republic, Chad, Congo (Brazzaville), Gabon and Cameroon. But in 1956, the French authority launched the process of balkanisation so that, at the time of independence in 1960, the two federations had been disbanded. In their place, 14 small independent (and economically unviable) states, including Togo, emerged. By so doing, France imposed a severe burden on these newly independent minuscule states. Fragmented and balkanised, they sought refuge in regionalism through economic cooperation, even though this was a poor substitute for federalism, particularly as the phenomenon of irredentism and separatism soon began to rear its ugly face. Hence the large number of economic integration entities established in West and Central Africa and subsequently in other regions of Africa.

For these regional cooperation arrangements to succeed and become sustainable, an increasing measure of collective inter-country self-reliance is imperative. This is required for the formulation and application of autonomous decisions needed to generate and implement independent ideas, identify problems and analyse and solve them regionally, while taking full account of the national dimension.

The third cardinal principle is people-centred democracy: a democratic system which is more than the competitive struggle for the people's vote. The ease with which the international community has conferred its seal of approval on any semblance of free and fair elections in Africa has validated the equation of democracy with elections and multipartyism. Because of this, there is a strong feeling that the recent apparent spread of democracy in Africa is a sham: the staging of elections is no guarantee that there are people-centred democratic governments with well-engrained democratic cultures. What is pervasive is low-intensity democracy – a compromise between pseudo-democratic institutions and dictatorships which enjoy little popular support (Adedeji, 1997). However, this type of democracy is acceptable to aid donors whose support is essential for African leaders. Hence cynics have christened it 'donor democracy'.

Donor democracy or low-intensity democracy excludes the generality of the people from any critical and significant contribution to national directions. Lack of popular participation in governance encourages gross mismanagement of the African economies, massive capital flight, unproductive use of resources, anti-rural bias, poor resource mobilisation, distorted priorities and extensive interventions by the IMF and the World Bank in national economic management. The absence of popular democracy also accounts for the lack of effective political accountability and financial transparency (Adedeji, 1990).

For democracy to survive, grow and thrive, it must derive from and be inspired by a deep-seated culture of popular participation; that is, in essence, the empowerment of the people and their organisations to involve themselves in creating structures and in designing policies and programmes that serve the interests of all and contribute optimally to the development process. In other words, popular participation is the *fons et origo* of a people-centred development vision that embraces the transformation agenda.

Thus, democracy in terms of the ballot box and multipartysm is only a subset of popular participation. On its own, it is far from being adequate for good governance. Popular participation must be the foundation of a true and genuine democratic culture. It is also a must for sustainable human development and human security to become a reality. While human development is a process of widening the range of choice of the people, human security enables the people to exercise these choices safely and freely with every certainty and confidence that the opportunities that the people have today will not be lost tomorrow. The two main aspects of human security are safety from such chronic threats as hunger, disease and repression, and protection from sudden and hurtful disruption in the patterns of daily life. It is these threats to human security – personal, economic, political, food, health, environmental and community and cultural insecurity – that sustainable human development is to eliminate.

In other words, sustainable development is development that not only generates economic growth but also distributes its benefits equitably; that regenerates the environment rather than destroying it; that empowers people rather than marginalising them. It is development that gives priority to the poor, enlarging their choices and opportunities and providing for their participation in decisions that affect their lives. Sustainable development is development that is pro-people, pro-nature, pro-jobs and pro-women (Speth, 1994).

It is these four cardinal principles that have informed and guided the five landmark strategies that during the 1980s and early 1990s have been crafted to forge the future of Africa and its people. These are:

1   the Lagos Plan of Action for the Economic Development of Africa, 1980–2000 and the Final Act of Lagos (1980);
2   Africa's Priority Programme for Economic Recovery 1986–90 (APPER), later converted into the United Nations Programme of Action for Africa's Economic Recovery and Development (UN–PAAERD) (1986);
3   the African Alternative Framework to Structural Adjustment Programmes for Socio-Economic Recovery and Transformation (AAF–SAP) (1989);
4   the African Charter for Popular Participation in Development and Transformation (1990);
5   the United Nations New Agenda for the Development of Africa in the 1990s (UN–NADAF, 1991).

Unfortunately, all of these were opposed, undermined and jettisoned by the Bretton Woods institutions, and Africans were thus impeded from exercising their basic and fundamental right to make decisions about their future. This denial would have been ameliorated if the African leaders had shown the commitment to carry out their own development agenda. But given their excessive external dependence, their excruciating debt burden, their narrow political base, the pervasiveness of donor democracy and their perennial failure to put their money where their mouth is, the implementation of these plans has suffered from benign neglect. Lacking the resources and the will to soldier on self-reliantly, they abandoned their own strategies, including the two – UN–PAAERD and UN–NADAF – that were crafted jointly with the international community under the aegis of the United Nations General Assembly.

Instead, perforce, the implementation of the exogenous agenda has been pursued because the operators of the development merchant system (DMS) have been ready to supply foreign-crafted economic reform policies, turned into a new kind of special goods largely and quickly financed by them regardless of the negative impact of such policies on African economies and polities. Assistance is readily available from the DMS to operationalise the paradigms emanating from its strategists and favouring the development route that they have mapped out for Africa, including the mode of its integration into the global economy. African governments have always felt obliged to conform to the norms, whims and caprices of the DMS. Needless to add, the overarching vision of the DMS sees the African canoe as firmly tied to the apron strings of the North's neoliberal ship as it sails serenely on the waters of globalisation. All these matters have been discussed *in extenso* in Chapter 1.

In such circumstances – even as indigenous effort is intensified to come up with African paradigms, strategies and policies capable of forging the continent's future in the right direction; even as the opposition of African governments to the neoliberal model of the structural adjustment programme becomes strident; and as globalisation continues to breed violence and conflict by exacerbating poverty, inequality, environmental degradation and unprecedented concentration of political and economic power in the hands of a few, while the majority are marginalised, impoverished and excluded – Africa remains firmly in the grip of the orthodoxy of the DMS. Without doubt, sustainable development in Africa will not begin until this struggle over development paradigms, strategies and agendas is resolved in favour of its people (Ake, 1996). Is the apparent warm welcome accorded to NEPAD by the major donor countries and the IFIs the beginning of a new approach to Africa's development or the triumph of DMS?

Why a New Initiative for Africa at the Dawn of the 21st Century?

What reasons have compelled at first two and subsequently five heads of state to take two further separate initiatives, leading to two more development strategies for Africa? The main reason, to put it bluntly, was the urge felt by the two initiators – President Abdoulaye Wade of Senegal and President Thabo Mbeki of South Africa – to be innovative, based on their shared belief that the strategies of the 1980s and 1990s had been initiated by African experts, and not by heads of state; hence they 'were made to be put in drawers and there wasn't even an attempt to implement them. Not even the simplest attempt! This time, the plan is drafted by those who decide, the decision makers' (Wade: 2002: 49): that is, the two heads of state themselves. In fact, the pamphlet *Introducing NEPAD,* produced and published by the Senegalese authorities, overreached itself when it derisively referred to the 'uselessness of the long studies and plans that are never actually completed, which pervade our (Africa's) history since the independence era' (NEPAD, 2002).

While President Wade put forward his Omega Plan, President Mbeki, joined by President Abdelaziz Bouteflika of Algeria and President Olusegun Obasanjo of Nigeria, launched the Millennium Partnership for the African Recovery (MAP).

Indeed, the OAU at its 1999 Summit in Algiers had mandated Algeria, South Africa and Nigeria to engage the industrialised North on the total cancellation of Africa's external debt and promote efforts to close the 'digital divide' between Africa and the industrialised countries. It is also worth noting that Wade's Omega Plan was first presented at the Franco-African Summit held in Yaoundé in January 2001. In June 2001 it was formally launched at the International Conference of Economists on the Omega Plan, attended by a group of selected Africans and non-Africans. The Plan identified the need to develop physical and human capital as the key prerequisites for sustained and balanced growth and argued for investment in priority sectors to be brought under the purview of a single international authority whose membership would include debtor and creditor countries' representatives, the World Bank, the IMF and EU representatives. It was no doubt the technical inputs of the experts that gave President Wade the confidence to boast that his Omega Plan was 'rigorous with almost arithmetical strictness in its objectives and pragmatic in its method' while the MAP by President Mbeki was marked (or marred?) by his 'romanticism and inspired by the end of the struggle against apartheid' (Wade, 2002: 50). Significantly, no acknowledgement was made of any of the several attempts at developing regional infrastructural systems like the pan-African highways and telecommunications systems. There was no mention even of the United Nations Transport and Communications Decade for Africa (UNTACDA) proclaimed by the UN General Assembly in the 1980s and 1990s – the first of its kind in the United Nations – whose cumulative impact has been quite positive in spite of limited support by the international community.

It has become evident that NEPAD's mapmakers have not informed themselves about the processes that culminated in the adoption of the five African landmarks mentioned earlier: the LPA and FAL; APPER and UN–PAAERD; the AAF–SAP; the African Charter for Popular Participation; and UN–NADAF. These straddled some twelve years and involved people at all levels – expert, political, national, regional and interregional. All of them, with the exception of UN–PAAERD and UN–NADAF, were subjected to the approval of African Heads of State, while the two exceptions were endorsed by the General Assembly of the United Nations.

The MAP was, right from the beginning, entirely an Mbeki affair: he had embarked upon mobilising support for it with the external powers even before it was drafted and before it was tabled at the OAU Extraordinary Summit held in Sirte, Libya, in September 1999. No doubt President Mbeki perceived MAP as being part and parcel of his African renaissance project, with South Africa as the fountainhead of the renaissance.

Thus MAP was intended to be a detailed project for the economic and social revival of Africa, involving a constructive partnership between Africa and the developed world. President Mbeki therefore concentrated on consulting with some of the leading world leaders (Clinton, Putin, Bush, Blair, Yoshiro Mori, the Nordic prime ministers, the European Council and business leaders at the World

Economic Summit) in 2001 before consulting even with the African National Congress (ANC) of South Africa. It is unnecessary to add that he also consulted both the World Bank (Wolfensohn) and the IMF (Horst Kohler). It was after all these consultations that he briefed his colleagues at the OAU Summit, not with a view to making it an all-African initiative but simply to welcome aboard as many countries as were willing to join in the actualisation of his proposals. Countries that were not ready would join later, and he hoped that participation would be as inclusive as possible. He was more concerned to have the commitment of a critical number of African countries, at least to begin with, than to canvass the entire universe of the OAU's membership. However, at the OAU Summit in Lome, Togo in July 2000, it was agreed that the presidents of Algeria, Egypt and Nigeria should join hands with President Mbeki to prepare the draft of MAP.

This account of how both MAP and the Omega Plan came into existence, and the exclusive rather than inclusive process that has been pursued in their preparations and merger, shows how far they trail behind the all-inclusive effort of the 1980s and 1990s. Both in conception and in architecture, indeed, NEPAD is more élitist than any of the five landmark strategies. In fact, it is in contrast to them. The manner in which MAP and the OMEGA Plan, and ultimately NEPAD, have emerged is the very antithesis of the postulates of the African Charter for Popular Participation. Of course, politicians are men and women who strive very hard for fame. Indeed, they have never striven harder than they do today. Emerging African leaders are only too willing to rediscover the wheel. They are tireless in pouring old wine into new bottles. Of course, with the help of the media, fame is created instantly. Yet never has it been more transitory and elusive.

Is NEPAD a Vision, a Programme or a Strategy?

MAP and the Omega Plan were merged into the New African Initiative. In its preamble, it claims to be Africa's strategy for achieving sustainable development in the 21st century. When in October 2001 the initiative was renamed the New Partnership for Africa's Development (NEPAD), it became a development programme 'anchored on the determination of Africans to extricate themselves and the continent from the malaise of underdevelopment and exclusion in a globalising world' (NEPAD, 2002: paragraph 1). It was further explained in the document that NEPAD 'is envisaged as a long-term vision of an African-owned and African-led development programme' which 'differs in its approach and strategy from all previous plans and initiatives' (ibid.: paragraphs 59–60).

To leave the confusion worse confounded, NEPAD is perceived in some quarters as an African version of the Marshall Plan. For example, the Canadian Prime Minister, Jean Chrétien, during visit in April 2002 to a number of African countries – Algeria, Ethiopia, Mozambique, Nigeria, Senegal and South Africa – asserted that NEPAD has been modelled on the Marshall Plan. In some African countries the expectation was that the new African initiative would lead to a Marshall Plan for Africa. Fortunately, President Wade in his interview published in the quarterly magazine *African Geopolitics*, to which reference has already been made, replied in the negative when asked if NEPAD is a new Marshall Plan and added, 'In post-war Europe bombs had destroyed everything, but the people were there. The human resources were! It was simply necessary to resolve the problems of real investment. In Africa we have no human engine. But, just as for the Marshall Plan we do need massive investment' (Wade, 2002: 56).

The fact that NEPAD is a different thing to different people, even among its protagonists, is significant but not very important. What is crucial is whether it presents a discernible vision of development with an integrated agenda for its realisation – as was the case with the Lagos Plan of Action, which was crafted around the basic principles enunciated earlier. While it can be argued that grand strategies of development are now of less interest than specific policy options, it is also true that sustainable development and socio-economic transformation will be next to impossible, no matter how high GDP growth rates are, unless in the context of national and collective self-reliance and self-sustainment. NEPAD is ambivalent in this crucial area. There are no linkages – either forward or backward or even lateral – between and among its five priority areas in the productive sector: infrastructure, energy, education, health and agriculture.

First, it is most telling that industrial development and manufacturing is not accorded high priority. The absence of any serious macro-economic analysis prevents due attention being given to the nature of sustainable development. Even the target growth rate of 7 per cent per annum was put forward only to justify mobilising external resources in the light of the resource gaps which are expected to be filled from external sources. In other words, NEPAD is more concerned with attracting foreign investments than with wealth creation on a sustainable basis. To reduce the proportion of the population living below poverty level by 50 per cent by the year 2015, as required under the United Nations Millennium Development Goals, would require, as perceived by NEPAD's authors, a growth rate of 7 per cent per annum and an investment rate of about 30 per cent of GDP. Since, historically, the evidently available rate of investment from domestic sources has averaged only 18 per cent of GDP per annum, the resource gap of 12 per cent of GDP will have to be filled from external sources.

Had the nature of development transformation through wealth creation been the primary concern, the centrality of domestic savings and the imperative of the reduction of capital wastages and of plugging capital leakages would have been prioritised. Such an analysis would have led inevitably to the urgent need to integrate Africa's production structures and its markets. Indeed, as has been argued in the LPA, the regionalism sought by African leaders involves the mutually interdependent integration of production structures and markets with the physical, institutional and social infrastructure.

Table E.1 Matrix of Strategic Actions in the Food and Agriculture Sector

Timeframe	Strategic objectives		
	Eradicate poverty	*Adopt sustainable development strategies*	*Participate effectively in the global economy*
1 Short-term	a. Establish micro-credit institutions targeting the poor (e.g., Grameen bank) and involve the poor in the management of those institutions; b. Strengthen local-level governance, so as to ensure *equity in access* to resources (e.g., land, water, extension services, etc.) by the poor and other vulnerable groups, such as women; c. Promote smallholder (herders, crop growers, etc.) associations; d. Support restoration and growth of traditional networks of communal engagement that provide coping mechanisms and social safety nets during crisis.	a. Support traditional community-based natural resource management institutions; b. Legalise traditional systems/institutions of common property resources (e.g., land, water, forests, etc.); c. Promote sustainable patterns of resource use; d. Promote indigenous knowledge and protect associated intellectual property rights.	a. Make use of the US–African Growth and Opportunity Act to promote the marketing of African high-value food products; b. Strengthen commercial/trade sections of African embassies in Europe and North America, so as to promote African high-value food products;
2. Medium-term	a. Train women in extension services; b. Promote forward and backward production linkages; c. Develop the skills of the poor through targeted training in management, marketing, storage & packaging, advocacy and awareness raising about basic human rights; d. Promote medium-scale farming, range and dairy management enterprises; e. Promote investment in high-value food production;	a. Promote replication of best practices and gender-sensitive production techniques; b. Facilitate establishment of community-based ecotourism operators, e.g., Community Areas Management Programme for Indigenous Resources (CAMPFIRE) in Zimbabwe; c. Promote investment in organic farming through appropriate incentive systems; d. Promote private sector development and	a. Elimination of food aid as both relief and development assistance instruments; b. Establishment of a new protocol between African countries and the UN World Food Programme (WFP) to purchase its relief supplies from the continent and to put in place a complete ban on food aid from Europe and North America for WPF operations in Africa; c. Establishment of sub-regional food banks/reserves to deal

Timeframe	Strategic objectives		
	Eradicate poverty	*Adopt sustainable development strategies*	*Participate effectively in the global economy*
2. Medium-term (cont.)	f. Allocate at least 1% of GNP to agricultural research and farming systems focusing on the eradication of poverty; g. Establish robust legal frameworks to allow African women to have equal access to resources, e.g., land, and to have full control of other resources such as cows and savings in their own names; h. Allow free move-ments of African agricultural products (e.g., live animals) between African coun-tries and markets; i. 'Africanisation' of all the agricultural initiatives; j. Establish an Internet website-e-Farm Africa to enable smallholder farmers to have access to the most appropriate production techniques as well as markets for African farm products.	investment in the key areas of harvesting, processing, storage, marketing, packaging and export of African agriculture products; e. Strengthen national agricultural research systems through the improvement of working conditions for African scientists and experts; f. Promote investment in agro-based manufacturing.	with both human and nature–induced emergencies and famines; d. Create institutional arrangements for collaborative research in farming systems between Africa and its partners in the rest of the world.
3. Long-term	a. Regional integration and establishment of regional centres of excellence in agriculture research and associated network of extension services with particular mission of eradicating poverty; b. Adopt a coherent regional macro-economic framework that calls for: (i) removal of barriers to trade between member states of a subregional organisation, (ii) free	a. Regional integration and establishment of regional centres of excellence in agriculture research and associated network of extension services; b. Adopt a coherent regional and agriculture-focused macro-economic framework that calls for: (i) removal of barriers to trade between member states of a subregional organisation, (ii) free movement of goods	a. Regional integration and establishment of regional centres of excellence in agriculture research and associated network of extension services; b. Adopt a coherent regional and agriculture-focused macro-economic framework that calls for: (i) removal of barriers to trade between member states of a subregional organisation, (ii) free movement of goods

Timeframe	Strategic objectives		
	Eradicate poverty	*Adopt sustainable development strategies*	*Participate effectively in the global economy*
3. Long-term (cont.)	movement of goods and services, (iii) free movement of people, (iv) harmonisation of monetary and fiscal policies, (v) harmonisation of exchange rates policies through free forces of demand and supply, (vi) unification of tariffs on goods and services entering a sub-regional market from the rest of the world; c. Formulate and co-ordinate regional poverty reduction strategy based on national poverty reduction strategy papers; d. Put in place a robust evaluation and monitoring system for a continuous assessment of the proposed anti-poverty measures and their impact on the specific objective of reducing by 50% the number of Africans living below the poverty line by the year 2015.	and services, (iii) free movement of people, (iv) harmonisation of monetary and fiscal policies, (v) harmonisation of exchange rates policies through free market forces of demand and supply, (vi) unification of tariffs on goods and services entering a subregional market from the rest of the world; c. Allocate adequate resources (say 5% of GNP) for investment in physical infrastructure, especially rural roads, storage facilities, information communication technology (ICT) facilities, and a chain or a value-added ladder between farm-level production and processing industry/ manufacturing gate.	and services, (iii) free movement of people, (iv) harmonisation of monetary and fiscal policies, (v) harmonisation of exchange rates policies through free market forces of demand and supply, (vi) unification of tariffs on goods and services entering a subregional market from the rest of the world; c. Promote global trading partnerships.

Source: L. A. Deng, 'A Reflection Paper on the Sectoral Priorities of NEPAD', presented at the African Forum for Envisioning Africa: Focus on NEPAD, Nairobi, April 2002.

Second, this over-dependence on external resources has also led to the neglect of the strategic importance of agriculture as the lever of development and transformation. Unless agriculture, food processing and agriculture-based manufacturing industries are accorded the highest priority, neither sustainable human development nor an end to the poverty of one-half of the poor population in Africa by 2015 will be achievable. Table E.1 (pp. 241–3 above) presents a matrix of required strategic actions in the food and agriculture sector for achieving food security and sustainable human development.

Africa urgently needs its food and agricultural revolution. The green revolution in East and South-East Asia in the 1970s laid the foundation for the Asian Miracle of the 1980s. Could Africa focus its attention on achieving a similar feat during the first decade of the 21st century by maximising the mobilisation of domestic savings for investment in the promotion of revolution in its food and agriculture sector? For a region with the highest population growth rate, this is the most important strategic option that is calling for actualisation, as has been argued again and again in the LPA, UN–PAAERD, the AAF–SAP and UN–NADAF.

NEPAD and Governance

NEPAD separates political governance from economic governance. This is no doubt for the convenience of its architects, because in the real world both are not just interrelated but also intertwined. They are like the horse and the carriage – you cannot have one without the other!

On the other hand, democracy is crucial to both political governance and economic governance. In other words, rather than have two governance initiatives – political and economic – there should be one democracy and governance initiative. This is important if Africa's fledgeling or nascent low-intensity, donor-driven democracy is to evolve into a proper democratic culture which is grass-rooted and all-pervasive. Democracy is as critical in politics as it is in economic development and management, just as governance is as important in the political domain as it is in the economic domain.

Thus, as we have already pointed out at the beginning of this epilogue, the democracy that is one of the four pillars for the construction of Africa's socio-economic and political order is much more fundamental than political pluralism, the ballot and the competitive struggle for the people's vote. It is a way of life, a culture which enhances and upholds human dignity and guarantees human freedom in all its different manifestations. Democracy must become internalised in all the social institutions if it is to grow and become ingrained in all aspects of human relations. This does not happen overnight. Unlike instant coffee, there is no instant democracy. A dictator or an autocrat yesterday cannot 'miraculously' become a democrat today. Democracy must grow from within a society and from within a polity. And for this to happen, there must be an enabling environment in terms of political freedom, political stability, social justice, equality of opportunity and the capacity and opportunity for people to participate in policy formulation and in discourses on policy issues.

The democratic culture cannot begin to take root, let alone become sustainable, in a Pharisee society of self-interest where the rich and the powerful are getting richer and more powerful and the poor and the powerless are becoming poorer and marginalised. The prospect for sustainable democracy in a stagnating and declining economy is dim. Above all, democracy cannot thrive in a situation of persistent political crisis and polarisation (Adedeji, 1992). True democracy will bring in its train long-term peace, stability and development. True democracy will be achieved only when those in power have respect rather than contempt for those they govern, while the latter develop trust and confidence in their leaders. People will never fully comprehend Africa's crisis so long as they continue to assume that it is mainly an economic one. What confronts the continent is primarily a political crisis, albeit with devastating economic consequences.

It is therefore imperative that an integral part of the democratic process must be the democratisation of the development process. A democratically determined development process immerses the entire populace in the struggle for socio-economic transformation and in turn transforms the people themselves by significantly modifying their values, their attitudes to work, saving and investment, their sense of self-reliance and human dignity and, above all, their perception of citizenship. Participation in citizenship constitutes the basis of all other forms of participation in development (Adedeji, 1997). A democratic economic development strategy is one that puts people in a position to participate in decisions affecting them and enables them to effectively exercise political power over their economic lives. It puts people in a position where their lives are not dominated by either the market or the state. The democratisation of the development process also delivers the benefits of development to the population equitably, thereby enhancing their power (MacEwan, 1999). In other words, democratising the development process enhances the political democratic process, while political democracy provides an enabling environment and infrastrucural base for a people-centred, participatory economic development and social transformation process – thus setting in motion a process of cumulative causation with the combined spread effects of both becoming overwhelming and impacting most favourably on human security and human development in all their ramifications.

In such circumstances, the quality of governance in its holistic form – political, judicial, economic and social – will be enhanced, and universal democratic values will become fully internalised. But it cannot be overemphasised that there is no one form of democracy that is universally appropriate and therefore the question of *deviation from the norm* does not arise. It is only in Africa, where mimicry has become a way of life, that democracy as practised in Western Europe and North America (and there are fundamental differences between the two models) is taken as the norm. In fact, given the African heterogeneity one cannot expect uniformity in democratic practices. Due allowance must be made for diversity, provided the universal democratic values are always respected. Therefore, the very idea of a single norm for democratic systems and practices must be treated with a grain of salt, if not with disdain. What does this norm comprise? What are its principles and characteristics? And who is to judge deviations from it? And will whatever mechanisms that are set up to bring the so-called deviants to book work effectively without exacerbating divisiveness in Africa's leadership?

Is the peer review feasible in Africa, or anywhere else for that matter, where there is a lot of sensitivity about sovereignty and the heads of state tend to herd together like trade union leaders? Of course, its proponents have hitched it to the wagon of external resources, particularly foreign direct investment (FDI). If the peer review system is not voluntary; it becomes a sanctions-imposing and blackmailing device in the hands of the donor community and the international financial institutions (IFIs) (Yash Tandon 2002). If it is voluntary it provides donors and the IFIs with a ready-made African policy instrument for discrimination, exclusion and divisiveness. Indeed, the G8 has already linked its support for NEPAD with the ability of African leaders to keep their commitments to utilise the peer review effectively to pursue the Western type of liberal democracy and free market strategies. Finally, there is no doubt that whatever peer review mechanisms for African leaders are put in place, the donor community will always try very hard to influence them. If current practice of adjudging performance is any guide, it is the judgement of the donors rather than that of the recipients that will prevail. It is the standards of the donors that will continue to be imposed on Africa, and whenever they conclude that their standards are not met they will withhold aid. And every time the behaviour or performance of an African country or a group of African countries is adjudged unsatisfactory, a cloud will hang over the whole of Africa, not just the erring country or countries. The whole continent will be lumped together and collectively vilified. The African peer review system will work as long as the judgment of the African reviewers falls in line with the *a priori* position of the G8. Whenever it does not, aid will cease to flow and trade will become less free. Rather than loosening the noose of the donor countries and institutions, peer review will tighten it.

NEPAD and Resource Mobilisation

Regrettably, NEPAD sees the issue of resource mobilisation in the very narrow sense of massive investment and hopes that the new money will come from Africa's 'partners' particularly in the form of foreign direct investment. Hence it postulates that increased private capital flow to Africa is an essential component of a sustainable long-term approach to filling the resource gaps (NEPAD, 2002: paragraph 153). It is important to note that NEPAD is not optimistic about aid or credit as sources of finance from the West. In fact, it looks at these rather unfavourably:

> Historically, the credit and aid binominal has underlined the logic of African develop-
> ment. Credit has led to the debt deadlock, which still exists and hinders the growth of
> African countries. Concerning the other element of the binominal – aid – we can also
> note the reduction of private aid and the upper limit of the public aid, which is below
> the target set in the 1970s. (NEPAD, 2002: paragraph 3)

Yet the proponents of NEPAD are sanguine about the flows of FDI to Africa.

Increased ODA and debt relief, together with additional mobilisation of domestic resources, are considered as complementary resources in the short-to-medium term. The FDIs occupy the centre stage in NEPAD's development strategy and resource mobilisation. On the basis of the target annual growth rate of 7 per cent required to meet the millennium development goals in Africa, it estimates the annual resource needs of Africa as US$64 billion. Attracting this huge sum, principally through FDIs, is seen by NEPAD as the challenge ahead. It is in order to attract such huge investments that NEPAD has made the commitment to Western-type liberal democracy and liberal economics in the form of free market strategies, and has proposed the peer review which we have just agreed is a dangerous double-edged tool.

Why did the distinguished experts who drafted NEPAD not explore all the possibilities of resource mobilisation, particularly as their starting point was to assert that Africa has been the indispensable resource base for humanity? (NEPAD, 2002: paragraph 8) If it still is, why speak of a resource gap that must perforce be filled by FDIs? Why limit resource mobilisation to money and capital? How were the resources gaps arrived at in any case? How was the incremental capital/output ratio calculated?

The fact that NEPAD has opted for the classical two-gap model of economic growth has given the greatest concern to the critics, and credence to their criticisms. To postulate in the 21st century, more than four decades after the unsuccessful effort at promoting development on the basis of the neoclassical model propagated by the operators of the DMS that the *deus ex machina* is massive injections of capital, particularly foreign capital, is to ignore completely all the lessons of experience. If only African governments could reduce the wastage of their domestically generated resources by just 25 per cent and plug capital leakages and capital flight by another 25 per cent, these two would add up, on the average, to between $30 billion and $40 billion per annum. Second, if commodity and debt problems were seriously addressed by the donor/creditor community, additional resources as large as $35 billion per annum could be released for development. While these targets may be difficult to achieve, they are do-able.

According to the World Bank's *African Development Indicators 2001*, the terms of trade index dropped from 158.3 in 1980 to 96.5 in 1999 (1995 = 100).

Specifically, sub-Sahara Africa's export unit value fell from 121.8 in 1980 to 89.4 in 1999 (with 1995 again the base year), whereas its import unit value during the same period rose from 77.0 to 92.6. Africa's export commodities are characterised by highly income-inelastic demand, with supply being price-elastic. The inevitable consequence is the boom-and-bust cycle which results in severe damage to the economy and reduction in the provision of essential public goods.

The reactivation of the two-gap model is also unfortunate because it was precisely the cause of the current debt trap and the exacerbation of the continent's dependency syndrome. What Africa needs is not to add to its debt burden but to reduce it and eventually be relieved of it. In any case, there is an element of oversimplification of a rather complex problem in the postulate that to achieve a 7 per cent growth rate per annum in Africa requires an investment of about 30 per cent of GDP. Given the abysmally low level of productivity, is it new investment or the raising of productivity that is urgently needed? How can countries that year in, year out are unable to implement their modest capital budgets be pleading for massive investment? Where is the executive capacity coming from? No doubt it will be imported, but this will result, as usual, in growth without development. This approach throws overboard the proposition that development has to be engineered and sustained by the people. It ignores the cardinal principle of national and regional collective self-reliance. Sustainable development is the organic outcome of a society's value system, its perceptions, concerns, endeavours, sweat and labour (Adedeji, 2002). In any case, how can African governments ensure that FDIs go to NEPAD's priority sectors?

In a poll on FDI in Africa conducted by UNCTAD and the International Chamber of Commerce at the end of 1999, the transnational companies (TNCs) that responded to the poll gave clear profiles of their assessment of investment profile priorities by region as follows:

- North Africa – petroleum, gas and related products, telecommunications and tourism;
- West Africa – petroleum, gas and related products, agriculture, forestry and telecommunications;
- Central Africa – mining, quarrying and forestry;
- East Africa – tourism and telecommunications;
- Southern African – tourism, transport, telecommunications, pharmaceutical and chemical products and agriculture.

The picture of the overall preferences of sectors for FDI by potential investors, the TNCs, is presented in Figure E.1. It shows that (1) tourism, (2) telecommunications, (3) petroleum and gas and (4) mining and quarrying are top of the preferences list as offering the best opportunities for FDI in Africa in the foreseeable future. Indeed, if (3) and (4) are combined, these extractive industries overtake tourism by a wide margin. This is seen by many observers of the

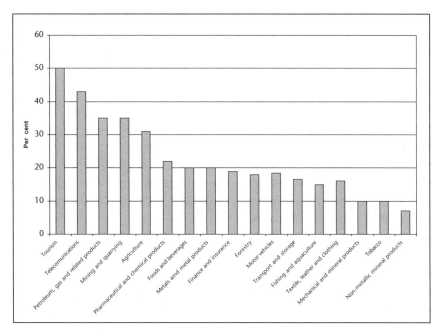

Figure E.1 Industries Offering Best Opportunities for FDI in Africa, 2000–3 (Frequency of Replies)

Source: UNCTAD/ICC (Geneva, 2000)

geopolitical situation as a pointer to the future. Led by the United States, the West is quickly moving to diversify its sources of imported oil away from the politically high-risk areas of the Middle East to places like West Africa. Strategically, West African oil is closer to the US than Middle Eastern oil and can be delivered via open seas unobstructed by canals or narrow straits. It is accordingly projected that oil companies like Exxon–Mobil, Chevron–Texaco and BP–Amoco will invest some US$10 billion per year in African oil, NEPAD or no NEPAD. American oil companies have never allowed politics to influence their investment programmes in the vital oil sector. For example, when Nigeria was under international sanctions during the Abacha military regime of the late 1990s, FDI in oil soared!

If, as has been correctly claimed, Africa's inability to harness the process of globalisation is a result of structural impediments in the form of resource outflows and unfavourable terms of trade (NEPAD, 2002: paragraph 34), how will FDIs help tackle these problems – particularly as it is generally admitted that globalisation has 'increased the ability of the strong to advance their interests to the detriment of the weak, especially in the areas of trade, finance and technology' (*ibid.*: paragraph 33) Would not FDI increase the power of the globalisers in relation to the globalised? Is the idea of capital from abroad filling the gaps not the very antithesis of the principles of self-reliance and self-sustainment?

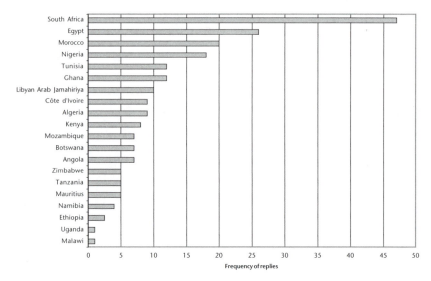

Figure E.2 African Countries Ranked According to Their Attractiveness for FDI, 2000–3 (Frequency of Replies)

Source: UNCTAD/ICC (Geneva, 2000)

Figure E.2 shows that, in terms of the attractiveness of individual African countries for FDI, at the end of 1999 South Africa ranked the highest, followed by Egypt, Morocco and Nigeria, while Namibia, Ethiopia, Uganda and Malawi ranked lowest.

Of course, if the authors of NEPAD have undertaken *a priori* a commitment to uphold and strengthen the DMS and its neo-economic liberalism, perpetuating economic dependence instead of fostering economic self-reliance and self-sustainment, then FDI in particular and external finance in general, in spite of their disregard for NEPAD's priorities, are the only alternatives. In such a circumstance, NEPAD's Capital Flows Initiative is both consistent and appropriate and the peer review and monitoring to ensure the operationalisation of the Initiative is quite logical.

NEPAD and the AU

Although the AU and NEPAD initiatives were commenced in 1999 and 2001 respectively – by different Heads of State – they have ostensibly evolved as separate and parallel entities and their receptions have been significantly different. While NEPAD has been warmly welcomed by the international community and more particularly by the G8, the AU has received scant attention outside Africa. The marked difference in their reception has two principal reasons. The Western enthusiasm for NEPAD is no doubt due at least in part to the fact that it has been initiated and promoted by African leaders who are considered to be pro-West and are seemingly friendly with and traditionally dependent on the West for survival. Not surprisingly, NEPAD's orientation and thrust are in conformity with the Washington Consensus, whose credibility has been severely undermined by the persistent economic instability in Latin America, the debacle in Russia, the Asian 'Flu which began in the late 1990s and the widespread development failure in Africa, where an African alternative was put forward as early as 1989. In spite of all these, NEPAD is still based on orthodox economic liberalism. That, at the dawn of the 21st century, African leaders can distance themselves from the AAF–SAP and the LPA, and declare their intention to conform to the norms of the DMS, must have come as a welcome surprise to the West.

On the other hand, the Constitutive Act of the African Union came from an entirely different source. Its genesis, supranational pan-Africanism, has for long been the idealistic aspiration of the people of Africa and of Africans in the diaspora. Although the first Pan-African Congress was not held until 1900, the pan-African movement stretches back to the eighteenth century when pan-African conscious-ness began to germinate. Between 1900 and 1945, a series of five seminal conferences of the Congress took place, the best-known being the 1945 Manchester Congress. The OAU was established in 1963 in the spirit of pan-Africanism, even though by that time, with a growing number of emerging African independent countries already enjoying the privileges of political sovereignty, pan-Africanism had been supplanted by nationalism and regionalism. When virtually the whole of continental Africa became politically independent, separatist movements within the newly emerging states and irredentist movements by national minorities became widespread. Violent conflicts have become pervasive and Africa has earned the dubious reputation of a violent continent at war against itself.

That is why the revival of pan-Africanism by the Libyan leader, Colonel Muammar Ghaddafi could not be opposed by any true African, and why the Constitutive Act of the African Union that emerged from the OAU's Sirte Declaration of 9 September 1999 provides the historic opportunity for a major breakthrough. If it is successful it will accelerate the operationalisation of the processes of self-reliance, self-sustainment, the democratisation of the develop-ment process and sustainable human development. If it is successful it will rekindle African peoples' aspiration for stronger unity, solidarity, and cohesion in a larger community of peoples, transcending cultural, ideological, ethnic and national differences.

Unlike NEPAD, the AU enjoys universal support in Africa, even if some people are worried that it has been hurried. Its potentials are as enormous as they are multidimensional. Like NEPAD, the AU's success will depend on good govern-ance, stakeholder participation and human rights, but it will do more: promote the African renaissance and restore to its people their integrity and self-confidence.

In any case, NEPAD as a programme will, sooner or later, be integrated into the Commission of the AU. With the launching of the AU at Durban, South Africa on 9 July 2002, the NEPAD Secretariat in Midrand, South Africa must be transferred to Addis Ababa and be integrated with the AU's Commission. This will be mutually beneficial to both. Once this is done, the door to the ownership of NEPAD by the African civil society will be wide open.

NEPAD and the G8 Africa Action Plan

The G8 formally responded to NEPAD at its Kananaskis Summit in July 2002 with a 12 paged document entitled *G8 Africa Action Plan* whose main features are as follows:

- Building a new partnership – but as individual countries, not collectively as G8; and not with Africa as a whole, but on a bilateral select basis. This will enable the G8 countries to base their action on their own performance review of individual African countries, and not rely on the peer review mechanisms of the AU. To this end, an OECD Development Assistance Committee peer-review process is being put in place. This will be in addition to the support the G8 will provide to African regional organisations in developing tools to facilitate their own peer-review processes.

- However, commitment to the Development Goals of the United Nations Millennium Declaration – regarded by the G8 as an integral part of their commitment to address the core issues of human dignity and development, including situations of humanitarian need – will be independent of particular regimes. In other words, democracy, good governance and peer review conditionalities will not apply in such emergency circumstances.

- Reiteration of the commitment made at Monterrey in March 2002 to increase ODA to US$12 billion per year by 2006, with an indication that if Africa demonstrates strong policy commitment between now and 2006, an aggregate half or more of the new development assistance could be directed to African nations that govern justly, invest in their own people and promote economic freedom.

- While inviting other donor countries to join them, the G8 also expressed the hope that South–South cooperation will manifest itself in the implementation of NEPAD. The African leaders promoting NEPAD have not only neglected their own civil society and business sectors but have also accorded no importance to the South in the implementation of NEPAD.

- Undertaking engagements in support of:
  1   Promoting peace and security specifically in the resolution of armed

conflicts so that by 2010 Africa will become self-reliant in peacekeeping and peace building;

2 strengthening institutions and governance, especially peer-review arrangements and measures to combat corruption, bribery and embezzlement, including securing the early establishment of a UN Convention on Corruption and the early ratification of the UN Convention Against Transnational Organised Crime;

3 fostering trade, investment, economic growth and sustainable development by providing, *inter alia*, greater market access for African products including concluding by 2005 further trade liberalisation in the Doha round of multilateral trade negotiations and applying the Doha commitment to comprehensive negotiations on agriculture aimed at substantial improvements in market access and in particular working toward the objective of duty-free and quota-free access for all products originating from the LDCs, including the African LDCs;

4 implementing debt relief through the HIPC initiative, which will reduce by US$19 billion (net present value terms) the debt of some 22 African countries that are following sound economic policies and good governance;

5 expanding knowledge and digital opportunities;

6 improving health and confronting HIV/AIDS;

7 increasing agricultural productivity and improving water resource management.

On the whole what the G8 countries have done is not to pledge new resources but simply to reiterate their existing international commitments and undertake to accord African countries of their choice most-favoured treatment. They are applying *mutatis mutandis* the commitments made at the Monterrey UN Conference on Financing for Development held in March 2002. What emerged from that Conference was the absence of any radical changes in policy and attitude. Rather, the Monterrey Consensus represents a surrender by the UN to the economic neo-liberalism of the Bretton Woods institutions; and now that their policies have such a UN imprimatur, the Bretton Woods institutions have been encouraged to continue to do more of the same. Even the US$50 billion per year estimated as the additional resources required for achieving the 2015 Millennium Goals worldwide is a non-binding and best-endeavour commitment. The US bluntly refused to accept this or any other target. In fact the environment of falling official development assistance (ODA) is projected to persist and even fall further in the foreseeable future. Yet Africa alone is hoping under NEPAD to attract US$64 billion every year – for an unlimited period!

The damaging surrender by the UN to the Washington Consensus manifests itself most glaringly where the Monterrey Consensus endorses the discredited

HIPC initiative. No new and innovative proposals achieved a consensus. Consequently, in spite of Monterrey, the creditor nations retained their right to continue to keep the debtor countries on a short leash with the powers of the Paris and London Clubs of creditor countries remaining intact. The HIPC Initiative will provide debt relief of only US$19 billion out of a total US$230 billion owed by Africa. The *G8 Africa Action Plan* has reiterated this position.

The Way Forward to Claiming the 21st Century

While the initiation of NEPAD is unique in the sense that African heads of state now contemplate facing squarely and proactively the challenges of African development, the establishment of the AU has raised high hopes and expectations throughout the continent. If the AU design falters, the cost of disappointment is bound to be prohibitive. Succeeding African generations will never forgive those who have raised Africa's hopes so high. The AU offers the people of Africa the historic opportunity to claim the 21st century. It is therefore imperative that the AU must become a thriving reality.

NEPAD can and should play a strategic role in furthering the continent's political and economic integration if it is fine-tuned to be consistent with the paradigm strategy and policy framework agreed upon in the 1980s and 1990s. The integration of NEPAD with these will go a long way towards making it more acceptable to the people and their organisations. Without strict adherence to the four cardinal principles on which these strategies have been built, structural transformation and socio-economic diversification will continue to elude the people. It is strategically important for the AU to enjoy the full support of the G8 and the entire international community – but not at the expense of the LPA and FAL, the AAF–SAP and the African Charter. Similarly, NEPAD should be able to garner the support of all stakeholders and civil society once it is seen as a genuine initiative which will not exacerbate Africa's dependence and dispossession but rather will deepen democracy and popular participation in the fragmented continent that Africa is. It is not enough for NEPAD, through the peer-review process, to help break down the destructive solidarity between African rulers who for too long have supported each other in clinging to power by rigging elections, banning opposition parties, intimidating the press and worse (*Economist*, 22 June 2002). NEPAD, as an integral programme of the AU and properly harmonised with its vision and mission, should become a major factor in building democratic cultural and political structures that empower people and trigger a virtuous cycle for human development.

Bibliography

Adedeji, Adebayo (1989) 'The Evolution of the Monrovia Strategy and the Lagos Plan of Action: a Regional Approach to Economic Decolonisation', in *Towards a Dynamic African Economy*, London: Frank Cass, pp. 321–34.

—— (1990) *The African Alternative: Putting the People First*, Addis Ababa: ECA.

—— (1992) 'Sustaining Democratic Rule for Nigeria's Economic Growth and Development: 1993 and Beyond', text of a special address delivered at the 32nd Annual General Meeting and Conference of NACCIMA (Nigerian Association of Chambers of Commerce, Industries, Mines and Agriculture), Abuja, May.

—— (2002) 'From Lagos Plan of Action to NEPAD', lunchtime keynote address delivered at the International Peace Academy Seminar on 'NEPAD: Toward an African Renaissance?', New York, July.

Adedeji, Adebayo *et al.* (1997) *Nigeria: Renewal from the Roots? The Struggle for Democratic Development*, London and Ijebu Ode: Zed Books and ACDESS.

Ake, Claude (1996) *Democracy and Development in Africa*, Ibadan and Oxford: Oxford University Press.

MacEwan, Arthur (1999) *Neoliberalism or Democracy? Economic Strategy, Markets and Alternatives for the 21st Century*, London: Zed Books.

NEPAD (2002) *Introducing NEPAD*, Dakar: Senegal Government.

Speth, James Gustav (1994) *Human Development Report 1994*, New York: UNDP.

Tandon, Yash (2002) 'NEPAD and FDIs: Symmetries and Contradictions', paper presented at the African Scholars' Forum on NEPAD, Nairobi, April.

Wade, Abdoulaye (2002) 'Africa, an Outcast or a Partner?', *African Geopolitics* (Spring).

Index

Abacha, Sanni 74, 76
Abdulsalami government 76
Abuja Treaty 22, 69-71, 193-4, 197, 200-1
accountability 12-13, 22, 25-6, 28, 47, 68,
    78, 95, 104-5, 111, 118, 137, 221, 235
Adamawa, Mt 214
Adedeji, Adebayo, and the African
    Development paradigm 191; career
    xvi-xvii, xix-xxii, 191; and the African
    Economic Community xx, 70; at
    AAF–SAP drafting session 52; and the
    African Charter for Popular
    Participation in Development and
    Transformation 52-3; and the Centre
    for African Regional and Border
    Studies 225; and the Millennium
    Symposium 64; SAPs critiqued by 74
Afregios 207
Africa Gas Pipelines Project 196
Africa, Central 87, 113, 201, 234, 248; see
    also ECCAS; Eastern 87-8, 196-201,
    224, 248, see also COMESA, EACC;
    Great Lakes region 87, 92, 215, 222;
    Horn of 87, 92, 127, 199-200, 215, see
    also IGAD; North 201, 223, 248, see
    also AMU; Southern 196-201, 224,
    248, see also COMESA, SADC; West
    25, 113, 195-8, 214-15, 248-9, see also
    ECOWAS
Africa's Priority Programme for Economic
    Recovery 1986–90 (APPER) 236,
    238-9

African Agenda 20, 23, 25-8
African Alternative Framework to
    Structural Adjustment Programmes for
    Socio-Economic Recovery and
    Transformation (AAF–SAP),
    accumulation model neglected in 50;
    achievements assessed 40-7, 49-53;
    African leaders distance themselves
    from 251; civil society participation in
    70; and debt repayment 161;
    economistic in emphasis 51; food and
    agriculture revolution in 244; funding
    for 52; and Lagos Plan of Action (LPA)
    64, 67; as landmark strategy for Africa
    236, 254; NEPAD compared with 238-
    9; in Nigeria 30-47; origin of xv-xvi,
    21-2, 37, 49, 191; policy directions of
    38-9, 50-2; and restructuring Africa's
    economy 71; SAPs compared with 67;
    theory of 37-8, 50-2
African Capacity Building Foundation
    (ACBF) 14
African Centre for Development and
    Strategic Studies (ACDESS) xx, 64, 70,
    126, 192
African Charter for Popular Participation
    in Development and Transformation
    21, 51-3, 64, 68-70, 236, 238-9, 254
African Common Market 195
African crisis 1-2, 5-6, 10, 20-1
African Customs Union 194
African Development Bank (ADB) 225

256